SPECIAL OPERATIONS EUROPE
Scenes from the Anti-Nazi War

BY THE SAME AUTHOR :

OLD AFRICA REDISCOVERED

BLACK MOTHER

AFRICA IN HISTORY

THE AFRICANS

THE LIBERATION OF GUINÉ

IN THE EYE OF THE STORM:
ANGOLA'S PEOPLE

AFRICA IN MODERN HISTORY

SPECIAL OPERATIONS EUROPE

Scenes from the Anti-Nazi War

by

BASIL DAVIDSON

LONDON
VICTOR GOLLANCZ LTD
1980

© Basil Davidson 1980

ISBN 0 575 02820 3

PRINTED IN GREAT BRITAIN BY
EBENEZER BAYLIS AND SON LTD.
THE TRINITY PRESS, WORCESTER, AND LONDON

Snow doesn't fall
to lose us all:
But so that every creature
however frail
declares its trail

           Serbian saying

PART I

ONE

I

ON A PERVERSELY pleasant day in the middle of 1941, with the second world war nearly two years old and going worse than ever, I was travelling by rail through the south of France to Spain. I was hoping to get back to England: provided, of course, that Hitler did not get there first. The day was full of sunshine, but not the outlook.

There was said to be beer on the train but nobody offered any, and it was better in any case to sit still. I sat still in my corner while the summer scene of the French riviera jolted past: the neat red roofs and soft blue sea, the stations with flowers in pots and baskets, Nice, Cannes, Toulon, Sanary; and I considered the outlook. It would be a pity to be tripped up now.

I had come by various means from Central Europe in this second summer of defeats, and the question, general but also personal, was where would Hitler go next? Would he still have a go at England, or would he hit out somewhere else: at Russia, perhaps?

It was to emerge afterwards, long afterwards, that Hitler had already missed the invasion-of-England bus; but this was hard to know at the time. Even the wilder branches of the British secret service kept their agents to the job on hand, allowing no inspections of any crystal ball. I expect they do it still.

There were signs and portents; but who could tell what they might be worth? As long ago as the previous February, László had returned to Hungary from a look at Slovakia, one of Hitler's puppet states, and I could report from Budapest, capital of neighbouring Hungary, that all mainroads in that Slovakian "republic" were newly signposted west-east for *Wehrmacht* traffic. They were signposted, that is, straight at the new Russian frontier established in 1939. Had the German Army done all that for fun? It seemed unlike them. Yet going East, against the Russians, seemed a crazy thing for Hitler to attempt. After all, he had an alliance with Stalin, or what seemed to amount to one. László's report might simply indicate a false trail.

But if it did, then England's turn would be next for sure; and among problems this would pose there would also be one, somewhere down the line, for such as me. Go to ground in Franco Spain if one couldn't get home? Disappear in Salazar Portugal? It would be safer here in Vichy France, right under the lantern. But hide here with whom? Anti-nazi resistance in the south of France, with England invaded, would be no great shakes: if, that is, there was any at all. And even if resisters were already at work in these pleasant towns and harbours, how would you find a way to them?

Nice, Cannes, Toulon, Sanary . . . the train jogged quietly at my elbow.

2

As it happened, an Italian then on the run in the south of France, and whose name would become Marzo, was about to ask himself the same question and was going to find the answer in Sanary. A widow who admired artists took him in. He was not an artist, but unvarnished truth cannot always be expected from a man on the run. Besides, he looked like an artist, or so the widow thought. A lean Italian with luminous blue eyes and the fine hands of a craftsman, a little *farouche* with black upstanding hair and caved-in cheeks, and yet gentle in his way of talking, off-hand, unhurried, interested, he was probably a painter and certainly a poet. She had a biggish house in Sanary and she took him in.

Sanary . . . I barely remember more than the name of the station, a glimpse of respectable villas climbing a grey hillside, a rattle of points and a scatter of power pylons, and then the train swinging once more westward beside the sea.

But the gods, for all that, had fixed the chances: though not for many months later. This is what happens now and then. You feel a twitch of fortune's prompting, and you have no idea why or what it may signify. It is called good luck, and you have to have it: even if the outcome, when it arrives, will be nothing you expect.

That was in July 1941, and good luck was hard to come by. I stayed on the train, and eventually I got to England. The Italian in Sanary was also lucky for a while.

He was a revolutionary who had fought for the Spanish republic and then, with others of the International Brigades around the time of Franco's rehearsal in Spain and the run-up for the real thing, had taken refuge in France. The Italians among them, with other Italian political exiles in France, meant to form a nucleus of united resistance to Mussolini's fascist dictatorship in Italy. It soon seemed a pious hope. In June 1940, France fell to Hitler's armies and Mussolini came into the war on Hitler's side. By the middle of 1941 there was not a single Allied fighting unit left in mainland Europe, and most people in France, by all the signs, thought the nazis had entirely won the war.

All the same, Italian exiles in France came together at a secret meeting in Toulouse during September 1941, and made an alliance for the future. They were members of the Italian communist and socialist and Action parties, illegal of course in fascist Italy, who had long bickered and dogmatised. Now at last, and long after what then seemed to be the twelfth hour, they reached common ground. They called for a union of all Italian democrats around a programme aimed at building a new Italy. They called for a separate Italian peace with Britain, the Soviet Union, and other countries assaulted by fascism; for the removal of Mussolini; for the renewal of all civic freedoms suppressed by fascism; and for "the restitution to the Italian people of its sovereign right to choose a government consonant with its own will and interests".

Spoken in the tempest, these were brave words; but the tempest continued. Only towards the end of 1942 did the wind begin to turn against the nazis and fascists: but very distantly, and not yet in France.

3

So the Italian exile in Sanary, as he told me long afterward, was happy to have found his widow. His luck held all through that grim year of 1942, and even till early in 1943. But by this time the enemy in southern France had fears of a landing by British and American troops coming from North Africa: something that was going to happen, in fact, only a year later and more. Renewed efforts were made by the Gestapo and its French friends to arrest all persons suspected of anti-fascism. One of the prisons they filled with anti-fascists was a grey old Napoleonic fortress called the Essaillon. You can still find it in the mountains which stand along the frontier between southern France and northern Italy.

The police missed him, as it happened: but not the security service of the Italian Army then in military occupation of this south-eastern corner of France. Through some mischance they found him and turned him over to the civil authority. The alpine roads were blue with cold when the police brought him into the Essaillon. This was bad for him; and yet he found that it might have been worse. He was forty-six, but the Italian commander of the Essaillon was older still, a reserve major who could see, by the early months of 1943, that things were not as simple as they had seemed. All of the major's prisoners were French save the Italian whose name was not yet Marzo. The major sent for this Italian.

The major was not exactly the widow in Sanary, but still he proved useful. Fascism in Italy was cracking up: or so, if still quite privately, it could now seem likely to a reserve major long past the enthusiasms of youth. His Italian prisoner might be a wicked anti-fascist but he was still an Italian and could as well become the prison librarian. There were few books to hand, but prison regulations provided that there should be a library, and therefore someone to look after it. This Italian would at least be able to move around the cells, as the other prisoners could not, and find a little company.

Granted a useful privilege as librarian, the prisoner extracted from the toes of his boots a sum in francs just large enough to convince his own particular warder that a service could be worth money, and set to work. The service in question, soon enlarged by the sheer rhythm of conspiracy and suitable if whispered lectures on the approaching fate of unrepentant warders, was to purloin newspapers. These arrived in packets addressed to the major who began, now, to receive them with some delay. They went first to the librarian, and the librarian composed from them a regular news bulletin. This he took round to prisoners whose political ideas were such as to make them probably reliable.

Any dissemination of news or newspapers among prisoners was severely forbidden by the regulations. But the librarian's arrangements evaded the ban. So that when things happened in the world they became quickly known, and, being known, discussed. This was going to prove more than useful.

TWO

THANKS TO THE librarian's arrangements, the "politicals" in the Essaillon at once got to hear about the fall of Mussolini on 25 July 1943 and the formation of a "post-fascist" government of Italy under Marshal Badoglio. It was heartening news for them and considerably discussed; but the details, of course, came out only later.

Meeting in Rome on 24 July, the Grand Council which governed Italy under Benito Mussolini's personal rule decided that the game was up: British and American invading forces were already in Sicily, and would soon be on the mainland. Some of these veteran leaders of fascism wanted to try for peace with the Allies on an "all-against-bolshevism" ticket. A few wanted to continue with the war on the side of the Germans. None of them, no matter how they voted that evening, wanted any more of Mussolini. At two in the morning of 25 July they voted for his removal by nineteen to seven, with one abstention.

A final scene was still required. It was managed by the King of Italy, to whom Mussolini now turned for support. A prudent man but possessed by a strong passion, the love of himself and his kingship, this king had long sheltered happily behind Mussolini's Blackshirts and their strong-arm squads. For twenty years this "national front", as Mussolini's movement liked to call itself although neither national nor a front, had filled the jails and cemeteries of Italy with any who dared to oppose its dictates: whether these protesters were revolutionaries like the librarian of the Essaillon, or liberals, or merely Christian patriots. And the king, enjoying this care for Mussolini's law and order which was also his own law and order, had found it sensible and right that jails and cemeteries should thus be filled. But now it became a rather different matter. The question now was how to save the king, not from the disasters of revolution but from the disasters of the dictator.

The king had therefore consulted the generals of an Italian Army that was nominally his to command; and the generals had agreed upon a plan. They would ditch Mussolini, promise the Germans to go on with the war against the Allies, but secretly bid for a separate peace with Britain and America. As it fell out, the

Fascist Grand Council obliged by sacking Mussolini first, and the question of knowing how to save Mussolini's law and order without Mussolini became a very urgent one. Late on the afternoon of 25 July the king received the deposed dictator in his Roman palace and confirmed that Mussolini would have to go. Marshal Badoglio would form a new government.

It stands on the record of this moment at which Mussolini's edifice of rule crashed about his ears that the man of destiny, super-nationalist builder of an empire and bosom friend of Hitler, had nothing to say except about himself. "Then it's all over," he said; and having said it, he said it again. Then turning to the king, a short man about his own size only not so fat, he asked in a plaintive voice not heard for decades: "And what about me? And my family?"

The king gave him soothing words, glad enough to have got it over with so little fuss, but the real answer came outside the king's palace. About to get into his limousine, Mussolini was stopped by a captain of carabinieri and led to an ambulance. It would be safer, said the captain, if the limousine were not used. It might be recognised, and already there were jubilant but angry crowds pulling down fascist emblems in the city. Mussolini got into the ambulance and found himself under arrest. Italy's "head devil", as President Roosevelt called him, was thus removed, while his régime melted away overnight. The big fascist bosses showed no fight, but ran to the German embassy in Rome or fled across the frontier into Hitler's Reich. The little bosses burned their uniforms and sought refuge where they could.

The "politicals" in the Essaillon heard at least the bare facts of Mussolini's fall. For them, and for others like them, a chance of freedom might now be near. As the summer months passed by, and Allied fighting units stormed into southern Italy, the chance seemed to grow continuously bigger. Yet the chance was smaller than they thought. It was really very small.

Badoglio formed his "royal government" with the intention of changing sides: of making a separate peace with the Allies and then continuing the war, but against the Germans. This would save the king by making him into an ally of those who, pretty clearly, were now going to win the war. The king would have nipped out of the frying pan, but without jumping into the fire.

It was a nice little plan, but too clever by half. Hitler did not fall for Badoglio's protestations of continued loyalty: on the contrary, he saw that Badoglio was almost certainly trying to betray him. All the same, he needed time to assemble the German divisions now required to occupy Italy and fight the advancing Allied armies there. So Hitler pretended for a while to believe what Badoglio promised, and meanwhile went on gathering troops to pour into Italy.

Hoping that he had fooled the Germans, Badoglio sent envoys to Lisbon where they were ordered to begin secret talks with the British ambassador to Portugal, a man of experience and good sense called Sir Ronald Campbell. These envoys told Campbell that Italy would turn against the Germans upon condition of being accepted as a full member of the anti-nazi alliance. Nothing doing, replied the Allies through Campbell: let Italy work her passage by fighting the Germans during and after surrender to the Allies, and then they would see. Other conditions must be met. The Italian fleet must be saved from German hands. There were tens of thousands of British and other Allied prisoners of war in Italian camps; these must also be saved.

Badoglio replied that his government would meet all Allied conditions provided that, after surrender, Italy and its king were at once accepted as an ally. Deadlock.

Fateful days slipped by, while Badoglio's envoys continued to argue their case in Lisbon. North of the Alps the German divisions gathered for Italy were soon numerous and ready to move. South of the Alps the Italian Army, confused and increasingly demoralised but still a considerable force, looked to its generals for a lead. A clear call to fight the nazis on an anti-fascist programme might have rallied most of these Italian divisions, and, as events soon showed, would certainly have rallied many of them. But the extraordinary truth is that no such call ever came. On the contrary, Badoglio and his generals preferred the destruction of their army, and German occupation, to any real support for anti-fascism. They feared the people of Italy a great deal more than they feared a nazi triumph.

On 27 July, only two days after Badoglio had formed a "post-fascist" government to save the king and his kingship, his chief of staff, the veteran fascist General Mario Roatta, issued a confidential circular to all Italian army commanders. Although Roatta must have known of Badoglio's plan to change sides, this circular said not a word about preparing for resistance to German invasion. Instead, it ordered Italian troops to shoot into any anti-fascist demonstration that might occur. The saving of Italy from German occupation, and an eventual peace with the Allies on favourable terms, would obviously have to depend upon supporting and encouraging precisely that kind of demonstration: anti-nazi resistance could only be anti-fascist resistance, whether in the army or among the public at large. But Roatta's confidential order said the reverse. "Any disturbance of public order, however minimal or motivated," Roatta ordered, "constitutes betrayal. It must be ruthlessly put down." Street cordons, warning whistles, appeals for dispersal were "antediluvian systems": they must be "utterly abandoned". Instead, the troops were to "march against demonstrations in battle order, open fire at a distance, also with mortars and artillery, and without the least warning, in the same manner as though they were marching against the enemy".

This was said at a time when Italy's anti-fascist parties, whether left-wing or liberal or Christian-democrat, were about to become legal once more, and were already preparing to join together in a committee of national liberation, aimed at building a democratic Italy on the basis of war against the fascists and the nazis. Great demonstrations and supporting strikes signalled the birth of this movement of liberation. But none of them found any favour with Badoglio and his generals: on the contrary, these generals agreed with Roatta that anti-fascist demonstrations must be "ruthlessly put down". It was even with the greatest difficulty that the democratic leaders were eventually able to extract anti-fascist "politicals" from jail. Many of the "politicals", like the Italian in the fortress of the Essaillon, stayed under lock and key.

Looking for arguments to convince the Allies, Badoglio's envoys in Lisbon made a virtue of this refusal of any concession to anti-fascism. Pull the rug from under Mussolini's law and order, they argued, and Red ruin was going to follow. Nothing in fact was further from the truth: nor, in the circumstances, could have been further from the truth. The choice was not between Badoglio and bolshevism, or anything remotely savouring of bolshevism. The choice was between winning a new national unity on an anti-fascist front against the nazis, or, short of that, unlimited disaster. But Badoglio and his envoys had served fascism for decades. They continued to wave their red flag of warning while the Germans, well informed of all this, grimly awaited their moment for invasion.

On 5 August, passing it along for "what it may be worth", Prime Minister Churchill in London relayed to President Roosevelt in

Washington the latest available statement of Badoglio's case. According to this, reported Churchill, fascism in Italy

> is extinct. Every vestige has been swept away. [Italy was said to have] turned Red overnight. In Turin and Milan there were Communist demonstrations which had to be put down by armed force. Twenty years of Fascism had obliterated the middle class. There is nothing between the King, with the Patriots (that is, Badoglio and company) who have rallied round him, who have complete control, and rampant Bolshevism.

The argument failed to persuade, if only because the Germans had still to be defeated and it was the Russians, as Churchill reminded any who might prefer to forget it, who were tearing the heart out of the German Army. Alliance with an Italy led by Mussolini's beaten generals was never on the cards. Yet Badoglio's envoys, as it also happened, were not the only persons who thought their argument made sense. Churchill wrote later on that the South African prime minister, Field Marshal Jan Smuts, had served as one of his most trusted advisers during the war. And on 20 August of that same year of 1943, though referring now to the possibly perilous consequences of British support for anti-nazi resistance in Greece and Jugoslavia, Smuts wrote to Churchill that

> With politics let loose among those peoples, we may have a wave of disorder and wholesale Communism set going all over those parts of Europe.
> This may even be the danger in Italy. . . .

As an insight into Smuts's mind, it may scarcely be surprising that the prospect of "letting politics loose among those peoples" must have seemed a daunting one. Smuts had taken very good care, after all, to make sure that no such dreaded liberty was let loose among four-fifths of the South African population. But out of this frame of mind, little by little, there was to emerge the great and central equivocation of the second world war. On one side, it was a fight against tyranny and racism. That is how the peoples, increasingly, saw and fought it. On the other side, it was a fight to preserve the interests of powers and potentates. And this is how crucially important leaders and governments saw and fought it.

Much sorrow and defeat was to come from this equivocation: and for Italy, now, a pitiless disaster.

Pitiful lies preceded it. On 1 September the king gave his formal consent to unconditional surrender to the Allies. On 3 September the surrender document was signed secretly in Sicily, but for publication only on 8 September. On that same day, 3 September, Badoglio in Rome repeated to Hitler's representative that Italy would remain loyal to Germany. Hitler was not misled and at once set going his preparations to disarm and destroy the Italian Army. But the comedy continued. At noon on 8 September the king again assured Hitler's representative that Italy would never surrender to the Allies, but would "continue the struggle, to the death, at the side of Germany". Then at 5.45 the same afternoon the Germans learned from an American broadcast that Italy had surrendered to the Allies. Hitler's man in Rome at once telephoned General Roatta, who replied: "This report from New York is a bare-faced lie of British propaganda, which I reject with indignation." Less than two hours later, the Italian foreign ministry had to tell the Germans it was true.

What was now to happen to the 75,000 Allied prisoners of war in Italian camps in the north of Italy, to the Italian fleet, above all to the Italian Army? What was to happen to the anti-fascist "politicals" in Italian jails?

By the next morning, soon after dawn, new German divisions were flooding southwards into Italy from the passes of the Alps.

THREE

1

THANKS TO THEIR librarian, the prisoners in the Essaillon had news of the Italian armistice, late on 8 September, almost as soon as the Germans heard it. The news swept through the grey old fortress with a blast that bid fair to open all doors, abolish all keys, and put the fury of escape into everybody's feet.

The librarian's prudent warder, who brought the news from the major's radio, also brought other information. This was that the major and his adjutant had taken their car and hopped it, leaving orders that the troops who had held the fortress were to move at once by a forced march over the neighbouring pass of the Mont Cenis into northern Italy: where God knows what was to happen to them, but never mind. Meanwhile the prisoners were to remain locked in their cells until a German replacement garrison, duly alerted by the major with a message to a German unit installed at the foot of the valley, could arrive in the fortress at dawn the next day.

The librarian, whose real name was John-Baptist Canepa, lost no time. He rushed from locked cell to cell, shouting the news, and the prisoners set about making their opinion known. While the guards were getting ready to go home to Italy, they broke up their beds, smashed such window panes as still existed, hurled themselves at locked doors, and raised a chorus of protest that sounded like the hounds of hell: as Canepa remembered afterwards, *un vero finimondo*. And such was the situation that the major's lieutenant, left in charge, ordered all doors to be opened at the moment when his troops began their march.

And so the Essaillon was that night emptied of its inhabitants. The troops marched out of the open gates and down the fortress slope to the little bridge that joins it to the main road, and wheeled leftward up the valley towards the Mont Cenis and Italy. The last among them opened two or three cell doors and threw down the keys to the rest, and the prisoners, who were French, fled after them to the bridge, where they turned rightward down the valley into France. And Canepa, now their ex-librarian, came last.

Someone ahead of him shouted, "You'd better hurry." But he

did not want to hurry. He wanted to linger for a little, which was scarcely wise. It was not the habit of prison, of this prison or other political prisons he had known, in Naples, Milazzo, Lipari, Ponza through all the empty years of defeat, all the years since his youth in the 1920s, that made him want to take his time. It was the sheer immensity of the event: within a few hours the world had changed, and the future, just possibly, could be different from the past. He walked through the open gate of the fortress, and saw the last of of the troops disappearing up the valley road towards the Mont Cenis and Italy: and there opened before him the prospect of a chance, a possible chance, whose scope and limits seemed enormous in the falling night. He told me, long afterward, that he could not bring himself to hurry. Fascism had collapsed: but were the fascists really finished? The nazis remained in the war: could they still be defeated? In any case, what part could there now be for all those who, like himself, had fought against fascism and yet survived the years of defeat?

He tried to grapple with these questions as the walls of the fortress stood back behind him. Impatient by nature, impulsive by preference, life had taught him to bridle the demons of haste and his nerves were strong. Hurry, and you might be going the wrong way. There had been so many wrong ways: the very years they had survived were mutilated with the wounds of error. He lingered, knowing what he meant to do but hesitating to begin.

Then he pulled himself together and stumbled down the cobbles that ended in the bridge to the valley highway. Down to the right, towards Chambéry and France, two or three of his former readers were still in sight: they would be among the politically awake, taking their time, considering the snares ahead. They might avoid recapture. Up to the left, beyond the rim of the mountain cliffs, the last of the troops had vanished into darkness. He came out on to the highway and turned left. And now he began to hurry.

Huge in shadows high above, the cliffs closed in around him. But the road went right up through these cliffs to the other side of the pass, and for a few hours this road might stay open. The panic of escape that had filled the Essaillon still gripped and swirled, back there behind him, and his legs were as bad as they had always been, these last five years since the wound in Spain; but he set himself to push them.

Some time in the small hours of that night without stars, pushing up the canyon to the plateau below the long ascent to the Mont

Cenis, he caught up with the soldiers who had stopped for a breather. They were all poor devils now, and no one made objection when he rested beside them and joined the last of their marching ranks. The officers, in any case, were up in front and perhaps even they would have accepted his presence. It was hard to be sure, but he would be safer with the soldiers than without them. Later on, when there was a little time to talk, he might be able to sound their mood. Over the pass, in Italy, they would recover more than their wind. This was an army in flight, but it was still an army. There was a chance: just possibly there was a chance.

2

But the major who had commanded the Essaillon, that aged sceptic fleeing ahead, had known better. Or at any rate guessed better: for the details once again came out only later.

Instead of preparing to fight the German invasion which all knew was bound to bring new nazi divisions to the reinforcement of other nazi divisions already south of the Alps, Badoglio's generals prepared the ruin of their army.

It died a merciless death.

On 4 September, one day after the armistice with the Allies had been signed secretly in Sicily, and four days before that armistice was due to be announced and take effect, the Italian high command issued its operational Directive 44. This informed army commanders that they should be ready to resist any attack by German troops. But it also informed them that they were not to act on this Directive 44 until they received a confirmatory order. The confirmatory order was eventually issued, but only on 11 September when it was far too late. Directive 44, to resist the Germans, never took effect.

The order that did take effect, at least so far as the Germans were obliged to notice it, was issued on 6 September, two days before the armistice became public. Signed by General Ambrosio, this put paid to any hope of organised military resistance to a nazi take-over. It instructed army commanders to act towards German units in whatever way they thought best. It ordered them to "tell the Germans that if they commit no acts of violence against Italian troops, then Italian troops will not take up arms against them, and will not make common cause either with the rebels or with any Anglo-American troops who may eventually disembark."

Afterwards, use of the term "rebels" for all or any Italian patriots would be confined to the Germans and their fascist puppets in the north. But Badoglio's General Ambrosio used it first. Like Field Marshal Smuts, Ambrosio and his kind knew who their real enemy was: like him, they thought the worst possible fate must be "letting politics loose" among the population at large. The first draft of the inoperative Directive 44, telling commanders to prepare for resistance to the Germans, had carried a tell-tale error of composition. In place of "the Germans", it had specified "the communists". The error was corrected, but the outcome was the same.

Hitler had in any case decided to eliminate the Italian Army; Italy's generals now helped him to do it. In Milan, on the day after the armistice, civilians armed with weapons taken from disbanded soldiers were able to stand firm against a German unit trying to seize that great city's main railway station. On the same evening, in spite of this and other acts of patriotic resistance and all that these might imply for a new national unity, the Italian general commanding in Milan, Ruggero, signed an agreement with the Germans. This provided for the disarming of all civilians against the German concession that Ruggero's own troops should remain, provisionally, in possession of their arms. Ruggero, in short, acted on Ambrosio's order, and preferred the nazis to the population. Within days, nothing remained of Ruggero's troops save men in flight or in prison trains going northwards through the Alps. But just to make sure of this, General Ruggero issued a "proclamation to the Milanese" on 10 September, the day after his agreement with the Germans. This provided that

> any person who uses arms against any other person will be summarily shot. From this moment all meetings, even in closed places except in church services, are most strictly forbidden. No meetings in open places may take place with more than three persons. The armed forces will open fire without warning on any larger meetings.

In this and other ways, all but a handful of Italy's commanding officers helped to dig the grave of their army. The commanding officer in Turin, Adami-Rossi, simply handed his city to the

Germans in order "to avoid a useless massacre", and without making the least effort to oppose the German grip. It was just the same in another great northern city, Genoa, while in Trieste the commanding general, Ferrero, whose force was no smaller than an army corps, first promised the national democratic parties that he would arm the people and then, on 10 September, abandoned Trieste without doing any such thing.

A few resisted. There were courageous attempts at rallying resistance to German units now flowing into Italy as a regular army of occupation. But wherever Italian troops showed fight they found themselves in isolation and abandoned by their senior command; the Germans set upon them without mercy and tore them in pieces. The fate that befell resisting Italian troops on the Greek island of Cefalonia was worst of all, but in some measure it may stand for all other examples of resistance in those catastrophic days. Here a plebiscite among the troops of the Acqui Division forced their general to refuse surrender to the Germans; and already, among these doomed men, there began to sound the first faint statement of a new defiance in Italy itself. Making contact with Greek partisans, units of this division turned to singing the old songs of the fight for Italian unity under Garibaldi a century earlier, the ballads of the *Risorgimento* that had carried Garibaldi's banners against dictators and invaders long before. The nazi reply was true to form.

After seven days of air bombardment the Germans put in ground assaults which eventually succeeded. Then they began a massacre of prisoners. According to the records, they executed about 4,500 Italian officers and other ranks on 22 September, and another 400 on succeeding days. Altogether, in the fighting and the massacres that followed it, some 8,400 Italians were killed on Cefalonia. Their bodies were strewn where they fell. Said a major of Hitler's "national front" on that occasion, a nazi called Hirschfeld: "Italian rebels deserve no burial". It was left for Greek peasants to think otherwise: when they could, these gathered the Italian dead in heaps and covered them with stones.

And what of the "rebels" who were not yet soldiers? The Italian communists certainly meant to resist, but those who could be counted upon to act were reduced by twenty years of persecution to the merest handful. The historian of the Italian communist party, Paolo Spriano, tells us that they may have numbered 3,000, but very few had any military experience and fewer still a pistol or a rifle. Active socialists and members of the Action party were in even smaller numbers, and in no better case to fight. Without the army, what chance was there for any of these?

The army died, but its last gesture was perhaps the most significant for what might have been, as well as for what the hidden future could hold in store. Abandoned by their commanders, huge numbers of Italian troops were rounded up at gunpoint and piled into prison trains for Germany, as were most of the Allied prisoners in north Italian camps. Altogether, some 615,000 Italian troops were thus interned in Germany, mostly after seizure within a few days of the armistice. To these, in later months, the Germans offered return to northern Italy if they would serve in the army of the puppet fascist state which Hitler soon established in the Italian provinces under German occupation. Conditions in the German prison camps were so bad that some 30,000 of these Italian prisoners died in the camps before the end. Yet more than ninety-eight per cent of all ranks preferred to stay in these lethal camps rather than agree to fight for Hitler and his puppets.

All that, as I said, came out later.

3

Some time around dawn on the day after the armistice they made a halt at a place where the valley widened before ascending to the plateau on the French side of the Mont Cenis. Moving off the road, men found a place to rest. Canepa, the man who was to become Marzo, climbed a brief mound to the top of a gorge with a stream of silver glittering far below in the first sunlight. Here on this mound there had once been trenches and an ancient earthwork, long melted into the meadow of alpine grass and herbs. He sat beside the lip of a crest that gave a view up and down the valley, and took out the bread that he had brought with him; afterwards, if there was time, he would climb down to the stream for a drink. A kind September dawn was full of the scent of thyme and lavender. Far above, as he lay on his back beside the lip of the old forgotten trench, he remembers even now that an eagle looped across the sky. A profound silence hung over everything; the war seemed far away.

Near him two soldiers told the odds.

"What'll there be at the top of the Pass?"

"There'll be ours. Military police, like that."

They were Piedmontese by their accents. He was from Liguria himself. Over the frontier, and then two days or three to Liguria: if the war would let him.

But which war? The griping of fear had vanished with the miles behind him, and he felt sorely misinformed. If one war had stopped with the armistice, another war evidently continued: but what kind of other war? They had looked for something different. They had thought that Mussolini would crash with Hitler in a grand continuous collapse. But no: it was not going to be like that. Now there was a new chapter shoved in between the collapse of the one and the collapse of the other: what kind of a new chapter?

In the Essaillon, discussing the future, they had abounded in calculations, and long before as well: there was no other wealth that exiles could find. They had come out of Spain as best they could, back in '39, and arranged themselves in France, keeping contact. Then the Germans had stormed into France and those who could had gone into hiding or what could pass for hiding. Meetings became more difficult; each crept into whatever hole that offered. Contact grew irregular, often lost. Now he was alone. He lay on his back and the mountains closed in and barred his thoughts, even now on a kind September dawn with an eagle flying free and a life to begin again.

What real chance was there now? The question as it seems to have presented itself to him that morning was a surprisingly general one. It concerned the possible future of Italy. Here was a collection of peoples, Piedmontese and Ligurians and northerners and southerners, abused and bedevilled by years of lies and foolishness, and now in huge and terrible defeat. What could the future hold for them, what could unite them, give them a new start together?

The answer, no doubt, had to be a vision or a dream: with sight restored to the blind, and hearing to the deaf. My own view of the matter is that he did in fact see this vision in that kind September dawn, a vision of companionship, a guarantee of hope, an explanation of what to do and how to do it, now and in the months ahead, if need be in the years ahead. But he is not the man to admit to the seeing of visions; it wasn't and it isn't his style. The main thing, he insists, is that he was going home. He was going to find Maria, and Enrica would be six years old. After that, he would see. The fact remains that he knew now what had to be done: somehow or other, what had to be done.

He drowsed in the dawn but the soldiers woke him and said they were going. He went down to the stream and plunged his head into alpine water and rubbed his stiff black hair until his scalp tingled, and drank deeply, and, it appears, began to feel better.

They continued through the morning, marching hard for the summit of the Mont Cenis, and the mood of hope grew more definite in him. The army was not yet finished. The army would fight; and, in that fight, he and his kind would find their place.

4

There was news that would have pleased him if he could have known of it.

Some had already turned and fought, and in his native province of Liguria. There, at the naval base of La Spezia, General Carlo Rossi of 16 Corps refused the German demand for surrender and was backed by a division of Alpini, the Alpi Graie. Before they were crushed they performed a singular service. They enabled the main part of the Italian battle fleet, joined by other warships from Genoa, to put to sea under officers still prepared to carry out their orders. These orders were to sail for Malta and surrender to the British. They were carried out in those same hours that political prisoners were briefly open for escape. This did the Italian Navy much credit, for the orders required all the bitterness of courage.

But the kind September dawn and noon had no kindness for them. Near Sardinia a German air attack hit the flagship *Roma* and sank her with all hands; they numbered 1,500. Another battleship, the *Italia*, was badly hit but managed to keep steaming; the *Vivaldi* went down from hits by German coastal guns; the *Da Noli* foundered on a mine. Yet with other warships from Taranto, far in the south, the surviving fleet escaped from German hands.

There was other news that would have strengthened his mood of hope. As he climbed to the Mont Cenis on that critical morning of 9 September, a strong force of British and American troops, covered by an armada of warships and aircraft, got ashore on the beaches of Salerno south of Naples where they took the Germans by surprise. Still further away, and in an even greater clash of tanks and guns and armies of infantry, the Russians completed a decisive victory in the Kursk salient and, for the first time beyond any doubt, seized the strategic initiative on their long battleline from north to south. Farther away again, unthinkably far away in the Pacific Ocean, the US navy had meanwhile won a similar initiative over the Japanese in a string of sea battles, and American and Australian troops were recovering unknown islands in the southern sea.

There was still a weary long way to go and I think that most of us, in our millions scattered each in his own corner of this forest of confusion, thought more of that long way ahead than of anything else.

5

Canepa could know nothing of these huge events, but the day was fine and the marching troops were plucking up their spirits. They were all tired, but they swung along the plateau before the last steep ascent to the pass, and they came up that ascent in a mood which was not exactly jaunty, yet was not defeated either.

But they came too late.

A coil of hairpin turns awaits the traveller at the summit of the Mont Cenis. They came up these sturdily, looking for their first sight of home. Of their officers, most had made off by themselves during the night, but those who remained led cheerfully over the last crest. Walking at the tail of the column, he lost sight of them as the road abruptly flattened. In that moment the head of the column halted without warning, and men cursed as they crashed into those in front. Shoving up together, the rear saw what the front ranks already knew. The Germans had got here first.

The Germans were not many but they had two machine guns mounted above them on either side of the road with crews ready to shoot. As he watched, peering from around the tail of the column, a German officer came nearer. His words grated loudly in bad Italian. "Brothers," said this German, "the war's finished for you and your arms are of no further use to you. But they're of use to us because we Germans have to go on with the war. So put down your arms and we will let you through. Lucky you, you can go home."

The trap was obvious, but so were the machine guns. While the remaining handful of Italian officers argued with each other, soldiers here and there began to throw down their rifles. Still politely, German soldiers advanced and picked these up.

He waited for no more. Behind the barracks of the empty

customs office to the left of the road a wood of pines and juniper spread up the hillside. He reached the first trees while the argument continued. Hidden, he turned to watch. Within a quarter of an hour the disarmed column of Italian soldiers had become a column of prisoners, and was heading back between German guards the way they had come. He did not know it then, but this was the fate of every unit of what then remained of Italian 4 Corps spread along this north-western frontier.

All through that day he wandered in the woods, trying for tracks that led down the Italian side, not daring to use the road; and now he was near the end of his strength. Hunger and the thin air of these mountains were bad companions, but they stayed with him and there was no hope of losing them. Nobody lived in these solitudes, and it would be immeasurably far to the first villages below the pass.

Towards evening, beginning to grow light-headed, he seemed to hear voices. He went towards them, distrusting his ears. But they were real. In a clearing scooped among the trees he came upon three men around a fire. Peasants or spies set to watch the woods? But he heard their voices, and these were rich with the accents of the Bergamasco. He went towards them. They did not even stand up, merely turning their heads towards him. He walked to them and said that Italy had concluded an armistice, an end of the war with England and America; and that he was a prisoner from the Essaillon, and liberated by this armistice, and on his way home. His voice croaked from thirst and weariness.

The three men stood up and began swearing at him: but from joy not anger. They seemed to crowd around him. They made him repeat what he had said, and then a third time, and at each repetition their happiness expanded. Then they looked at him with peasant eyes.

"Poor devil, he's hungry."
"Yes, he's hungry, give him food."
"And he's finished."
"Yes, he's finished, give him shelter."

He heard it all in his weariness: that, and the rest. They were charcoal burners from the Bergamasco. Yes, but their truck was down the valley. They'd left it there while they filled their sacks in the woods. Tomorrow they would come back with their truck and take their sacks. As far as Susa: yes, but from Susa he could take the train to Turin. And meanwhile they had a hut; yes, and he could rest there till tomorrow: tomorrow when they would take him down to Susa. An armistice, an end of the war, did he really mean it? Their voices fluttered in his weariness.

They took him to their hut, helping him with their arms through his own, and shoved open the door and cleared a space among sacks of charcoal already in the hut, and found empty sacks and laid these on the floor. They brought more food out of their wallets, bread and a lump of bacon fat, and showed him where a spring lapped up among the heather; and then they went away, stamping on their peasant legs, shouting at each other in their dialect that he barely understood, promising to return soon after dawn.

After he had rested for a while, he hauled himself that evening to the spring and removed his clothes. The spring made a little pool that came up to his knees: sitting in it, he could freeze the whole of his body with mountain water. Its chill entered his vitals, gripped his stomach, made his lungs fight for breath. A baptism, he thought, and was annoyed with himself for thinking it. All the same he was free, and the world of tomorrow could be different from that of yesterday. Let it be a baptism.

Clothed again, his feet burning with the awakened sores of unfamiliar marching, he went as far as the fringe of the woods. What he saw was what you can see today. Reaching away down there to a pale horizon lit by the last of the day, the plains of Piedmont led onward to hills beyond the middle distance. Somewhere beyond these again there were his own mountains of Liguria, but far out of any possible sight. Those were the mountains that he had to reach. He doesn't remember, but I doubt myself if he had the least idea about how he was going to reach them.

Everyone should be allowed to dream in his own way. He was not a man given to dreaming, life hadn't shaped him that way. If he had been given to dreaming, he might at this point have considered a pleasant dream or so, a vision of the future. Such as that the long years of frustration and defeat, of prison, exile, and the rest could now be left behind; and that life would welcome him again; and that he would recover the lost years, justify them and forget them. I doubt if he considered any such vision, or dreamed any such dream. All that belongs to the fiction of romance. He was no kind of romantic, and he was living no kind of fiction.

What I think he did was to look down to those distant plains and wonder how the hell he was going to get across them. If the Germans were on the pass of the Mont Cenis they were down in the plains as well. If the charcoal burners kept their word, instead of betraying him, he might reach Susa. If he could get from Susa to Turin, he might also reach friends who could be trusted. If so, he might somehow get to Liguria. He might even find Maria and Enrica. A lot of ifs, and none of them promising. Meantime he was tired, hungry, and down to his last reserves of cash. It would be one blind step after another, and each of them tough.

He slept for several hours, more or less; and in the morning the charcoal burners kept their word. They returned and took him down to their truck on the road and stowed him among their sacks and jolted down the pass to Susa. Nothing went wrong, and in Susa there was helpful confusion. There was also fear, and even panic. Wishing him well, for this was as far as they were going, the charcoal burners set him down at the railway station. He left them quickly and was at once engulfed in a besieging crowd. All these people, it seemed, were determined to go somewhere else. Tumults of anxiety harried them with fearful rumours. There were no trains. Yes, there were trains, but only for the military. No, the military had buggered off; the trains were only for the Germans. The trains were bringing the Germans. The Germans were arresting everyone. A woman screamed into his face, clawing at him.

He pushed into the station, his head down, taking a chance that had to be taken. More confusion: but no Germans, not yet, and no uniformed fascists either. He wasn't going to buy a ticket; that was a risk that didn't have to be taken. He decided to wait, and meanwhile find something to drink. In a bar bereft of any supplies or service, he found a tap that worked. Above the tap there was a fragment of mirror: it's odd the things that are remembered. A face stared back at him, an unfriendly face beneath a shock of stiffened hair. In its sunken cheeks and bitter blue eyes there was only the assurance of despair.

6

Sixteen months later, when I reached him at last, his cheeks were hollow and his eyes were blue and his hair, in spite of all those years, was black and often bristling. But the bitterness and despair had vanished, and in all the time we were together I never saw them. Given the circumstances, one could think this surprising; but so it was.

7

There were, it seemed, trains; or, at least, there might be. There was none that day, 10 September, nor any on the day that followed. He slept in the station, just to be sure of missing no train, but found some food in a nearby trattoria. Towards eleven on the morning of the 12 September a train finally materialised and was at once assaulted by the crowd. It was said to be going to Turin, and he pushed in too.

It reached Turin on the afternoon of 12 September. Coming out of the main station he saw that the time of freedom was running quickly out. Fascism had been said to be finished even before the armistice, and perhaps this was true in the distant south. But it was not true here. He walked into the centre of the town and came as far as the via Po where arched colonnades on either side lead up from the river. He kept behind the colonnades, looking for Passoni's house. Open trucks crammed with shouting Blackshirts swept along the via Po. Soon they would be searching for him and his kind.

Passoni's was nearby. With enormous luck, he had remembered Passoni's address. They had shared detention on the island of Ponza years before, but he remembered the address. It was a kind of miracle. He did not believe in miracles: never mind, let it be one.

He turned off the via Po and found Passoni's building, a tall front of stucco covered with the grime of years. Third floor: no, fourth. Passoni's name was on the door. He knocked and rang, and there was silence. Then footsteps: another miracle, Passoni was at home.

They stared at each other and then embraced, uttering extraordinary words.

"There's no time."

"No, but you can stay. You must stay. Then eat, at least. There's only my wife. You don't remember my wife?"

He thanked Passoni and embraced Passoni's wife and ate their food. Then he asked for Neri's address.

"You must have it, he's a lawyer like you."

"Neri's? Yes, of course I have his address. But you can stay here."

"Caro amico, it's not a question of staying. I have to find Neri. And at once."

"Yes, perhaps you'd better lose no time. The fascists have taken over again. They even say that Mussolini will be rescued by Hitler."

"Mussolini, how's that possible?"

"Well, they say a lot of things. You can see how it is."

They parted with grey faces, and he went to find Neri. A decent socialist, Passoni understood that. A man in this situation needs his own party. He has to know what he is expected to do, even if he knows it already.

He found Neri that evening. Not really a miracle: people on such evenings stay at home unless, of course, they are already on the run. What must a communist do in this situation? Neri would have contact. Neri did have contact.

"The party," Neri said, "has decided that each comrade must go to his home region, or wherever he is normally settled, and work there." Work at what? That would be made clear in due course. Naturally, but all the same? He sat in Neri's kitchen with Neri's wife and teenage daughter, a sallow child with glowing eyes, and listened to Neri's capacious voice and wisdom. He must get to Genoa, and then twenty kilometres down the riviera coast to Chiavari. Neri said it could be done: the fascists were everywhere, and the Germans too, but it would have to be done.

"And Mussolini?"

"No, that's impossible."

FOUR

I

IT SHOULD HAVE been impossible.

After arresting Mussolini on 25 July the Badoglio government sent the fallen dictator to internment on the island of Ponza. There they put him into a cottage lately vacated by an Ethiopian leader, Ras Imeru, whom Mussolini's fascist armies had captured during their invasion and occupation of Ethiopia in the 1930s. But now Mussolini was singing small and talking of the pleasures of retirement. Yet the Italian Navy, whose responsibility it was to guard him, feared a German rescue raid and decided early in August to move him to the more distant island of La Maddalena, which is near Sardinia. As Badoglio continued his double game with the Allies on one side and the Germans on the other, and the atmosphere of plotting thickened, the navy lost its nerve again. On 28 August, six days before the armistice was signed in secret, they flew Mussolini to a hotel high in the southern Appenines. There he was guarded by an Italian military police contingent of 250 men.

Hitler had at once decided to get hold of him by a daring commando raid. On 10 September, on the day when the prisoner from the Essaillon was hiding in the woods of the Mont Cenis, twelve gliders and 120 paratroops were allocated to the mission. But General Student, who commanded this operation, thought it well to avoid a shoot-out with the military police at Mussolini's hotel. To that end he commandeered an Italian police general called Soleti. This man's task was to order the military police to surrender their prisoner without resistance. He is said to have done his best to avoid it, but his best was not impressive. On 12 September, and as it happened while the prisoner from the Essaillon was on the train between Susa and Turin, eight of the gliders landed successfully and General Soleti jumped from the first, as it slid to a stop, and ran to the hotel guards, shouting at them not to shoot. There were no German casualties, save in one crashed glider, and Mussolini was hurriedly packed into a light aircraft which took him to Practica di Mare, and then, in a Heinkel detached by Hitler's orders, across the Alps to Vienna. It proved as easy as that.

Two days later Mussolini was greeted by Hitler at the latter's afterwards famous bunker in Berlin. The meeting is said to have been cordial. Hitler told his ruffled friend to set up a new fascist government in northern Italy. Under German orders, this would govern all that part of Italy which still lay north of the German-Allied front line. Mussolini would raise Blackshirt militias and other forces so as to deal with any civil unrest, leaving the Germans with the military task of getting on with the war. And this was the beginning of a neo-fascist republic that became known, after its headquarters on Lake Garda, as the Republic of Salo. Here in Salo for the rest of the war, as Churchill was going to record, a "squalid tragedy was played out. The dictator and lawgiver of Italy for more than twenty years dwelt with his mistress in the hands of his German masters, ruled by their will, and cut off from the outside world by carefully chosen German guards and doctors."

Squalid it might be, but the tragedy was real. For with this development there opened a prospect not only of Italian resistance to nazi occupation, but also of a civil war, throughout northern and central Italy, between Italians determined to destroy fascism and the last-ditch fanatics of Mussolini's strong-arm squads.

Not thinking of civil war, others meanwhile were taking personal decisions. In that chaos many went to ground, but at least a few had other ideas. On the same 12 September which saw Mussolini's release from captivity, a group of eighty disbanded soldiers walked out of the ancient Piedmontese city of Cavour in the plains west of Turin, and made their way into the hills. Nearly all of them were from the southern provinces of Italy, as was their leader, a young Sicilian lieutenant called Pompeo Colojanni whose partisan name was to be Barbato, the bearded one. Though heavily hit by German reprisals in the following weeks, Barbato and his group refused to stop their war. Northward and eastward, all round the great amphitheatre of the Alps, others were following the same decision. Unknown leaders emerged and men joined them: Cino Moscatelli above Cervarolo, Francesco Moranino in the Biellese, Filippo Beltrami in the valley of the Ossola, and more of the same elsewhere. Harried and scattered by self-confident German troops and newly formed fascist militias, these bands lived hard and died easily. Within weeks they were hungry and bereft of supplies. And the winter now lay before those of them who managed to survive.

2

Neri could have no information about any of that. The night of 12 September he spent in running around, with the news of Mussolini's escape now rattling at his nerves, for the fascist radio was already baying with triumph. Some time in the early hours he came back to the flat with a railwayman's jacket and cap, and a grin of satisfaction at a job well done. "Here you are, Canepa," he said, "it's organised."

Canepa travelled to Genoa on the footplate of an engine hauling a train to the Ligurian capital, and from there it was simple to reach his native town of Chiavari. The fascists were strongly in control but he melted into the crowd: easily, for the dialect of Liguria was the speech of his childhood. He went through the town and found his grandmother's house in the old arcades where the odours of cheese and wine made another homecoming. But his grandmother's house was no place for him, and he continued to the home of his friend Rambaldi, a painter of his own opinions. Maria and Enrica, he learned from Rambaldi, had gone into hiding at Favale.

That was a day's walk into the mountains behind the riviera, and he knew it was Maria's shrewd choice. Many years earlier the village of Favale had given refuge to dissenting Protestants who had passed for revolutionaries in those times. They were used to dissidents in Favale. Leaving Rambaldi's in the small hours of 14 September, on the day that Hitler was receiving Mussolini in Berlin, Canepa walked up into the hills. And there, hidden in a cottage on the cliffside of Ramaceto, a cottage perched above Favale like the proverbial eagle's nest, he found his wife and daughter.

3

Drawing their battleline rapidly across the peninsular south of Rome, the Germans thought there was bound to be trouble in their rear. That was the sense of their promoting Mussolini's Republic of Salo: its last-ditch fascists would be useful against their own population. Hitler's SS chief Himmler was urgent on this point, arguing that such police troops as he could spare from other occupied countries would be too few for the job in Italy.

The Germans were right to expect trouble in their rear, but they were understandably sure that it would be little. In Rome on

9 September, with the Germans not yet quite in occupation of the city, the six democratic parties came together in a committee of national liberation and issued a call for armed resistance to the nazis. But who was going to listen to them save a handful of romantic hotheads? The Italian Army was now disbanded or in flight, except for occasional units here and there, or else was being herded in huge numbers into cattle trucks for transport to internment across the Alps. Only the long-outlawed communists, and to some extent their anti-fascist comrades of the socialist and Action parties, possessed any organisation that would lead their members into action; and they, as everyone well understood, were few and scattered. They made a start, but under fearful conditions.

Genoa, like other northern cities, showed this. On the afternoon of 9 September the local leaders of the six democratic parties met in a bombed house on one of the city's main streets, and formed their committee of liberation for the region of Liguria. Representing the communist, socialist, Action, republican, Liberal and Christian-democrat parties, all of them illegal until a few weeks earlier, these men knew nothing of warfare. They were workers, traders, lawyers or architects who scarcely, until now, knew each other. But they too, like other such committees elsewhere, issued their call to resistance and gave out orders to collect weapons and begin the work of agitation. Their contacts were slender and their means of action, like their experience, very small. Meanwhile they faced an enemy determined to take no risks. Handed the city by its commanding Italian general, the Germans imposed a curfew and set about forming Blackshirt militias to police the streets and hunt down possible resisters. A wave of arrests at once followed. Knots of armed resisters were isolated and destroyed. Few escaped. But some escaped.

4

Up at Favale, it became an affair of waiting to see what might yet be done. Canepa began by inventing a ballad to be sung to the air of a Russian partisan tune that went all over Europe in 1943 and afterwards climbed, for all I know, to the top of the pops. Composed in the dialect of the Ligurian riviera, the words of the refrain became a password: "*Sutta a chi tucca,*" or, broadly, "It's up to you to get up there: to make for the hills and do your bit." He bowled this password discreetly down the valleys from Favale, especially those of Fontanabuona and Aveto, and awaited some response. By this time he had collected four army rifles and one pistol for distribution, as well as a pistol for himself.

Nothing happened for a while, and the outlook went from bad to worse. But late in September, while new fascist administrations and Blackshirt militias were sprouting along the riviera, news climbed to the eagle's nest at Ramaceto that four young men had walked into the village below, and were asking for the partisan command. Favale held to its dissident tradition and refused all knowledge of any such body until, despairing, the young men gave their password. This was the beginning of Canepa's band, the "band of Cichero" as it became known from a mountain village behind Ramaceto: Canepa, three Sicilians and one Sardinian, with Maria to cook the food the peasants brought them.

Next came Bini, a young communist from Genoa who was a student and a journalist, and Bisagno, an equally young Christian-democrat who was a junior officer of carabinieri; and then an English prisoner-of-war called Sam, who was among the many to escape from internment during the first hours of the armistice, and with Sam an escaped Russian called Mikayo; and gradually, one by one or in tiny groups, others of this kind or of that. By the end of October they were rising forty in number, though with fewer than a dozen weapons. Of various anti-fascist parties or of none, five were students, seven or eight were peasants, while the rest of the Italians among them were mostly from the shipyards and factories of Genoa.

They began planning small actions, trying to get the better of their fears and inexperience. They captured a few weapons; volunteers from the seaboard brought up several more. They assumed partisan names, and this was when Canepa became Marzo. But now the winter lay before them, and the Germans. By Christmas the forty of late October were down to six men and one woman; and the worst of the winter had still to come.

What remained of Marzo's band of Cichero vanished into snow and silence. It may be commendable to try the impossible; it will seldom be considered wise.

5

Elsewhere, the collapse of Hitler's Italian ally had various effects. At this point I am obliged to bring myself into the story, and change the scene from Italy to Jugoslavia: while apologising for this sin against modesty, I shall explain the reasons in due course. So abandon now all thought of heroism, and consider a worried man of twenty-eight in the hills of Bosnia, astride a horse all too well aware that its rider cannot ride in any manner proper to a horse, and least of all to a self-respecting cavalry horse lately taken from the enemy (but not by its rider) and still accustomed to the rules of regular service.

Now a horse of this background that is trying to make sense of its rider is liable to be intolerant at the best of times. For this horse, whose name was Mirko, it was not the best of times, that day when news of the distant Italian armistice came through.

For alongside Mirko was another horse, a fine prancing chestnut with the froth of enthusiasm at its bit. And astride this challenging creature, riding as to the manner born, sat General Kosta, one of the most justly celebrated of the fighting commanders of Tito's partisan army. And General Kosta, thin and lean and hugely capable of command, at thirty-two the victor of a score of skilful battles against a far stronger enemy, had fixed his thoughts at present on another battle that he was about to win. His chestnut pranced with the vigour of decision; and Kosta twirled, the master of his fate.

That horse Mirko suffered; but then, so did I.

PART II

ONE

THE ENEMY HELD all the towns, but Kosta had the countryside. From where we were that morning we could see the road to Sarajevo, the Bosnian capital, in a broad cleft of the hills to the south while back along it, northward, nestled the small town of Tuzla which Kosta's Third Bosnian Corps was about to attack. From the bracken and the brambles of that blue day of 9 September, Tuzla's smudge of white-washed cottages stood in the middle distance.

We were halted on a dusty trail between low hedges and were picking blackberries without having to dismount, or rather General Kosta was picking blackberries and I was trying to pick them. A courier arrived at a canter from along the track behind us. Halting in the usual sweat and clatter, for couriers like to make a fuss of their arrival, this young centaur handed his partisan general a written message. Kosta read it and turned to me with that smile of his which reminds me still of a man playing chess better than his opponent but not caring to admit the fact.

"The Italians," he said, "have surrendered, they've signed an armistice."

I am unable to recall what I replied; and there was this damned horse.

Kosta was almost excited: it was useful news, perhaps more than useful. The Germans would have to get out of Italy or else commit large new forces there: either way, the armistice was bad for them. Here in Jugoslavia there were many Italian divisions which, till now, had helped the Germans and their puppets to fight the Jugoslav partisans; these Italian divisions need be reckoned with no longer. Besides, new partisan divisions could be armed with weapons taken from them. Kosta thereupon gathered up his reins and kicked in his heels and put his chestnut to a trot and then a gallop, flying back along the road to his command post; and the outraged Mirko, not to be put down no matter what kind of a sack of potatoes he had to carry, did what every self-respecting cavalry horse ought to do. He followed; and somehow, I did too.

The situation was like this. A few weeks earlier, a parachute had landed me against the hump of a Bosnian boulder in a black night of scouring wind, high on the meadows of Petrovo Polje in central

Bosnia, roughly in the middle of Jugoslavia. With me came a wireless operator who proceeded, losing little time, to shoot the top off his right-hand index finger, the one he used for tapping on his key. He did this with an admirable precision but under the mistaken impression, as it transpired, that hospital treatment was to hand. It was a setback that turned out to be of inestimable value, such are the perversities of war, because base in Egypt then dropped me another wireless operator, Sergeant Stanley Brandreth, an expert at his work with all the courage and good sense that anyone could possibly wish to lean upon, as well as a heart-warming respect for the natural equalities of mankind. With me, too, there had come a veteran of the Coldstream Guards, Sergeant William Ennis; he possessed the same qualities but, sadly and sorely missed, was killed in action not much later.

Already here before us at a bivouac on Petrovo Polje was Major William Deakin, as cheerful as you could expect in a man who was more than lucky to be alive, and who had eaten no square meal for eleven weeks. He it was whom the British high command in Egypt had sent as its first liaison officer to the then mysterious Tito, founder and commander of the Jugoslav partisan movement and army. Deakin had arrived at a very tough moment, but I will get to all that a bit further on. His arrival marked in fact a turning point, for the Jugoslav partisans were about to receive British recognition, and, with that, eventual recognition throughout the Allied world. Resting in those August days after desperate battles with the enemy, Tito and his commanders could feel that their long isolation from any outside aid might at last be nearing an end.

Relaxed and welcoming, Tito received us in a tented shelter within a wood of birch and Serbian spruce, and gave in this welcome, I think, another proof of his greatness as a revolutionary leader, justly and foreseeingly to measure events and men. We talked in German, for my benefit, since a command of the Serbo-Croat language was among other helpful skills, including those of guerrilla warfare, which British Army training apparently assumed that any fool would master overnight. Admirably hard and fit for his fifty-one years, Tito talked and listened. I think that he was privately amused at our knowing so little, but at this early stage was still wondering what we British had really come for.

We arrived in due course at the reason I had come for, and which I now explained. Tito replied that success in this was unlikely, and the prospects of survival not especially bright, but if that was what the British wanted then he had nothing against my having a go: he merely thought that I should know what I was in for. The partisans would in any case help me on my journey, and in the meantime I could perhaps be useful to General Kosta, who happened to be going part of the way? We shook hands on that, and parted.

Tito having given the necessary orders, General Kosta announced that we should ride; and this was when the horse Mirko was produced. Compared with other Jugoslav horses that I came to know, and they were not few, Mirko was really a pearl, but I failed to understand this at the time. On the first day of our journey we rode for thirteen hours without a halt, after which kindly arms lifted Mirko's rider to the ground.

"It's the only way," Kosta said forgivingly, "I had to learn that way myself." But I more than doubt if Mirko forgave me.

And so I too disappeared into snow and silence, for the winter came with abundant blankets of both, although in circumstances very different from those of the band of Cichero.

At first we marched east through russet autumn days. Coming down green meadows, we crossed the Bosna river on the way to General Kosta's immediate objective, which was to take the enemy-held town of Tuzla. This was not yet a fighting mission, for our column included civilians and partisan nurses. As it happened, some "nationalist guerrillas" in the pay of the Germans —they were called chetniks—spotted our column as we came in twilight to the approaches of the river, and alerted the German garrison at Doboj along the railway line to Sarajevo. This garrison rushed up an armoured train. Our column was about half-way through the silver waves of the Bosna, riding or wading waist deep when the armoured train arrived and opened up at a few hundred metres with mortars and machine guns. But its gunners failed to get the range in time, and were left to the small mercies of Kosta's rearguard, the 5 Kozara brigade. These veterans blew up the track in front of and behind the train, and then destroyed its crew.

Beyond the river, having suffered only two wounded and nobody killed, we marched towards a hillside bonfire lit to guide us in the night. Towards morning, with Mirko practically a friend by now, I rode past the ashes of that beacon and came into a village where Kosta's second in command, the admirable Todor Vujasinović, was awaiting our arrival. I want to record that I dismounted by myself, and joined the others as though it were nothing in the least to be remarked. They looked after me and gave me food and drink. Luckily for Mirko, there was also someone who knew how to look after him.

So far as Kosta and his units were concerned, this was only a run-of-the-road night march whose purpose remained unknown to the enemy. But within days it led to an all-out assault on Tuzla and the taking of that town against stiff resistance, chiefly by puppet troops from Croatia, then a region of Jugoslavia that formed one of Hitler's fascist states. Tuzla was important for tactical reasons that do not matter here, but chiefly because its taking would protect the eastern flank of Tito's main forces and open a new field of warfare and partisan recruitment. It also opened, incidentally, good communications with the small partisan groups who lived in the plains to the north, groups upon whom my further mission must depend. Kosta's men took Tuzla with immense success, capturing 2,167 prisoners and twenty-nine pieces of field artillery as well as much to eat. Among the last was a pile of sugar; and the hungry fighters of Kosta's corps were eating Tuzla sugar for a long time after.

Perhaps needless to insist, I played no part in any of that affair, and was little more than a passenger whose usefulness turned on an ability to bring in British supplies by parachute. This meant selecting a piece of ground to which aircraft from North Africa could drop containers, and then informing base of its map references and the pattern of fire-signals that the aircraft should look for on the ground. All this was simple, and sounded promising to our partisans whose view of the matter, forcefully expressed, was that their requirements need only be wirelessed to the Allies for all to be at once fulfilled. The rest of the operation was less simple. For whatever the Allies may have thought about their duties, base was in Cairo across the Mediterranean, some 1,500 kilometres distant as the aircraft were obliged to fly; and at this time, as I was well placed to know, base possessed only the merest handful of the long-range bombers of those days that were capable of making the return journey. Besides, this handful of Liberators and Halifaxes had to serve the "dropping needs" of all our Balkan missions in Greece as well as Jugoslavia. So a sad routine developed. We arranged signals and pinpoints and waited through pale autumn nights, straining ears for aircraft whose approaching hum would give the sign to light our fires; and then, returning empty-handed in the dawn, we tried next day to explain why nothing came.

Little came in those autumn weeks, and nothing in the snow-bound months of an immense winter which followed. The hills were lost in snow, and the plains to the north liquefied in mud and swamp, and the enemy turned once more to trying to eliminate the partisans. The weeks grew wearily into months, and it seemed the war would never end. Silence fell, and for many it became the silence of the dead.

All the same, as I proceeded on my journey and in due course reached the pale long plains that lie along the southern rim of central Europe, I have to admit to beginning to feel better. There were complex reasons for this which will also be explained. Let me only say, at this point, that everyone must be allowed his own lunacy. But to explain how it came about that an anxious passenger in the midst of those bitter and ferocious battles could begin to feel a lift of the heart and a fulfilment ahead, I shall have to cast back a little. Have patience: I will be brief.

TWO

I

KARL MARX SAYS somewhere that history repeats itself, but as farce. At least for the earliest years of this story, the 1930s, I rather think that the great man got it the wrong way round. The farce of the 1930s continually repeated itself as history: for those, of course, who were able to enjoy a sense of humour.

In that decade of the 1930s there was the hugely funny spectacle of millions of workless British people whose rescue from poverty, according to the best available opinions, must depend upon reducing what the public had to spend while raising the cost of what the public had to buy. There was the ingeniously humorous experience, for the unemployed, of having to pass a "means test" before receiving what became known, with a brilliant touch of the comics, as "transitional benefit", but universally as the dole: a dole you could receive only when the "test" had found that you were living in the same house as no relative, whether father, mother, brother or sister, who happened to be "in work" and could thus support you: or, alternatively, only when the "test" had found you without marketable assets, so that a lady down the way where I was living then, along Tyneside, had to sell two cherished chairs (hard brown sit-up things, but she got five bob for them: forgive me, twenty-five pee) before her husband, out of work for five years, could receive the weekly handout. Bracing days, if comical: and no question of mollycoddling idlers.

Later on, around 1936 or so, there were other amusements to be found, such as the "national front" of Sir Oswald Mosley and his Blackshirts (not a laundry saving as to colour, except incidentally, but a copy of Mussolini's) who discovered, thanks to unfurling the Union Jack and other curious inspirations, that Britain's real trouble was not unemployment, the world depression, the rise of nazism or even the policies of prime ministers MacDonald, Baldwin or Chamberlain: but, purely and uproariously, the Jews and especially the Jews of London's East End. Great stuff: and then, a little later again there was the heartening spectacle of Mr Chamberlain's umbrella returning from an interview with Hitler, and promising a happy peace beneath its shelter. This was followed by Britain's promising to guarantee the safety of Poland from nazi aggression in a situation where there was not the faintest hope of Britain's being able to do any such thing. It was no mean performance, one might concede between the laughs, that could produce this rabbit from the prime minister's top hat; and the studio audience, composed of a selection of leading comics chosen from among the writers of *The Times* and such, understandably gave it a big hand. Or a little later, for those whose appetite for public entertainment was still unsated, there was the British communist party marching down the Strand with banners calling for peace with Hitler on the grounds, no doubt because the best of farce is always logical, that Stalin had made peace with Hitler and so we should do the same. The history of the 1930s was all that and more; and yet, ungratefully enough, it was often quite difficult to laugh.

Personally, the decade had begun on a serious note. Having graduated from putting stamps on postcard-advices to wholesale buyers of bananas for the lucky wage of sixteen bob a week (forgive me again: eighty pee), I was singled out at the age of seventeen, naturally on outstanding merit, for promotion to an altogether more advanced technique and skill. This consisted in blazoning the windows of all the fruit and mixed-grocery shops of northernmost England with stick-on transfers proclaiming that a Fyffes banana was "a meal in a moment": for anyone, that is, who happened to have a penny to buy one with. Needless to insist, this hard and crafty art required intensive training; and a benevolent company gave initiates at least half a week, on full pay moreover, to an explanation of its secrets and psychology.

Persuasion of reluctant shopkeeper was the first thing. Once successful, borrowing shopkeeper's steps, or neighbour's if none possessed, was the next. Mounting steps with a smart gale from the North Sea curling up your backside, or the winds of Westmorland lifting your hat a mile away (for without a hat you must have risked the company's reputation, not to speak of your own), and affixing aforesaid transfers in tasteful art and pattern to the detriment of rival transfers, formed the crowning moment of achievement. Not for nothing did you receive two pounds a week for this intriguing labour, and carry home in lavish wealth a lot more than half the male population of those regions. Bright prospects also lay ahead. The wise providers of Fyffes Bananas would take notice of your imaginative toil, and would even allow you, quite possibly, to go on doing the same thing for halcyon years ahead.

But the young have no sense of gratitude, and I was very young. A perverse ambition nagged for more. Only in London, as it seemed, could that be found; and besides, as I thought, down there in London a beautiful radiographer waited for me in the hanging gardens of Earl's Court. Let us pass over that, for this is not a sentimental tale. The jagged shores of love and longing beckoned with the waves of youth and shipwreck naturally followed. We were sitting in deckchairs on a sunny day in Hyde Park when my raven-haired radiographer announced that she was going to marry a psychologist, whatever that might be, and as I wept she wisely walked away. Other single-handed shipwrecks just as naturally came thick and fast but they seemed to matter less: for when you feel that you have lost everything, and even the last sight of land, you become inexcusably careless. All the same, my radiographer had done me a good turn: she had brought me to London.

I would have worked for the devil to get to London then. As it turned out, I began by doing almost as well. I used to do two days' stick-on work in one, spend two nights in the Newcastle-London train, and the intervening day in London looking for a job. A first world war patron of my bedsitter landlord in Newcastle, a retired colonel in the employ of the Coalowners Federation of Great Britain, gave me an introduction to a gentleman called Major John Baker-White who ran an organisation called the Economic League. This was housed in a rather impressive office on Millbank along the Thames by Lambeth Bridge, and was devoted to the cause of defending capitalism, whatever that might be. The honourable and gallant major required a speaker. As I knew nothing of politics and had never addressed any public gathering save mixed-grocers, housewives and unemployed Tynesiders assembled to applaud the banana lad's acrobatics on the steps, especially when he fell off them, my qualifications appeared adequate. It proved to be a bold and daring operation, notably at venues such as Bristol Bridge and Clapham Common, and there were memorable moments of confrontation. But the task, after a few spellbinding weeks, proved beyond me. I reached this sad conclusion one day on Camberwell Green when a lawyer-looking type in a black hat came up behind the handful we had managed to attract from a neighbouring dole queue, mainly by the trick between the two of us of heckling each other, and demanded to know what about the Liberal party? I had simply no idea.

But I did have intimations of literary greatness, however mysterious, and so I drifted into journalism. Drifted is not quite the word. No editors seemed to understand the value of what they were being offered. Besides, was journalism a respectable employment for a future Dickens or a Tolstoy? Some rather grave doubts about this were confirmed during an interview with the assistant editor of a then prestigious London daily called the *Morning Post*. After boring through the usual barricades, I informed him that I was prepared to work for his paper in a suitably serious and literary way: but was there not a danger, I inquired, that doing this would degrade or even ruin my literary style? Yes, he said, he thought there was, and smiled in a kindly way: the *Morning Post* was really not the place for me. I thanked him for his advice and got back on the train to Newcastle, this being before my three months with the Economic League.

All the same, in the manner of the otherwise unemployable, I wandered into journalism as the 1930s pursued their way along the primrose path. Thanks to a Cheeryble brother known as Mr Hutchinson of the *Colliery Guardian* in Furnival Street, I once held a job for as long as twelve months, being editor and in fact sole employee of a distinguished journal. This was called the *Quarry and Roadmaking*, and its circulation of some 600 copies a month included no more than 200 given away for advertising purposes. But more often the exigencies of national policy found it impossible to retain me for as long as a year. I went from this to that, passing through various disasters of the radiographic sort and others of my own silly making; and I also spent a year in looking at Italy and the Balkans, something you could do in those days on practically no money at all. When 1938 came, and then 1939, I completed my education with a spell on the *Economist* thanks to the patience of a memorable editor, Geoffrey Crowther, and his long-suffering assistant, Donald Tyerman; and I was doing quite well by the time that war with Hitler became certain.

War was declared with another shipwreck waiting on the rocks ahead, yet this was no surprise by now. "My heart belongs to Daddy", they were singing at the time, and Daddy got the girl. This girl was beautiful beyond words, but all the same Daddy did me a singular service, although I am not so sure if he did himself one. He was, I believe, rather short of wind.

2

The war came early in that September of 1939 with barrage-balloons floating over London and air-raid sirens liable to scream before they were hurt. Many thought that London would be laid waste overnight but nothing much happened except to Poland, which disappeared. In Fleet Street they were saying that an oil blockade would finish off Hitler in high old time and so the building of any army to fight the nazis, when you came to think of it calmly, was a probable waste of money. In Paris, where the *Economist* sent me to report on the progress of our ally, posters throughout the city assured us that we were bound to win because we were the strongest: "Nous vaincrons parce que nous sommes les plus forts," a statement announced as so obviously true as to call for no supporting evidence. Since there was no supporting evidence, this discretion was no doubt wise. Farce should not be grudged its climax; and this was still the 1930s, just.

Only one man in Paris of those I managed to interview spoke a language different from the posters. He was Georges Mandel, a senior minister in the government of the day. This lion-hearted Frenchman, whom the agents of betrayal afterwards murdered, received me on the grounds that an envoy from the *Economist* must have the ear of the banks and lords of Britain, and therefore of the government of Neville Chamberlain. And when he saw this pale young character placed before him he was too polite, and also perhaps too desperate, to revise the message that he had.

"You tell them," he said, "that the spirit we have in France is not good, not good at all. They must do more for France, they must do more for themselves." But the spirit they had in France did for him instead.

In October it seemed well to volunteer for active service on the principle that the first in would stand a healthy chance of being, with luck, the first out. My dear mother, far away in the country, thought that this new war was something to have as little to do with as possible: and reasonably, for she'd lost my father during the last one. My stepfather advised me to find a safe niche, but his advice I had long regarded as a passport to disaster: it would certainly be right to do the opposite of anything that he could think of. Besides, in March 1938 I had witnessed Hitler's legions marching into Vienna, and that was a spectacle quite convincing even for a muddled middle-of-the-roader. I'd seen Jewish women dragged into the street and made to scrub pavements, the Gestapo squads moving in on suspect houses, the oncoming shadow of the brown battalions; and theirs was a world that I did not wish to share. Standing among a crowd on the Ringstrasse while Hitler made his entry, an angry enthusiast had shouted at me: "Warum jübeln Sie nicht?" But I had not rejoiced; and I explained all this to my mother.

And then I didn't want to spend the war as a journalist: the war, it struck me, must be worth something more than that. Really, if the truth be told, I wanted to come in from the wasteland of the unwanted, I wanted to belong, I wanted to be wanted. Only belong, only be wanted: and wasn't this the chance that the war must give? The army thought otherwise: the army was not recruiting yet. I applied to the airforce, and answered a glittering call for middle-aged tailgunners. A beady-eyed recruiting team in Kingsway, men of no friendliness, were not amused; and the only alternative seemed another try at landing on the jagged shores. I was recklessly inviting further shipwreck when, early in December, rescue came.

At this time I was working in the mornings for the *Star*, a London evening paper which has long since vanished, as its diplomatic correspondent with, of course, a crafty ear to the gossip of all the chancelleries of Europe. The money was good but the tenure seemed less so, and I was wondering where to go next. One day that December its editor buzzed for me.

This editor did not love me; and the revulsion was mutual. He was in truth a conscientious newspaperman of small talent married to a lady of large ambition: the newspaper trade is known for this effect on wives, it is a question of compensation. I found him tedious and pedestrian; no doubt with better reason, he found me cheeky and pretentious. Nearly six years later, returning from the war to look for work again, I asked him for an interview and he refused even to see me. But he had much to contend with and perhaps one should not blame him.

"I hear that you want to get into the Forces."

His was the patient sarcasm of a man being asked to believe, once again, that you wished to bury your grandmother.

"All right, the War Office wants to see you."

I replied that I would go there at once. After all, they had to win the war. At last, it appeared, they were at grips with the fact.

"No, you won't."

We stared at each other.

"You will go tomorrow, at a quarter to one, to Simpson's in the Strand. And there you will find a man reading, I am sorry to say, the *Evening Standard*." He paused for me to take this in before adding: "And you're to keep it strictly secret."

I objected that Simpson's was a restaurant where half of London was liable to be lunching at a quarter to one, and they all read the *Evening Standard*, its tone being higher than the *Star*'s.

"Your problem," he said.

3

But it proved enchantingly easy.

I pushed my way through the mob at Simpson's and the *Standard*'s serried sheaves and harvests, and there I found nobody who seemed to answer the prescription. But up on the first floor the lobby in those days had a solitary chair, and in this chair there sat a man of saturnine allure, and with the right newspaper. I recognised him at once as a character from Eric Ambler. Later on he turned out to be one of the gentlest persons you would wish to meet, even though a former chief sub-editor of a Fleet Street daily; but just now he was a super-spy.

Over the soup we chatted journalism. The War Office seemed oddly well informed about it.

During the beef he asked, "Do you know anything about explosives?"

Now the prospect of losing a likely job in a period of mass unemployment is one that wonderfully concentrates the mind.

"As a matter of fact, I do."

He lifted a black eyebrow and I hastened in with proof. Was I not a veteran of the *Quarry and Roadmaking*?

"Explosives," I said, "one's dealing with that kind of thing all the time."

Though perfectly untrue, this seemed to please and comfort him. He grew a little more expansive. "Do you know anything about the Balkans?"

Child's play: had I not made a long tour through Jugoslavia a year or so earlier, and done some subsequent reporting there and in other Balkan countries? I enlarged on this mastery of Balkan affairs, dropping the right hotel names along the way: the Majestic in Belgrade, the Athenée Palace in Bucharest, even the one in Sofia whose name I have since forgotten.

Several days later another meeting followed, this time with superior though equally nameless persons. And around the middle of December, nicely in time to avert more wreckage on the usual shores, they informed me I should join.

And this is how at last I managed to leave the wasteland of the unwanted and belong; and how for the first time in my life I landed a safe job bound to continue, so far as all the evidence could show, oil blockade or none, a good bit longer than a year. I was immensely comforted, and, bursting with untellable news, journeyed to the woods of Wimbledon Common where I shouted my fortune to the four winds. Not only did I now belong to the community of the nation, I belonged to the heart and core of the innermost state machine. The secret service, no less.

This was not quite the case. What I now belonged to was a war-emergency organisation called Section D, commanded by the amiable Major Laurence Grand and formed in 1938 with half a dozen people. Designed to grow into a means of promoting resistance in countries over-run or overawed by the nazis, Section D eventually developed into a large and many-sided organisation called the Special Operations Executive, or SOE for short, whose full strength in the end, according to its historian M. R. D. Foot, was to reach some 10,000 men and 3,000 women.

Apparently an easy con, Section D had kept a little trick in store for me. After some ten days of intensive preparation, passed in an office near Victoria Street where nothing serious could be explained because everything was strictly secret, and out of which you came as innocent as you went in, they said to me: "You'll leave on the first of January. For Hungary."

"But Hungary isn't in the Balkans. I don't know a thing about Hungary. I'll be lost there."

They received this with a proper impatience. Hungary or Jugoslavia: could one boggle over such trifles? Wasn't there a war on? "Hungary," they said.

THREE

NEED IT BE recalled that there were next to no airlines in Europe then? You went to Hungary, or anywhere else in Europe that you could still go to, by train. Italy not yet being in the war, I went by way of Milan. There I was joined by a colleague in Section D, a tubby man with a charming air of boredom and a corresponding tendency to sleep. We came to know each other well in after times, and his company would prove a pleasant relief from anxiety. He was really one of the unsung heroes of the 1930s, being the high priest and chief attendant of Saint Rock, the patron saint of dogs. Do you remember the patron saint of dogs? Perhaps not, for the 1930s are distant now: yet countless thousands of small tin canines, built in miniature after a genial Saint Bernard and painted tastefully, were sold to grateful ladies in the suburbs and villages of England. The priest of Saint Rock should have made a fortune; only, it transpired, somehow or other he had not. This being so, he had taken to promoting pugs in New York. Joe Stillman's gym on Eighth surely knew him well, even if Damon Runyon surprisingly failed.

Our train crossed the northern plains of Jugoslavia, not yet invaded by Hungary, an invasion still sixteen months ahead, and soon approached the frontier of the Magyar kingdom of the crooked crown. South of Subotica, rather near the frontier by now, my companion awoke and looked at me with a happy smile. He pointed to the rack above my head.

"Those blue sacks. We can't have them inspected."

But if the Hungarian customs should insist?

"You'll make a diversion. Throw a fit, threaten to jump out of the window, almost anything may do. I've got diplomatic immunity, so don't worry about me."

Money passing, there was no inspection.

Trundling through southern Hungary towards Budapest, I asked him what was in the sacks? He smiled again, and with an expansive secrecy. "Plastic and such, a few toys. The sort of thing, you know, that D goes in for." I looked wise, but the *Quarry and Roadmaking* had never heard of plastic, let alone of toys.

At the Budapest terminal we got hold of a taxi, loaded the sacks ourselves, and took them to the British legation near the old castle on the Buda side of the Danube. Thereby, later on, and after the import of more blue sacks, a tale would hang. But for the moment they were none of my business.

I found a hotel and felt very lost. Outside my window, across the street, a neon sign flared after dusk. Balefully it said: "Központi Takaréki Pénztár", and no language that I knew gave any help. Afterwards, having persevered with the Magyar tongue, I learned that this meant no more than central savings bank; but in those early days I used to stare at it without hope. Belonging, it seemed to tell me, was not going to be so easy after all. This was the beginning of 1940, but the 1930s still had a chain around my leg and it tugged hard; now and for many perplexing months.

D's man in Hungary, arriving there in January 1940, had two immediate tasks. The first was to found and operate a legal and above-board news agency for the distribution of British news to the Hungarian press and radio. This was acceptable and even welcome to the Hungarian authorities. Although already under German pressure and infiltration, the Hungarian régime and government still hoped to be able to stay reasonably neutral. Gestures to the Germans were the main thing, but gestures to the British were feasible on a minor scale. Permitting this British news agency was one of them.

Kicking the 1930s out of my way, I threw myself into the work. It proved a grand experience; being wanted and belonging began, for a while, to seem easy again. I was no longer seeking employment, after all: I was now an employer myself. At the age of twenty-five, this was really something. I leased offices, comfortable and even spacious, on the Petöfi-tér beside the Danube. I took on staff, one and two and three and eventually half a dozen. Obtained from D by way of a diplomatic contact in the British legation, money proved to be no problem. It was like winning the Irish Sweepstake and the war into the bargain. I acquired an executive desk, and I sat down by the waters of the Danube and rejoiced.

The second task, below board and illegal, was less exhilarating. This was "to promote resistance". Hungary's passage into the nazi camp might not be avoidable; but it might be delayed.

"There is," said my legation contact, a few weeks after my arrival, "this parcel of money for you." This contained a hundred crisp fivers of the large white kind of those days. The decoded instructions said that I was to use them for bribing politicians.

I sent them back, explaining that I had yet to know any

politicians, bribable or otherwise, and in any case could not hope to bribe them with five-pound notes. The fivers came back again with a curt message. "Do what you are told," this barked. Anxiety deepened; in the end I spent them in a variety of ways and felt guilty for a time.

Another part of this second task was to find a printer willing to produce, secretly in exchange for payment, the kind of anti-nazi propaganda too hard for the régime to stomach. One useful target would obviously be the local pro-nazi party, the Arrow Cross led by a crook called Szálasi who was hoping to rule Hungary on an outright nazi pattern. Thanks to an ingenious and bold acquaintance, a scion of the old Austro-Hungarian imperial family who had once known Parvus Helfant and acquired the taste for conspiracy, a printer was found who was willing to do this work at night, when his plant was otherwise silent. A good Hungarian friend called George Páloczi-Horváth volunteered to write anti-nazi leaflets, and very talented they were, while my Austro-Hungarian assistant organised a means of scattering them broadside. The idea was to suggest the existence of a large anti-nazi organisation. Around the middle of 1940 we began this work, and at least we repeatedly stung the Arrow Cross newspapers to furious protest.

So you might well think me fortunate: my own news agency, links with the "underground", plenty to eat and drink and money in my purse, a safe job if ever that existed: or safe at any rate for as long as one survived, and nobody can ask for job assurance in the after-life. All this I had, and more: for magically the shores of love now lost their splintering disaster. Here they were changed to gentler scenarios, transported to the hot-spring bathing pools of Buda ringed deliciously with snow as long as winter lasted, or in summer carried to the lilting lake-lapped beaches of Balaton and soothed in the wind of weekend walks through woods and meadows of the Dunantúl, hand in hand, or bejazzed and befumed in the dives and clubs of Pest, carried further in the candle-lit cellars of Három Csiri Kocza, that blessed Three Billed Duck, and other dining joints where gypsies from the Alföld strummed their violins and sang their purple songs, till brought at last to happy ending in the waiting beds of Buda. Could anyone want more, or half as much?

All this being merely by way of introduction, I will cut short these scenes of evident fulfilment. A worm, in truth, was in the fruit. Depression appeared, and gathered. Anxiety became chronic.

Belonging turned into a myth. There was a sense, both dim and sharp, of having missed the point: of being, and hopelessly, in the wrong place. For now in the middle of 1940 the 1930s flopped at last to an end; but the end was a bang. The Germans over-ran France.

There came Churchill's unforgettable response, reaching even as far as our lost little colony in Budapest. We should fight on the beaches, we should never give in. Yes indeed, but not on the beaches of Balaton.

For a while, even so, life continued as before on the merry-go-rounds of Buda and of Pest, only now the gilt looked tinsel and the music failed to convince. Shouldn't one be somewhere else?

Facing nazi invasion in that autumn of 1940, the Ministry of Information in London ceased sending the long daily news wires which fed my agency; and I formed a new habit. We had daily customers in most sections of the Hungarian press, and Budapest Radio also used our bulletins: were they now to be denied their diet of truth? One could do something about that, even if it wasn't fighting on the beaches. I began to get up at six every morning so as to re-create our news service before the staff arrived. I am glad to affirm that it was a better service than before. As the weeks passed I devised a world-wide range of sources, including many prestigious names, who revealed the facts of British victory and triumph on the distant fields of Africa, discussed the deepening crisis of Germany's oil supplies, divulged the inner frailties of fascist Italy, and won the anti-submarine battle of the Atlantic at least a year ahead of time. The good Hungarians who worked for our agency, translating and date-lining and distributing all this gilt-edged news from my early morning typewriter, gravely upheld our reputation for telling the truth and nothing but. We carried on. We never closed.

The remainder of 1940 and early 1941 fell about our heads. Sorrows came not singly. London was ferociously bombed for weeks on end. Nothing went right. Hopping on one foot that was still just legal and another that was not, I lived in a misery of mind and nerve that brought the curtain almost to the floor. One should be somewhere else. Others thought so too, and all the more for knowing nothing of Section D and their instructions. What was a fit young man about, jazzing in the dives of Pest while his country burned? He should belong, he should not be content to save his skin. Applied to by code through legation contact, D were unimpressed. "Continue," they replied to requests for transfer, "for as long as possible." But continue what?

The question was given another screw from an unexpected quarter. Called to our legation as that gruesome winter of early 1941 was drawing to a close, I was hailed before the British minister. This was an Anglo-Irish gentleman of impeccable diplomacy whose views by now, well known amongst us, were that the war was probably lost and that, this being so, nothing should be done to make bad into worse, above all nothing irregular. But he had just come upon something most irregular, and in his own legation. A cherished vision of quiet retirement to neutral Ireland seemed under sudden and wicked threat. He was terribly disturbed. He told me why.

The blue sacks had continued to arrive, every now and then, and their contents went discreetly into the cellars of the legation. The idea, evolved with a colleague in another secret branch, was to keep the stuff safely there while the two of us found means to carry out London's orders for its use. These were to distribute plastic, a conveniently malleable form of high explosive, to Hungarian volunteers who would use it against enemy shipping on the Danube as and when the local balloon went up, and when no further diplomatic considerations were involved. Some of this plastic, still more conveniently, was packed inside small metal containers, known as limpets, that were magnetised and thus affixable to the outside of hulls. More or less you simply clapped them on; and they stuck there quietly, not even ticking, till their time-delay detonators set them off. These limpet "toys" were said to work quite well.

Some progress was made in finding appropriate volunteers to stick them on, but the time for hand-out had still to come, though by now we thought it must be near. Meanwhile, given the legation's diplomatic immunity at least until the balloon went up, by which time the stuff would be elsewhere, the legation was perfectly safe. The cellars were capacious and little visited; the British minister, in any case, was not a man to give you wine. He was understood to be saving his expenses.

He allowed me to sit down opposite to him.

He was a man of natural pallor and pale blue eyes and pale spectacles rimmed in gold. All these he turned away from me, and told his indignation. His anger trembled, and with reason. He had ordered his military attaché, purely as a routine precaution, to search the legation. And this major of the British Army, whose name I will forget, had found our stuff in the cellars and informed the minister.

"I take it that this material is yours?"

There seemed nothing useful that one could say.

"Very well, I at once ordered my military attaché to take this material and throw it into the Danube. He has done this. He has thrown it into the Danube, you understand?"

What would D have said?

"And I warn you now that if you attempt to bring in any more of such material, or in any other way act in this manner, I shall denounce you to the Hungarian police."

His anger trembled into quiet enjoyment. I looked at him and lied, but of course he knew that I was lying; he also knew that I had no diplomatic immunity.

"I shall do that, do you understand?"

Mistake, you will think: with the enemy almost on the doorstep, I should have dared him to do his worst. My colleague in the other secret branch made the same mistake in the same kind of interview; after all, we were anxious too. But beyond that we were there to prepare for what might yet be done if Hungary should become entirely lost, and now, in this small but still useful matter of limpets and such, we had nothing to prepare with. The time had passed when blue sacks could arrive, no matter what diplomatic corners the acolytes of the priest of Saint Rock, travelling as king's messengers, might be willing to cut. The minister was concerned for his diplomatic purity: well enough, but to throw our stuff into the Danube? Yet there was nothing to be done.

I went back to my news service, and, through Kurt Wolhdran and friends, to the printing and scattering of anti-nazi leaflets. Surviving official records, which I have not been allowed to consult but which the proper authority in London has briefly quoted for me, state that we printed some 1,200,000 of such leaflets between September 1940 and February 1941. We certainly printed a great many although I think we began a little earlier than September; but there is nothing to prove it and apparently none of the leaflets has survived. The same confidential records say that our news agency in Budapest circulated 17,189 items between May 1940 and February 1941 to sixteen Budapest and seven provincial dailies, and to over one hundred provincial weeklies; the cuttings of items used by these papers, they add, averaged sixty a day by

August 1940. If paper was any use, paper had been used. But what could paper do? One should be somewhere else.

The end came then. Down the way in next-door Jugoslavia, a dithering government signed a pact with Hitler. Other Jugoslavs forthwith threw out this government and denounced the pact. No wisdom was required to see that the balloon, in these parts, was poised to rise: just as no wisdom, by the same token, could retrieve our limpets from the bottom of the Danube.

This anti-nazi *coup* in Jugoslavia occurred on 27 March 1941. About a week later I happened to be lunching with my chief contact in the Hungarian Foreign Office, Antal Ullein-Reviczky. His third-floor flat on the Danube quay looked across the river. Standing at his windows before lunch, I saw marching and motorised troops filing down the quay on the opposite bank, going south.

"German troops."

"Hungarian," Ullein reassured me. "There are manoeuvres."

He was misinformed. This meant war, and war meant an end to my mission in Hungary. After lunch I assembled those among my news agency staff who wished to leave, made other preparations, and ran for it, catching the train for Belgrade in Jugoslavia. That was on 3 April. The invasion of Jugoslavia opened on 6 April. I was about to put my right foot into the bath at the Majestic hotel in Belgrade when there came an unknown whistling noise and a thunderous crash, and more of the same. Here, too, the 1930s were well and truly at an end.

FOUR

I TOOK MY foot out of that bath, and understood that bombs were falling. They were going to fall for quite a while.

Hitler had decided to destroy the Jugoslav state, as the records have since revealed, in a campaign of "merciless severity"; he was outraged by a small country's daring to assert its independence, and especially because it interfered with his plans to invade Russia. This campaign of Hitler's was code-named, very nazi-like, Operation Punishment, and the bombing of Belgrade was the start of it. "When silence came at last on 8 April," Churchill was to write, "over seventeen thousand citizens of Belgrade lay dead in the streets or under the débris."

After the bombing, the troops: German troops over three frontiers, Italian troops, Hungarian troops, Bulgarian troops. Within two weeks a badly prepared and worse led Jugoslav Army had ceased to exist. Carved into pieces, trampled into the ground, Jugoslavia vanished in a welter of violence and ruin.

The German armies at once continued southward into Greece where they overcame, though not easily, the Greek Army and a British expeditionary force sent to help the Greeks. After that they began to clear the isles of Greece of any opposition. The large island of Crete remained in Allied hands. Reinforced by New Zealand and Australian units, the British meant to hold it. On 20 May the Germans began a strong attack with airborne troops under cover of their airforce operating from the Greek mainland. A long and bloody battle followed by land and sea. The Germans lost the sea battle but took Crete.

To Hitler in Berlin the whole situation now looked neatly cut and dried. Writing to Mussolini several months earlier, on 31 December 1940, he had already explained that the war in the West was won, saving only for a "final violent effort" that would "crush England". In the East, he added, his relations with the Soviet Union were at present "very good"; and well might he say so, for the Russians had stood aside in "stony composure", as Churchill recalled later, during Hitler's crushing of France and the Low Countries, just as they now stood aside while Hitler seized all of south-eastern Europe on Russia's doorstep. The Russians were to make up for this, and with an endless courage and self-sacrifice; but not yet.

Outside Europe the situation was somewhat different. All through the second half of 1940 and early 1941 the British Army in the Middle East dominated the scene there, and fought successful campaigns against Mussolini's fascist divisions in Cyrenaica west of Egypt. In the Atlantic Ocean the British Navy was beginning to win its bitter war against Hitler's submarines, and there, too, the American government of President Roosevelt was already proving a good friend, though not yet an ally. Would America ever come into the war? Not until 7 December 1941 did the Japanese imperial government provide the answer. On that day its naval airforces attacked without warning the main body of the American battlefleet, then lying in Pearl Harbor at Hawaii. Four of the biggest American battleships were sunk at their moorings, and every other damaged heavily save one in drydock. Telephoned by Churchill, Roosevelt confirmed the event, adding: "We are all in the same boat now." And so it was that Churchill could become convinced, not much more than a year after Hitler had reassured Mussolini to the contrary, that the West was going to win: no matter how long the winning might take or what catastrophes might come between.

All this was still distant or obscure while Hitler's armies rattled through the Balkans. Britain's chance of winning seemed small indeed. Inside Europe, after the loss of Crete in that bloodstained spring of 1941, nothing remained to fight with save survivors hiding from defeat and a tiny garrison at Gibraltar; nor was there the least prospect of landing anything to fight with. We were out of Europe; and it was hard to see how we should ever get in again.

And now, to make doubly sure that we never got in again even supposing that he could not crush England, Hitler conscripted huge quantities of captive European labour and set it to building fortifications wherever coastal landings might eventually be threatened. In complete control of all communications, he spread his secret police, Himmler's Gestapo and other agencies, in a tight-meshed net throughout the lands he had occupied, sent his agents into the two or three semi-neutral countries that were left, and ordered the security service of his *Wehrmacht*, his army, to cover all areas of direct military occupation with another net, known as the *Sicherheitsdienst* or SD.

This continent that Hitler now held in an iron grip was given a name. It was called *Festung Europa*, Fortress Europe.

We were going to have to get back inside it. Somehow or other.

FIVE

SOME OF US were still trying to get outside it, and leave as quickly as we could this continental fortress whose doors were slamming shut all round its shores. You will think this very wrong, and perhaps it was. Anxiety is no excuse; but anxiety was added to confusion, and the confusion was complete. Telly heroes of the future were to make short work of all such problems and save the day with marvels of artful skill; but they were absent at the time.

With Belgrade in flames, D's men gathered in a house near the British embassy and considered what to do: more properly, now, they were SOE's men, for D had grown into SOE some months beforehand. They included about a dozen assigned to Jugoslavia with a London commander on a visit, together with one from Bulgaria and one from Hungary who was myself. If the Royal Jugoslav Army could hold its ground, somewhere in the inner mountains, all might yet be well. Meanwhile we should leave Belgrade with the royal Jugoslav government.

But the Royal Jugoslav Army could not hold its ground, no more in the mountains than along the frontiers. Soon it was only a matter of running for it. Desperate Jugoslavs tried to find their units, and failed. Others stood in hopeless resistance, and died. Our British party, totalling with foreign friends more than a hundred led by the ambassador, Sir Ronald Campbell, headed for Sarajevo in the hills of Bosnia. Somewhere along the way, halted in his old Rolls Royce at the head of our trail of cars pushing night after night through the darkness, Campbell wirelessed for instructions. These came back on 13 April, and from Churchill himself.

Churchill informed Campbell that there could be no question of any British sea support for Jugoslavia by way of the Adriatic from the Mediterranean.

> The reason for this is the air, which did not exist effectively in the last war. The ships would only be sunk, and that would help no one. But [Churchill continued] we do not see why the King or Government [of Jugoslavia] should leave the country, which is vast, mountainous, and full of armed men. German tanks can no doubt move along the roads and tracks, but to conquer the Serbian armies they must bring up infantry. Then will be the

chance to kill them. Surely the young King and the Ministers should play their part in this.

If however they should be forced to leave and no British aircraft could be sent for them, then a British submarine might be able to take off those who mattered most.

But the Jugoslav Army was thoroughly smashed, and the country too. Already Hitler's puppets in Croatia, a region covering half of Jugoslavia or thereabouts, had declared an "independent state" under a Croat fascist called Ante Pavelić. We now learned what this meant. Driving south over the mountain passes from Sarajevo, heading for the Dalmatian coast, five of us in a car reached the little town of Konjić around the middle of the night. I had known this place in my pre-war wanderings and led the way to a hostelry where I had stayed. Hammering on its door brought no response. But as we waited for response we came aware of a ring of men closing in behind us. They were peasants with rifles, and were no friends. Here in Croatia, they said, they have declared an independent state and we have joined it. We are British, we replied, we are passing through. No, they said. But happily the "independent state" was only a few hours old and these peasants had received no orders. As they hovered we got back into our car, turned it smartly, and went back over the mountains the way we had come.

Another road, further south, led Ambassador Campbell's party to the coast of Montenegro and down the hairpin bends to the great bay of Kotor. Along the way we passed a now familiar scene of confusion and defeat. Churchill's instructions were sound but they were also premature: the fighting here, if there was to be any, was clearly going to come later. At Kotor we halted, for a flying boat was said to be coming up from Athens, and in fact it came the next day, a lovely bird landing on the water. Into the fat belly of this Sunderland we packed all our foreign friends, including for my own part George Páloczi-Horváth, the remainder of our Hungarian party having managed, earlier on, to reach Greece by train; and then we stood on the beach and waved them goodbye. They could have hoped for short shrift if taken by the enemy.

Then we continued on our way to a seaside resort called Herceg Novi and found a large hotel there and made sure we finished up the beer. Perhaps a submarine would come for the ambassador? But again, perhaps not, and in any case a submarine could take only a handful: what then would happen to the rest of us? Ambassador Campbell had an answer. He was a diplomat of serene and sensible courage, a pleasant change from the man in Budapest. You will all, he said to us of SOE, become press attachés on my diplomatic staff. It was not glorious and it would never do for the telly; but it worked.

A day or so later large motor cycles mounted by Italian soldiers arrived up the coast from Italian-occupied Albania, and, just as they came into Herceg Novi, a British submarine surfaced outside the port and steered towards the beach. Its commander had made a risky journey through enemy minefields in the mouth of the Adriatic, and now was not to be baulked by finding the Italians in possession. These had nothing but small arms to fire at the submarine, and agreed to send an officer on board while the commander put one of his own officers ashore to parley for the ambassador: each officer would be a hostage for the other. But the Italians also phoned the Germans up the coast at Dubrovnik, and within a short while three Stuka dive-bombers came in to the attack. The submarine had to leave in a hurry, and without the ambassador.

This was lucky for us. Unless the ambassador remained with us and stood firm for us, the outlook was bound to be bleak. But Campbell had no thought of letting us down. He took it all quite in his stride, and stuck to his story when the Italians had loaded us into trucks and taken us down to Albania for internment. Italian interrogators demanded to know who all these people were? They are all, he said, my staff. *All* of them? Of course. A pleasant little scene ensued. Rightly unconvinced, the interrogators lined up all of us who were manifestly not diplomatic, having no such passports; we included, as I recall, an amiable but most undiplomatic Maltese trader who had somehow tagged along. Step forward, said the interrogators, all who are not diplomats. Nobody moved; but they let us be.

The reason for this kid-glove treatment transpired in due course. Over the way in Rome the Italian foreign minister, Count Galeazzo Ciano, was happy to have the prestige of holding a large party of British diplomats, and the more the better. The Germans demanded that he hand over those who were obviously not diplomats: those men, they said, are British agents concerned with our Balkan sphere of action. But Ciano refused. He was Mussolini's son-in-law and servant, but disagreed with Mussolini's sub-

Scenes from the Anti-Nazi War

servience to Hitler. He enjoyed his little act of defiance and even sent his wife Edda, Mussolini's daughter, to look us over in our Albanian camp.

We had good grounds for being grateful to Ciano, whom Hitler afterwards shot for lacking in enthusiasm. He saved us from the Germans. But our good luck held, and this time thanks to a British Army in distant Ethiopia. While the Germans were wrecking the Jugoslav Army, this British Army in Africa was doing the same to Mussolini's troops which had invaded Ethiopia in 1935 and turned that country into an Italian colony. A few weeks after our internment in Albania and later transfer to central Italy for further internment, these British divisions in Ethiopia chased the fascists into rout and captured the commander of their armies, the Duke of Aosta, who was also the Italian king's cousin. The Italian king now wanted him back, and in exchange for our ambassador.

The Italians would have released Ambassador Campbell and his authentic staff in any case, though no doubt with some delay. But a duke, surely, was worth more than that? Campbell thought so, and the Foreign Office agreed. It was stipulated that the duke should be exchanged, but for our whole party. Perfectly astonished, we were entrained one day for Spain and eventually reached Portugal, passing along the French riviera on the way.

Several of SOE's men were ordered to go to Gibraltar and await aircraft in that place: there were, it seemed, strings that SOE could pull. This sturdy garrison received us without asking questions, and in any case they had other matters on their mind. Most of the troops there had fought in France during 1940, but had managed to get back across the Channel from the Havre peninsula in the débâcle of that defeat. In England they had enjoyed a fortnight's leave and had then received immediate orders for Gibraltar. Ever since, they had sat on the Rock, expecting Hitler's divisions to come at them through Spain. But Hitler's divisions had not come, and a different problem had emerged.

In the Highlanders' mess which generously took me in, they discussed this problem over the port. No women were allowed across the border from Spain, and no troops were allowed off the Rock: security was firm on both points. Quite right: but in that case what to do? A stocky Highland major who presided over our mess summarised the tactical choices that were open. One was to tell the men to grin and bear it; the other was to open brothels.

The British Army did not license brothels and, he held to general consent, we were not going to begin now. The men must grin and bear it. I do not know what the men thought about this; the officers, though of course strictly for a little walking exercise, could go across the Straits to Tangier. These officers were a friendly lot, and puzzled by their plight.

Another and larger decision reached us on about the same day, and we discussed this too. Over the radio from London came news that seemed impossible. But the BBC could not tell a lie, and we were obliged to believe it. On this morning of 22 June 1941, said the BBC, Hitler's armies have invaded Russia. Why Hitler's armies should do this when Hitler had the whole of Europe west of Russia at his feet, and when Russia so far as anyone could tell was ready to accept this situation, might surpass all understanding. It surpassed ours, but it was true.

The Highland major opined that now we would see. Someone said that the Russians would last three weeks. You under-rate them, said the major, they'll go for three months if a day, those Russkies, they'll take Old Nosey's mind right off Gibraltar.

They took Old Nosey's mind off a lot more than that; but it was only in the aftermath that anyone could see how nearly the major had got it right. Many warnings were given to Stalin of Hitler's treacherous intentions and Churchill was among those who gave them, but Stalin ignored them all. They were Allied provocations to embroil him, he decided, with his friend in Berlin. Taken by surprise, the Russians suffered fearful defeats through the early months of Hitler's invasion.

All the same, we had a new ally.

This fact strengthened the big question: how to get back inside Fortress Europe?

PART III

ONE

WINGING IN FROM wherever they were able, D's returning men found the London of mid-1941 another world from the one they had left at the beginning of the war. Previously housed in an office on one floor, their headquarters were now transformed into the Special Operations Executive, and occupied a several-storeyed hive and hierarchy on the left-hand side of Baker Street as you go down from the Marylebone Road, a location kept so secret that there was still an occasional taxi driver who failed to share it. Growing since the middle of 1940 as Hitler knocked off one country after another, and placed under the remote control of the Ministry of Economic Warfare, SOE had acquired an enduring character. As between military and civilian, this character was neither one thing nor the other or else it was both at the same time; but the ambiguity proved good for its work.

Distrusted by the War Office and deplored by the old pros of secret intelligence, SOE was all the same an extremely English organisation: no other country's rulers, I should think, could ever have evolved it. It was, in short, a triumph of deliberate amateurism. Its uppermost ranks were filled, at this stage almost to a man, by senior businessmen and bankers or others aspiring to be such when the war was over. Now this might be anything but amateurish in terms of economic warfare: if you wanted to know what to do about Roumania's oil wells, then call in the men who had managed or financed them. But it was wonderfully amateurish in terms of political warfare. For SOE's chief aim and job, more and more after 1940, was promoting armed resistance, a work which took SOE straight into the middle of politics: and politics of a special kind. This was the politics of upheaval and protest, of the subversion of conservative order, even of revolution: the kind of politics, in short, that was rightly held in horror by senior businessmen and bankers. They knew absolutely nothing of such matters, having previously regarded them as the business of the police. Now, quite suddenly, they had to act—in other countries, of course—against every good conservative habit and belief.

This setting of respectable grouse-shooting City men and squires to the work of helping poachers led to strange confusion and many tears, and may well seem a silly way of trying to win the war. In fact the silliness was only apparent. Its rationale, from SOE's point of view, was part of the whole idea. If you had to dabble in protest and upheaval—and how else were you going to promote resistance to established order?—then you had better get it done by persons who would limit the damage, and prefer, wherever possible, to help people like themselves.

Told to sup with the devil of disturbance, SOE was thus provided with a long spoon to ladle out the food. If a lot of the food then went astray, this was understandable: in helping the devil's disciples, the holder's hand naturally wobbled. Inefficiency had little to do with that, for SOE became remarkably efficient at what it really wished to achieve. An air described by Professor Foot as "raffish, amateurish, disreputable" certainly gathered about its doings, but as often as not this was deliberately encouraged in the interests of discretion. By the end of 1941, as Foot says, SOE and its personnel were ceasing to be any more ineffective, let alone disreputable, than those of the legendary secret service or, come to that, the German SD. Of course this may not be claiming all that much.

Baker Street was deep in enterprises when we at last got home from Fortress Europe, and high reputations were on the way. Yet on the chief question of getting back inside again, problems remained. Sherlock Holmes no longer being a neighbour, Baker Street found the answer difficult in several over-run countries, and more than difficult in others. Fortress Europe was very much a fact by now. The bombers could go there and they did, blazing out of East Anglia in the darkness and returning, when they were able to return, through a questioning dawn. But our problem was to go there and stay there, and this required firm friends and allies on the ground. Who and where might they be? Could anything be heard of them?

What was beginning to be heard from inside the Fortress, though confusedly as yet, were sounds of a different sort. Some time in that autumn of 1941 an agent coming out of Turkey, a neutral country on the south-eastern glacis of the Fortress, brought sombre news. German troops in Jugoslavia had lost soldiers killed in a clash with Jugoslav guerrillas near the small Serbian town of Kragujevac. Whereupon these troops, it was said, had seized some 7,000 men between sixteen and sixty, arresting them in streets and shops and homes, and proceeded to shoot them in groups of a hundred at a time. Could that be true? After all, *seven* thousand? When these Germans were not thugs of the Gestapo or the nazi party, but soldiers commanded by officers?

Yet the order for this massacre was produced in due course. It was then seen to be in pursuance of a directive issued by Hitler's chief of staff, General Keitel, which laid down that: "In reprisal for the life of one German soldier, the general rule should be capital punishment of fifty to one hundred communists. The manner of execution must have a terrorising effect." It was further seen that the regional commander in Jugoslavia had stipulated that a hundred civilian hostages must die for each German soldier killed, and fifty for each German soldier wounded; and the total seized for death at Kragujevac, give or take a dozen either way, came out at 7,000. These were driven out for killing to a wooded hillside near the town on 21 October 1941; and there they died, with 300 schoolboys numbered among them. The pattern was set.

Such things came out of the Fortress in fragmentary reports; and they were scarcely believed. Then other things began to be heard about the fate of Jews. Even when allowing for what was known of nazi racism, these things also appeared over-large, exaggerated, or likely to be aspects of all that inflation of wild rumour which had impaled Belgian babies on German bayonets during world war one. Many thought like this; but wrongly.

Geared to its programme of genocide, the Hitler state was now moving quietly forward with its general extermination of Jews, gypsies, free-thinkers, masons, trade unionists, radicals, revolutionaries and other forms of sub-human life. This was the time, onward from 1941, when the destruction of such "categories" acquired a fully bureaucratic hand and face. Gone were the slap-happy days when booted droves of Hitler's "national front" were encouraged to show love of their nation by mashing up its citizens with club and cosh in a manner very wasteful, after all, of energy. Order was now brought into the toil of purification. With proper rules for extermination, its sounds grew muffled.

Yet a little of all this began to be heard outside the Fortress, and conclusions could be drawn. If there was repression, and clearly there was, then there must be protest. The task was therefore to find the protesters; and, having found them, produce means to help them. This was bound to be difficult except in one or two countries of northern Europe where D had disposed of enough time and backing to carry out part of its original mission, and lay on means of contact capable of surviving enemy occupation; and where, in any case, clandestine links with Britain were helped by these countries' being relatively close at hand.

Elsewhere the barricades proved very tough, as did life inside them. During the last days of April 1941, in the ruins of the Jugoslav Army and State, the future leader of Jugoslav resistance had narrowly escaped arrest. Tito was living discreetly in the city of Zagreb at the time; but Zagreb was now the capital of a puppet fascist state and sown with its agents. When the police ordered the requisitioning of all private cars, Tito decided that it would be better to hide his "tin lizzie" rather than hand it in and risk questions of identity. So he hired builders to brick up his garage with the Ford inside it. One of the builders told the police.

Fortunately not at home, Tito took the overnight train to Belgrade. In that shattered city he continued to gather his party comrades and prepare for war against the enemy. Already the first uprisings had broken out. By September the partisan movement had become a fighting force and held the town of Užice, where they organised a small rifle factory. Meanwhile Serbian officers of the routed royal army also gathered in the hills south of Belgrade, and for a little while proved ready to fight the enemy alongside the partisans.

Little or nothing of all this could be known in London. More was learned about Greece. But generally, as was shown even in the nearby case of France, contact with men and women ready to resist had become a puzzle to which very few of us had any key; the French experience is rich in stories that illustrate the problem. The man who became Colonel André, afterwards a crucial figure among many in the fighting resistance of the French, was a soldier in a French colonial regiment when the Germans attacked France in May 1940. Cut off and out of ammunition, this regiment was chopped to shreds on 10 June and its survivors taken prisoner. Young Ouzoulias, who became André, was lined up along a wall with other Frenchmen while the captured black soldiers, he recalls, "were shot at once".

Taken with other prisoners to a camp in Austria, he failed in a bid to escape during April 1941 but succeeded three months later. The method chosen was to hide in a train taking a group of liberated prisoners-of-war back to France. Ouzoulias and two others lay beneath the compartment benches until one of them was discovered by the passengers. But their fellow countrymen did not give them away. They reached Châlons, where railwaymen helped them further. Within a few days the future André got to Paris and there, on 2 August, he made his own contact, in his case with the French communist party, in a restaurant long famous even then, La Closerie des Lilas.

Many such contacts were now being made. But they remained very much "inside the inside".

TWO

RETURNED FROM OUR holiday in Italy, the Balkan contingent of SOE was given a week's leave. For me, at least, it proved too long.

London was strange, unknown, obsessed with itself, the victim and the victor of fifty-seven nights of continuous bombing and discontinuous bombing ever since. For critical weeks of late 1940, awaiting German invasion, the front line of the whole war had run through London streets, and cratered acres of jagged ruin were there to show what this had meant. The war had crashed into everyone's home, violently or not, and everyone had a rending or extraordinary tale to tell for which, however, the local audience was growing thin. It was hard for a newcomer to get a word in edgeways, and the effect was lowering.

"Where was that you said you'd come from?"

But not a single bomb had fallen on Budapest, while Belgrade's ordeal had endured no more than three days.

"So what did you say you were doing?"

But the orders were to say nothing.

Only in Baker Street was there any refuge. Depression thickened.

The girl that Daddy got proved kind and promising; but also married. "That doesn't matter," she said, "I won't let it matter." But of course it mattered; the 1930s were behind us now, the 1940s already had a different edge.

Other friends wished to be welcoming but were busy with the thousand problems of a life that left one out; and once again there was no belonging. At a party one night in Cliveden Place, home of Francis Meynell whose genius was for kindly friendship, a lovely actress sang ballads of happy hope. You would find her, she sang, while her golden hair was hanging down her back. Fat chance, I thought, and went away into the black-out offended by all those people with a sense of humour. I was still worrying a great deal, you see, about myself.

In Baker Street, praise be, they had no sense of humour. Off, they said, you're needed in the Middle East; and in this at any rate there was comfort. One's immediate return to the Middle East, for dispersal to such other destination as might yield contact with "inside", was considered indispensable. The outcome of the war could well depend on it: or so one could imagine if one wished.

Hungary might be locked and barred behind five hundred miles of nazi-occupied territory, as well as by the waters that also lay between; but even Hungary was not forgotten.

Other colleagues were similarly notified, and two or three of us were given immediate movement orders. Among these was the distinguished historian who afterwards became Professor Hugh Seton-Watson, and who now shone as the inventor of the unofficial emblem and armorial bearing of SOE. This tasteful design was an arrangement of tennis equipment entitled "Rackets and Balls". I have never found, however, that it was officially adopted.

Aircraft ferried us from Poole Harbour to the estuary of the Shannon in the Republic of Ireland and from there to West Africa, where we hopped along the coast from The Gambia to Nigeria, and then across the continental grasslands to Khartoum in the Sudan, and finally by flying boat down the Nile to Cairo. I saw Africa for the first time; and I was almost happy.

Over many succeeding months I pass in silence, this not being a story about myself. With a passport under another name and some minimal disguise, so as to make it a little less easy for the enemy, I went up to Istanbul and lived in a flat near the Pera Palace Hotel and tried, without the least avail and sometimes with disaster to others than myself, to renew contact with "inside". All this, to put it mildly, became a time of mounting misery and frustration. Gradually, a burden of guilt and pointlessness seemed to accumulate, and merge with the wailing song of Turkish maidens whose hair, no doubt, was hanging down their back but could, for all I cared, go on hanging down it; or with the acid scream of trams on the Istiklal Çaddesi; or even, faintly heard, with the din of battles far away. Not even the sturdy priest of Saint Rock, who reappeared with his chuckle now and then, could bring appeasement.

He brought some light relief, all the same. One of his duties was to push "whispers" into public circulation. These were little lies designed by London to demoralise the enemy and his friends by sowing false information. Old Nosey's armies were having a bad time by now before Moscow, far worse than even the Highland major had foretold; and the winter threatened to make it worse again. With the Russian armies standing firm after their sore defeats at the beginning, this winter promised to be very bad for the enemy. A little ahead of the fact, one of the priest's "whispers" explained that it was going to be the coldest winter in living memory; and the proof was that the cranes, all along the Black Sea shore, were flying south. Which is what no sensible crane would ever have done otherwise. It seemed an unlikely story, but the priest duly put it round.

At lunch in the Istanbul Club, one day, we eavesdropped on our neighbours. An elderly gentleman of high neutral connexion was confiding in a friend. "The Germans," he said, "are in for bad trouble. There are cranes, don't you know, flying south." The priest of the shrine gleefully bubbled. So we were winning the war after all? It was even better than paper.

The news was not all bad. If Hungary stayed barred and silent up there in Central Europe, more important countries were beginning to respond. Our Greek section in Istanbul, thanks to the foresight and discretion of one of D's best men, had made contact with a Greek ally left behind near Athens, had set up a regular shortwave radio contact with an agreed code, and was busy using it to run a clandestine ferry across the Aegean Sea in Greek sailing craft of the type called caique. All subsequent British operations in occupied Greece were to flow from this early though obscure success.

Another such contact was made with Roumania; and something, it seemed, was going forward in Jugoslavia, although nobody knew exactly what. In September 1941 a British submarine once more went up through the Adriatic minefields, and landed a British officer on the coast of Montenegro with the mission of finding out. A man of serenity and strength, Captain D. T. Hudson was one of D's veterans; and both qualities were to be required of him. With him in *Triumph* went two royal Jugoslav officers whose instructions from their exiled government in London, not confided to the British, turned out to be altogether at odds with his own instructions. Much was to result from this contradictory mission, though little that SOE expected.

THREE

CAIRO WAS THE seat of the high command of the British forces in the Middle East and North Africa, and here a major branch of SOE had taken shape. This development was right and proper but the source of many sorrows for the lords of SOE in London, because, although "Cairo" was subordinate to "London", "Cairo's" commanders were far away, subject to urges and intuitions of their own, and liable to be sure of knowing better. A coolness came between the two, not to say a strong dislike; and London, periodically asserting its authority, instituted what became an annual August purge of Cairo's senior personnel. This carry-on did nothing to reconcile the high command in Cairo to the existence of a largely independent but evidently fruitless organisation, and bitter things were said. Nobody need be surprised. All available experience shows that the only real pleasure to be got from war is to quarrel with your own side.

The priest of the shrine of Saint Rock explained this point to me, later when I had finally escaped from Istanbul. We were sharing a flat during this puzzling period: or rather he was giving me a room in a flat which he shared with a beautiful Greek lady.

"Your trouble is that you're too damned miserable."

"Oh, I don't know."

"Yes, you are. You'd like peace and happiness between Cairo and London."

"It would help."

"On the contrary. Should we then be spurred to our best efforts? Would our imaginations take creative flight? Not a bit, we'd be a bunch of paper-shovers, document-circulators, humdrum, forgotten." He arranged himself more comfortably in his armchair, and drew my attention to the case of Captain Sleede.

"You'll see, if you manage to live long enough," said the priest, fixing me with his bright brown eyes, "that Sleede will be a big name after the war. Sleede will be famous, and how rightly, as one of the masterminds of the business. They'll send people from the Sunday papers to interview Sleede, they'll print big serials about him. Of course they will."

"You mean, he'll be classed with T. E. Lawrence?"

"My dear chap," said the priest in the withering tones deserved by an elderly client in Harrogate who had compared Saint Rock with a Pekinese, "T. E. Lawrence was a mere vulgarian who blew up trains. What creative imagination do you need for that, what fantasy? But consider Sleede. Now there's a giant for you."

So I did consider Sleede. This was possible in those early days before Sleede's reputation went, as it were, behind him. Possible, though not easy. The Cairo office was a block of flats called Rustem Building, an easy tramride down the street from "Grey Pillars", as general headquarters was familiarly known. But Sleede's hangout was hard to find and only to be got at through the right connexions, for Sleede insisted on a decent obscurity. His own appearance bore this out: a shambling figure out of focus, a large slow-moving uniform in duck and not in gaberdine that seemed to clothe a being whom you saw and then you didn't see. Mostly you didn't see him, for even then he was becoming legendary within the narrow circle of those admitted to secrets.

One can speak of these matters now. His speciality was secret ink. Very important persons arriving in Cairo to confer with others of their kind were taken, if greatly privileged, to see a little of Sleede's work; the idea was to unveil for them at least a tip of the iceberg of subversion. And there, having climbed many stairs, they were secretly shown the bottles. These stood in a row, as I seem to recall, upon a deal table. Usually there were three bottles; sometimes there were four. They were of the sort that pharmacists employ, great fluted bowls a metre high with tall and glittering stoppers. Each contained a liquid of a different colour, and with properties designed to serve a diversity of underhand purposes. Sleede said little about all that, for he wasn't a man to give much away; the real backroom laboratories were of course never revealed.

There came a time, though, when Sleede's patience began to fail. The visitors, he complained, were too many, their questions exhausting, their enthusiasm a nuisance. His creative grasp was being weakened, his imagination dulled. With ever more properties revealed to him in ink, he needed to get away, refresh himself, find space for meditation. Besides, one gathered, there was a danger that London might confiscate this man of various talent. All this, we saw, weighed upon him. His attendance at the office grew irregular. His uniform became more creased; there were days when he looked as though he had slept in it.

Sleede took his measures: silently, as was his way. He disappeared in search of an ingredient, a rare component of Damascus ink that was said to induce erotic aspirations in the user, and thereby, when palmed on an unsuspecting enemy agent, reduce willpower and concentration. Whether or not he found this ingredient, he was next heard of as having left Beirut in a caique for the distant island of Crete, a destination now within our system of clandestine communications. Naturally he made this disappearance under suitable cover, and the fact of it was discovered only through the arrival of a monster bill for Beirut nightclub expenses. He had left, it transpired, owing the kind of money appropriate to a credible cover story of this nature.

Malicious tongues inevitably wagged and jealousies were aired. Some small spy in another branch even claimed that the contents of the bottles, when tested, were only coloured water. But this was the sort of libel that serious operators in the underground must always expect and rise beyond; and Sleede had risen to the mountains of Crete by now. There was briefly some question of signalling him to come back and explain himself. But Sleede never explained himself. "Those who can," he used to say, "discover and invent. Those who can't, explain."

Sleede stayed in Crete. He never came back so far as any of the records show or have survived. He stayed there, meditating; and as the Sunday serials may yet reveal, he is quite possibly there to this day, retired among his mysteries while keeping strictly to himself the stories that cannot yet be told. On summer nights, the Cretan peasants tell, up there in the hills you will hear among the voices of the ancestors, echoing in cavernous consent, the gentle plashing of a liquid as it laps from stone to stone. It may well be so.

But in those days Crete was a risky sail from Beirut, beating round the lee of Cyprus and running for the cliffs of the southern shore; and the men who operated that link had little patience with jealousy or gossip. They were hard men and much inclined to despise paper, not to speak of ink. No Pay Corps potentate, however menacing, could have interested them in helping to elucidate the nightclub bills run up so reasonably by Sleede.

"And so you see the importance of Sleede." The priest of the shrine was talking on his balcony in Gezira while his Greek lady lay asleep beside him in the afternoon sun. "He knows what the future wants. He's sitting in his cavern over there, in the middle of Crete, and he's waiting for the recognition that one day, do you see, will come his way." He sketched a gesture to the sky. "A brilliant stroke, of course. But could it have happened if Cairo were a mere sub-branch of London? My dear fellow, fantasy in Baker Street? You'd be lucky." He paused, regarding Melina beside him. "But no fantasy, no myth, do you see? And what's the good of a war if it can't produce a decent myth?"

He waved his hand to generations yet unborn, gyrating there among the sun-dazed kites and clouds above Gezira. "This time we'll produce the cloak-and-dagger myth, and we'll do it a lot better than that boring fellow Lawrence. Melina, my dear, wake up, you'll get your bottom burned."

Though unnoticed then, save by the priest of the shrine, other great reputations were founded in those months, not least by one of Sleede's colleagues, a genius of magical invention who devised "Joe's fly button". I should explain that Joe in this case was not an actual person, but a generic name given to all personnel dropped on warlike missions into Fortress Europe. The fly button in question was magnetised and sewn to Joe's battledress trousers. Then with the aid of a pin or needle, which is what everyone always has about him, Joe could use it as a compass whenever captured by the enemy and aiming to escape. A simple device, you may think; but it's often the simplest discoveries that win great wars. Other cunning little things were thought of, but not until long after in the piping times of peace were any of their inventors to receive due recognition. Sleede and his ink, as it happens, have never had their series on the telly or even in the Sunday papers. Perhaps they yet will. If so, the priest of the shrine would have greatly enjoyed it: if only he, with many more good men, had not died too soon.

Down there in Cairo, after I had at last got free from Istanbul, there were other personalities to be found in the secret service. After the provincial quiet of Istanbul, Cairo had all the bustle of a strange and various metropolis. Forceful characters abounded. Among them was the future head of British secret intelligence, a man of misleading modesty and patience whose name will have to stay unmentioned. Another was Hugh Seton-Watson, only begetter of SOE's unofficial emblem and now the person to whom all applied for light and learning on a host of exiled European politicians who counted somewhere on the Cairo payroll. His special task, a noble one, was to succour these frustrated souls in the wilder phases of their emigrant delirium and persuade them that all, however improbably, might yet come right. A third was

Mrs Hasluck, a lady who had long inhabited Albania, then as now a land of mystery, and could tell you at a glance the difference between a Gheg and a Tosk, the two tribes into which, one learned, all Albanians were divided. Strange views and extraordinary instruction could be had from each of these and many more.

But in the corner of the secret war that became for a while my own, the SOE operational section for Jugoslavia, I found Lieutenant James Klugmann; and he, perhaps, was the least expectable of all. James resembled the priest of Saint Rock in possessing a shrine, but all likeness stopped there. James's oracle was altogether different in its message from the beaming brown-eyed consolation of the father of a million Saint Bernards, and was entirely human; there was nothing about it in the least bit doggy. James was an intellectual, and his oracle was History. What he preached on Clio's authority was not the need for sorrow-saving myth, but for liberating perspective. The kites of Cairo might float amid a cloud of future witnesses to the truths of Saint Rock. But James looked calmly down the avenues of time, and found his truths grounded there, very various but never mythical.

Was James of foreign origin, a European of Lorraine for all his absolutely English style, language, background and philosophy degree at Oxford? There is no good reason at all for thinking so, or for accepting any other of the odd theories that were eventually advanced about him. The certain fact is that James was very English, and yet also very European: and so in this respect, as well as in being an intellectual, he was pretty well unique in the Middle Eastern theatre of war. Beyond all that he was the only one of his kind, I should think, in another respect. He was a British communist who had arrived in the Middle East as a private in the Pioneer Corps.

Destined to the digging of drains and similar occupations, such being the fate reserved for communists in the British armed forces, James had sunk to officer's rank by sheer weight of literacy. The same handicap had taken him into SOE Cairo: another fact which may well suggest how rare was that particular handicap in those days, since any views to the left of the middle of the Conservative party were generally held, in SOE Cairo, to be plain proof of national betrayal. When I arrived there he was Lieutenant Klugmann, but the sheer weight of literacy later sunk him lower still; and if the war had gone on long enough he must unavoidably, I think, have fallen to the rank of General Klugmann.

He could talk with brilliance on almost any subject, but what he really liked to talk about was politics, because without understanding politics you could not understand history, and without understanding history you might as well retire from active competition. But if you wished to hear James talk, and no one ever talked better, you had to choose your time and place. He lived in those months in a large flat within the centre of the city; but there were reasons why a visit to his flat was useless. To begin with, James was held to possess an endless quantity of friends, so that his evenings could be reasonably compared with the smoke-filled corridors of an American political convention. For James was one of an English kind in quite another way than hob-nobbing with Europeans; he was an Englishman, and a British officer to boot, who hob-nobbed with Egyptians. It was reported that he actually liked Egyptians, enjoyed their company, and even ate with them. His evenings, it appeared, were filled with Egyptians. Navigating through a fog of smoke and persons dimly seen, you would find him in the heart and centre of an endless discussion, his spectacles beclouded with the steam of proximate bodies, his peering gaze obscured with the mist of a cigarette that he was never without, his stained forefinger pointing down the avenues of time, where, no matter how bestrewn with proximate bodies, the perspectives of the war stood clear and plain.

A better place for talk was out by Mena House in the shadow of the Great Pyramids of Gizeh. There, in a square-built villa behind a high stone wall, James spent some of his afternoons. The villa had belonged to a local purveyor of professional delight, and its interior was decorated with an appropriate shade of pink and plenty of standard lamps long since loaded with the dust of warlike misery, but still supplied with shades of watered silk. Fallen now upon junior officers' salaries, and even sergeants' pay, the place had once been fit for pashas. But James was undoubtedly happy there. He took off his cap and his belt and loosened the jacket of a uniform clearly made for someone else, and became, if that were possible, still more himself. Supposing you had the right of entry, you saw him then in all the secrecy of sheer enjoyment. Melina's lissom curves might soothe the priest of Saint Rock as the white breasts of Dover welcome the wanderer home from the sea. The consolations of Klugmann were on a larger scale, more fully rounded in perfection as the Scripture sayeth, and of a variety that could not cloy. An intellectual ascetic, he went naturally to extremes. He could be satisfied with a single partner, if one were all that came to hand, but reached his full elevation and relief only with the stimulus of many.

James, in short, lectured. He might talk to you later, but meanwhile you were patient while he sat upon a little table and talked to his assembled audience: choking from the smoke of the cigarette between his lips, raising sympathetic laughs, interrupting himself to wipe his spectacles, blinking encouragement at questions, fielding all disputes and continually adding to his edifice of explanation, to his tracing of history along the avenues we had lived and forward into those we were about to enter. In listening at the villa out by Mena House you were taken gently by the hand and shown the kingdoms of this world, and what they were, and how they worked: not in order to possess them, but to understand.

Closed to prying eyes behind a high wall, James's audience lived for his lectures. Hidden away, forbidden to go out, strictly clandestine, they considered him their only lifeline. A singular audience, they were craggy men with huge shoulders, hard of face, their hands clawed with toil, and as stubbornly powerful in their convictions. Difficult to sidetrack and impossible to persuade, they were open to an explanation only if it came from James. To other would-be mollifiers they returned a glare of steady disbelief. At Rustem Building, among the few who were allowed to know of their existence, there was fear of trouble.

And who were they, you may well ask, this audience of subversives? Why was security not upon their track? We might be in alliance with the Soviet Union, in this year of 1942, and officially in love with Russia and all things Russian: but even so, surely there were limits to irresponsibility? Matters were more complex than you might imagine. I will explain.

I heard of the people in the villa out by Mena House only after my Istanbul misery was over. Down the list of officers whom I was then appointed to command there stood the name of Lt Klugmann. Who was he, I asked, and what did he do? They hastened to explain that he looked after the Canadian Jugoslavs. "You'll find," they added, "that you can't do without him. Those Jugs will listen to nobody else, and they're very upset."

The facts, giving no room for fantasy at all, turned out to be these. Back in the worst days of defeat when Fortress Europe slammed its doors and Hitler built its fortifications, certain emissaries of SOE at work across the Atlantic had taken thought for the morrow. If Hitler's invasion of England should fail, they argued, there must come a time when the doors of Europe could be forced from outside. Among other things, this would call for parachuting missions into Jugoslavia, and these missions would best be manned or assisted by natives of that country who spoke the language as their own and could hope to find good cover. British officers and other ranks there were to volunteer for that, but only the merest handful knew Jugoslavia and its languages. One of these, Captain Hudson, had landed from the submarine *Triumph* on the shores of Montenegro in September 1941. His radio had functioned for a while, and he was still there; but little else was known of him. Captain Atherton, parachuted later, had been murdered by bandits.

So the emissaries of SOE across the Atlantic looked for volunteers among Jugoslav emigrants in Canada. They found some with difficulty and chose about thirty. All were miners of strong revolutionary convictions. Yet needs must when the devil drives, and these were brought to Cairo where they were kept in the villa out by Mena House until such time as they could be sent to Jugoslavia, together with a young Londoner of Jugoslav origin called Alexander Simitch. Later on, with Simitch as the indispensable wireless operator, a team of these volunteers would be dropped blind—without, that is, a pre-arranged reception on the ground— into the hills of Jugoslavia and make the crucial British contact with Tito's partisans. No one in British authority was ever going to thank them for doing it, of course, for they were unimportant persons and were only going, after all, where they had wished to go. But at this time their chances of going to join Tito's partisans looked so small as barely to exist; and this was why, being men of no fantasy, they were full of anger and dismay.

The fact is that politics moved in at this period, around the last months of 1942, and unavoidably; or, as James said, reality came home to roost. It could even be called the Klugmann period and it changed a great deal; even the priest of Saint Rock, for whom politics was the death of fantasy and consequently a bad thing, was affected by the change. Along the avenues of time this war of ours grew serious at last. The music and its meaning struck a sharp note now.

"We are involved in a contradiction," said James in the villa out by Mena House, "you have to understand that." Following his pointed forefinger, the Canadian Jugoslavs did understand it.

They also disliked it. While British policy and the BBC continued carefully to suppress all reference to the Jugoslav partisans, the Canadian Jugoslavs were acutely aware of their existence. That was why they had volunteered to come from Canada: they wanted to become partisans themselves. Now, it appeared, the British refused all contact with the partisans in favour of contact only with Royal Jugoslav Army officers commanded by the chetnik leader, General Mihajlović. But to get away from Royal Jugoslav Army officers and everything they stood for had formed one large reason for their having gone to Canada in the first place, and they were certainly not going to return to any kind of royal Jugoslavia. Craggily, they said so. Patience, replied James, and pointed down the avenues. All would be well; the dialectics of history were at work.

It seemed quite unlikely then that James could be right, and the villa out by Mena House growled with revolt. Yet the period of politics had none the less begun. In tremendous battles near and far, the war turned over on itself.

FOUR

I

A LITTLE EARLIER, although well into that summer of 1942, I had managed to get away from Istanbul. With Hungary motionless or almost so, and good men lost in trying to make it move an inch or two, a request for transfer was at last accepted. This seemed surprising. Along the avenues of time, even the name of Tito remained obscure for those of us concerned with Jugoslavia; while in Italy nothing stirred, or nothing that we knew of. Elsewhere, yes: the walls were breached in northern Europe, if very narrowly as yet, and here in the south our caiques steered for Greece across the wine-dark Mediterranean. But what could there be in any of that for me?

Awaiting transfer, one of Saint Rock's duties became available. The caiques needed high explosive, and someone had to fetch it for them. Just where and how the caiques were loaded in Turkey remains, I think, an item on the secret list. All I can say is that I went up and down between Istanbul and Palestine, armed with an illuminated parchment conveying the immunity of a king's messenger, and returned each time with a consignment of blue sacks. There was nothing remotely dangerous in doing this, but for an anxious man it brought a little comfort. Coming back, demon Arab drivers delivered the sacks and me to the Turkish frontier and the train across Anatolia.

Istanbul seemed more beautiful than ever the last time that I came there from Palestine: perhaps because farewell, as with the girl that Daddy got, could not help but make it so. The Anatolian railway went right up to the waters of the Bosporus, uncrossed then by any bridge, and terminated at the station of Haydar Pasha. I expect it still does. And from the quayside here on the Asian shore of the Bosporus, there was the unforgettable beckoning of Stambul on the other shore and the minarets of Aya Sofia and her companion mosques, slim fingers to the sky above the rig and ruck of ships in the Golden Horn, and along from these, moving east, the bridge of Pera choked with distant ferries and again, further along, the rising hill of Pera and the cliffs of old Byzantium all barely visible through mist and evening sunlight where they housed, white shadows in the dusk, the fretworked palaces of forgotten lords and pashas.

The ferry was approaching in a flurry of spray beside Leander's lighthouse with a scoop of gulls keening in its wake. Waiting for it, I stood among the blue sacks I had brought, eight of them this time, and counted timidly lest one should go astray. The ferry came in with a clatter of passengers and chicken coops and peasant bundles, and a porter helped me carry the sacks on board. By now the night was falling and the ferry moved towards a mist of stars. They seemed the symbols of an ancient and ingrained defeat presiding over the forgotten and the lost, including me. Even the war was far away.

Not elsewhere, though. Down in Palestine and Egypt a great stir was on that August. Rommel and his Afrika Corps with sundry of Mussolini's fascist divisions were approaching the valley of the Nile; and for a while it seemed that nobody would stop them. Huge quantities of paper were burned in Cairo instead of typed upon, and at Rustem Building the men of SOE prepared to withdraw to Jerusalem. In this hopeful moment London saw its chance, and pounced with a purge still more severe than usual. Everything was to be reorganised. Dignified lawyers and businessmen disguised as majors and colonels were to vanish from the Cairo scene, and others of their kind, likewise transformed, were to appear instead. But there was more: new military commanders were to be appointed by the army, and now, in this period when politics moved in, these soldiers were to exercise themselves in SOE Cairo. The period of politics began in wonderful confusion.

But good came with it. I received a new appointment.

In Jerusalem there was Colonel Guy Tamplin taking charge. He was, to begin with, an unnerving figure: tall and thin, greatly brisk, and carrying about him the air of a man who meant, at long last, to put some sense into this gang of wretched bunglers whom he was now entrusted to command. It turned out rather differently in the end, but the end was not yet. Now the moment was for crisp decision. "We are," he said, when interviewing the lugubrious transferee from Istanbul, "reorganising the whole bag of tricks." There was need for a new spirit of initiative, a sense of urgency, a will to get things done.

Listening to Tamplin, I felt ever more hopeless: he was obviously bound to turn me down. Had I ever got anything done? Was there the slightest evidence of a spirit of initiative? Illegal pamphlets, paper, newspaper bulletins: I hadn't the nerve to mention them. A remote regimental depot in the Middle East, last exile of the unemployable, was going to be my fate. But the avenues of time contain surprises, as James would certainly have said if James had been there to say it; and the colonel decided that the transferee should have the job.

"You will be G2 of our Jugoslav section."

He had a trick, while talking, of seeming to forget what he intended to say next. I became used to this, but in that first moment it was more than alarming. A G2, I learned later, was a GSO 2, or General Staff Officer second class, this being the rank of officer appointed to direct operational command of each of SOE Cairo's "country sections": for Jugoslavia, Greece, and so on.

I knew nothing of this at the time, and I kept my mouth shut, hoping for a clue or so, but Colonel Tamplin paused at this most anxious juncture and looked around as though some vital element were missing. I thought I knew what it must be; but it was only his cigarette lighter. Finding this, he lit up and rattled a silver chain and identity disk that he wore on his wrist. This seemed to bring the war a little nearer, but in fact, as I found out after, the disk was a relic of the Polish campaign of 1939 in which, being until then the manager of a British bank in Poland, the colonel had played some part. I had taken Tamplin for a regular of the truest blue; but this colour, as it came out later, applied only to his political opinions.

"Let's see, you're a captain. Well, you'll be promoted major, it goes with the job. You will take over the operational control, under me, of our links with Jugoslavia. Your experience, I repeat, will be useful."

He was indeed a kindly man, if sadly muddled.

With Rommel held and the flap over, we returned to Cairo almost at once. I put up my shoulder crown and occupied a five-roomed office in Rustem Building and inspected my new job.

Its chief duty, as it turned out, was to select volunteers among officers available from the army in the Middle East, and send them by parachute, together with wireless operators who were also volunteers, to groups of "nationalist guerrillas" in Jugoslavia. These were called chetniks.

It was the same old thing again, in short: sending others in and staying out oneself. Could one not go oneself? No, said Tamplin, one could not. Could one go later? Improbably. Proper soldiers, it appeared, were needed for that; there had to be an end to amateurish bungling. Could one, at least, do a parachute course? Very well, if that was all I wanted: Tamplin really was a kindly man, and hated to be badgered. So the newly-appointed G2 Jugoslavia went down to the Great Bitter Lake, half-way along the Suez Canal between the Mediterranean and the Red Sea, and swung from swings and threw himself from moving trucks and duly wrenched an ankle on his first jump, which seemed appropriate.

The sending in of others continued, and depression closed in again. An entirely fresh start now seemed the only hope. Duly approached with an offer to exchange a major's crown for the rankless sleeve of an aircraftsman bottom class, a senior group-captain reached by cunning and connexions thought the proposal a poor sort of joke. What kind of people did I think the air force wanted?

So the sending in continued. But the scenario began to change. It changed amazingly. When all hope for me seemed gone, life began again: more accurately, life began.

2

The Afrika Corps was stopped less than a hundred kilometres from the Nile and its crucial cities of Cairo and Alexandria, and was then attacked in force by British 8 Army on 23 October. On 4 November the battle of El Alamein was over and won, and the Germans were in full retreat to the west. They were followed hard. The great struggle for the Middle East, and soon for the whole of North Africa, was nearing an end.

Another decisive turning point came in Russia at much the same time. In August 1942 Hitler's southern armies, pushing ever more deeply into the backlands of the Soviet Union, reached the banks of the lower Volga and the outskirts of the city of Stalingrad, which they were ordered to take at all costs. But the Russians had the measure of their invaders by now. Holding house by house under a suffocating weight of bomb and shell, they clung to their city. As Russian and German reinforcements began to assemble, a tremendous contest continued to unfold. And the Russians won it. They encircled the besieging Germans late in November during a major counter-offensive planned by Marshal Zhukov. Hitler put his prestige into the balance, ordering his generals to stand where they were. On 31 January 1943, they could stand no longer and surrendered. The Russians, killing or capturing more than 300,000 of Hitler's troops, completed the greatest single victory of the whole war. Stalingrad became the symbol of nazi defeat.

All this, meaning for us the relief of Egypt and a practical guarantee that the relief was permanent, radically improved the prospect of breaking into Fortress Europe from across the seas. The strategic initiative in the Mediterranean swung decisively to our side, and this was now confirmed by the landing of an American and British army at the western end of North Africa, promising a rapid junction with the British shoving westward through Tunisia. With all North Africa soon cleared, the way then lay open to Italy and afterwards to southern France. On 10 July 1943, British and American troops were going to cross the Mediterranean and invade Sicily.

That is running ahead a little. Duly reorganised in August and September 1942 and known now to the outside world as MO4, SOE Cairo could see that its hour had struck. Already there were regular radio links with British liaison personnel sent to the chetnik groups of General Mihajlović in Jugoslavia, while other missions had joined fighting groups in Greece and Crete. The task was to reinforce these groups with arms and medical supplies, and despatch new British missions to other groups that were thought to exist or might now emerge. But SOE Cairo still had problems.

Transport was one of them. With the desert war drawing to a close, volunteers came easily to hand. But how to send them? Caiques went back and forth to Crete and even to the southern shores of Greece; but going further, and going inland, called for dropping men and supplies from long-range aircraft. These had to be big bombers; and all bombers were in desperately short supply. Those capable of going as far as ground signals in Jugoslavia or northern Greece had to be Liberators. Bomber command was prepared to allow us for this purpose, in those last months of 1942, precisely four such aircraft. Manned by staunch New Zealand aircrews, these four were driven back and forth on very long journeys, night after night; and soon enough the average number fit for service was down to one or two.

But a worse problem barged upon the scene. This was the politics I have mentioned. Armed resistance in Greece and Jugoslavia was clearly growing in size and strike power month by month. Nothing simpler, then: do all you can to back it up, and select, if you must, the most combative. Not so: for this resistance, we now learned, was divided within itself. There were right-wing forces or those who claimed to be such; and there were left-wing forces who certainly existed. Could you get them to work together? Not easily, it seemed; even not at all. Could you select the most combative? But this meant selecting the left-wing forces. Would high policy approve of that? Over, said high policy, its dead body. Problem.

It all grew gradually clear even to political innocents like myself. In Greece and Jugoslavia, and to varying degree in all other occupied countries, large and serious resistance came and could only come under left-wing leadership and inspiration. Whole ruling classes had collapsed in defeat or moved into compromise with the nazis. With notable exceptions, the beaten generals and all their kind followed their governments and kings into exile, went into retirement, or took service with the nazi occupiers. Some believed they could conciliate the conquerors; others despaired of any rescue; not a few shared the beliefs and aims of the nazis. Preaching the unification of a nazified Europe, Hitler was able to win fighting volunteers from every occupied country.

Again with exceptions, the right-wing sold out and the centre simply vanished from the scene. Here and there patriotic officers tried to stand against this collapse, and called for resistance in the name of king and conservatism. Yet the people to whom they called proved reluctant or quite unwilling to follow them. Plenty of ordinary folk were ready to risk their lives, but only, as it soon transpired, if they were not risking them for king and conservatism. In these countries of bitter pre-war dictatorships, it further transpired, the self-sacrifice and vision required to begin an effective resistance, and then rally others to the same cause, were found only among radicals and revolutionaries. Exceptions there were; but such was the general rule. And again, in practice, this leadership was found above all among the men and women of harried and clandestine communist parties whose remnants were still uncowed by persecution.

These communists were generally men and women of an unusual courage and moral purpose; lesser qualities would have ditched them long before. But they had problems of their own. For years they had operated, and been obliged to operate, as severely closed societies for whom all wisdom came, at every point of stiff decision, from the Comintern in Moscow: from the leaders, that is, of the Third International. We shall scarcely know what this meant to them until the archives of the Comintern become open for inspection.

But there is little doubt that what it meant to them by the early 1940s, if not before, was obedience to the personal decisions, or the personal changes of decisions, of Stalin himself. There, too, we are still pretty much in the dark, for while we have since learned much about Stalinist terror we have yet to penetrate the mechanisms and calculations of Stalinist policy. Who precisely was responsible for what, and why, and from which real motivations? This book is in any case not offered as a retrospective analysis. All that was clear at the time was the general effect.

Barricaded behind their obedience, and seeing in this obedience the acid test of their own value as well as the value of their internationalism, the communists followed Moscow through thick and thin. If Moscow said they must unsay today what they had affirmed the day before, they gritted their teeth and unsaid it. Even if Moscow took the lives of their comrades, they looked the other way. Nothing stopped them, or most of them: neither dreadful persecution nor fearful doubt. The faint-hearted were left by the wayside. The recalcitrant were cast into outer darkness. Orthodoxy had become all.

This was the discipline that shaped a whole quality of clandestine life; and this in turn was the quality, within the sealed ranks of these parties which had become sects, that engendered the will and courage to lead resistance to a ruthless and all-conquering enemy. Couldn't they have done far better with a democratic discipline? Wasn't their Stalinism a major obstacle, an invitation to disaster? It is easy to think so now, and some, as we have since learned, thought so at the time. But such questions are really beside the point: history is not a tale of might-have-beens. As matters actually stood, these communists were able to succeed both because of themselves and in spite of themselves. They had to win against a most powerful enemy; they also had to win against their own history, or a good deal of it. Which helps to explain whatever they did that was bad as well as whatever they did that was good.

This is not a history of the communist movement, and the antinazi war, in any case, could give no final answers. But it is barely possible, looking back, to exaggerate either the force of this communist discipline or its blindness, and very difficult to grasp the power of belief which gave it strength. It was not simply that the great Russian revolution of October 1917 formed, for these men and women, the source and origin of all useful social progress in our century. It was also that the further means of progress—the whole cause of a revolutionary internationalism—had become incarnate in the Soviet national State. Through hell or high water, the Soviet Union remained the workers' homeland whose defence must come first. And this view of things, arising in the years of foreign invasion and boycott of the infant Soviet State of the early 1920s, was systematically enforced by Stalin in the 1930s, or at any rate after 1935. It came to a point where those who argued against Moscow were not only denounced as enemies; they were also killed. As the terror worsened, many were killed whether they argued or not.

This happened to the exiled Polish communist leadership in Russia. It all but happened to the exiled Jugoslav leadership as well. While the royal Jugoslav dictatorship was persecuting communists inside Jugoslavia—and in 1935 alone nearly one-third of the existing communist membership, some 950 persons, were arrested by the police of the dictatorship—the Stalinist State was doing much the same, and sometimes worse, elsewhere. By the end of 1938 the executioners of the Soviet State are credibly said to have killed about sixty of the Jugoslav party's staunchest members in exile.

And even that, it seems, was not the end. There were also those who had fought for the Spanish republic. About 1,700 Jugoslav volunteers joined the International Brigades against Franco fascism and its backers, and of these about 700 died in action or of wounds. Many were communists; of these, among the survivors, some 300 eventually worked their way back to Jugoslavia after the nazi invasion of 1941. The most daring and determined of them became Tito's military commanders. But others worked their way back to Moscow, and of these too, it appears, an unknown number were duly killed by the NKVD.

Tito himself escaped Stalin's "purge" and was allowed back to Jugoslavia in March 1939. There, as the party's secretary-general, he set about reorganising his scattered party and preparing for whatever might lie ahead. It could be nothing good. But it was worse than anyone expected. In April 1941 there came the débâcle of the invasion, and, almost at once, the onset of a widespread massacre of Serbs and others by fascist Croats of Pavelić's newly-founded "independent Croat State".

Tito at once ordered party members to form small fighting groups for the defence of people against this fascist terror; and this was how the forerunners of the partisan detachments came into existence late in May. Hitler then invaded Russia, and on 1 July came orders from the Comintern in Moscow, received by a short-wave radio set concealed in a house in Zagreb, that the Jugoslav communists "must launch an open fight against the invaders". On 4 July Tito generalised this instruction into an order to form fighting groups in every region; and clandestine organisation, by this time, had become such that the order was followed.

That is how the partisan war took shape. In flight from enemy terror, multitudes of peasants or townsmen fled into the hills and forests; and there they found Tito's communists ready to organise and lead them. These communists were poorly armed and short of military experience until the "Spaniards"—the volunteers who'd fought in Spain—escaped from German camps and filtered home; but their real weakness lay elsewhere.

Called to lead a nation, they were still locked inside their conspiratorial inheritance. If they had a clear and firm idea of how to lead and how to follow, this was characteristic of the communists of the "Stalin period". It was, in short, authoritarian. Secret committees "at the top" took decisions; down the line these decisions had to be fulfilled without question.

Now much of this was "in the situation": it couldn't have been otherwise, given the deep clandestinity in which these communists had always been obliged to work. Much of it, again, was the product of the Stalin or rather Stalinist "phenomenon" whose weight in any final estimate has still to be measured by the verdict of history. How far was it inevitable? Where did the fatal fault really lie: how much in theory, how much in practice? The anti-nazi war could offer no final judgment on that. But it could and did offer a final judgment on something else. And this something else proved decisive.

What became clear, in these dramas of 1941 and after, was that these communists of occupied Europe had to face a choice: either they developed an entirely new approach to their methods and objectives, or else they would be erased from the scene. And it is easy to see why.

When invasion and resistance let politics loose among these peoples, those who took to arms were very soon found to be concerned with two aims. They wanted to fight the nazis and their puppets, but they also wanted more than that. Liberation had a dual meaning: liberation from the present enemy, but, no less, liberation from the past enemy—here in southern Europe, invariably, from crudely militaristic tyrannies installed in the 1920s and enduring through the 1930s.

And very soon, too, this second aim became as important as the first. Once again it is easy to see why. Who save an insignificant few were going to risk their lives and their families, their property if they had any, for the benefit of putting back those pre-war tyrannies or installing others? What the mass of volunteers and the still greater mass of their sympathisers saw as crucial was the chance to open the way, after the war, for a life that would somehow become free of old miseries and hatreds.

Deeply felt if often vaguely expressed, this was the real price that people placed upon their acceptance of the ferocious perils of armed resistance. It was above all out of this longing for a way of life that should be altogether different and better that there came the strong idealism and moral force, and sometimes the utopian hopes, that marked all the great movements of resistance. Men and women of no heroic pretensions accepted death or suffering not only as lying in the line of duty, for there could be no particular merit in doing that. Beyond duty, they accepted death or suffering as the price of a moral victory for whatever men and women think best in themselves.

This ran through all levels of thought and aspiration, and from the sublime to the extremely humble. "What do you want from this war?" I asked a peasant woman who sheltered partisans in the enemy-infested plains of the Vojvodina, and among others sheltered me; and she replied without hesitation: "The first thing is that men shan't any longer have the right to beat us." The people who gathered in armed resistance were certainly fighting for their very lives. Yet in every sense that was meaningful to their lives, they were just as surely fighting for more than that.

So they looked for people who could lead them in this dual liberation. Only the communists possessed the ideas, organisation, and disciplined self-sacrifice that could meet the need. But, just as surely, the communists could not answer the call as authoritarian conspirators. They had to earn and win their leadership in the broad light of argument and example. They had to discuss, debate, ceaselessly strive with doubt or disbelief. In a tough and everyday sense, they had to democratise.

In Jugoslavia and Italy, as events would show, they were able to meet this challenge with success. In Jugoslavia it was very much the merit of Tito's genius as a political and military strategist. The evidence suggests that he saw from the first that a movement of national liberation had to be and to mean just what it said: or else go under. It had to fight for the freedoms that people wanted, and it had to fight for the independence that could alone guarantee those freedoms; and Jugoslavia's eventual break with Stalinism, long delayed as it was by many circumstances, came only as the further logic of these needs.

Getting these ideas across as party policy, but even more as party practice, was obviously difficult. It called for a process of mental adjustment, necessarily hard to make; and meanwhile the absolute need for wartime discipline rendered the process harder still. As much later history was to show, the democratic conversion of minds and methods of work has had to be as long and painful as the promotion of a democratic consciousness. Yet this above all, or so it seems to me, is a process that history will remember from those years.

3

To us "outside", trying to get "inside", only one aspect among these developments was meanwhile coming clear.

In southern Europe, if not elsewhere as well, effective resistance on any scale was going to be left-wing. The accompanying fact, that this left-wing resistance could hope to succeed only in the measure that it faced and took the challenge of a broad "grass roots" democracy, was still buried from sight. It would probably have mattered little if it had not been.

For the whole development was inherently disturbing to the Allies, and especially to the British government and its operational departments. Britain was still the military leader of the team so far as Europe west of Russia was concerned, and Britain had alliances with kings and governments in exile. Britain was committed to restoring them to throne and power.

Besides, the alternative to kings and governments in exile seemed very awful. Usually, this alternative was thought of in

Smuts's term, "bolshevisation"; but even those with a far more subtle and informed understanding than Smuts ever achieved were naturally upset. The British government was predominantly conservative, as were Britain's generals and senior civil servants, not to mention businessmen such as the Lord Selborne who now became the political chief of SOE. They wanted resistance inside the Fortress, but they could not possibly want it to be left-wing. They wanted friends who would fight for a restoration of kings and governments in exile; but the friends they found were seldom any they could count on to do that. The military need clashed repeatedly with the political intention.

This raised what James, in a favourite lecture to the Canadian miners in the villa out by Mena House, liked to call a classical dilemma.

FIVE

I

JAMES USED TO pause at this point in his lecture and consider his audience with an especially owlish stare, meanwhile raising his right hand and extending the well-known index finger until it pointed, slowly and deliberately, straight ahead. Nobody in that stubbornly argumentative gathering was ever heard to speak at this juncture. They watched that elevating finger; I watched it myself. Drawing on a cigarette held in his left hand and savouring the drag and then expelling smoke in clouds, James now was fuelled and loaded for his climax. The tension was great, but, when it came, so was the relief. Suddenly the pointing finger stabbed forward, transfixing the dilemma, the classical dilemma, while the left hand and arm swept up and round and down again, enclosing in sorrow not in anger all those revealed to be upon its horns.

"You see, don't you? If we refuse to help the Left in Europe, that leaves us with no resistance worth helping. But if we do help the Left, what about our dearly beloved kings and governments in exile?"

And James smiled happily, benignly, at this demonstration of the lovely laws of history; and the audience shuffled its feet and eased its posteriors on their hard chairs beside the lamps of watered silk, and smiled back at him and thought they saw a tidy way along the avenues. It was a beautiful exercise in rapport; but James was not a teacher for nothing.

Clasping his hands together with the cigarette between his lips, he demanded greater mental effort: "No, you've got to see beyond that, haven't you? You've got to see that this war has become more than a war *against* something, against fascism. It's become a war *for* something, for something much bigger. For national liberation, people's liberation, colonial liberation." And now he tapped on the table with the flat of his hand, beating time to his words, while the cigarette between his lips flapped and trembled in the storm.

"So what does that mean? It means you've got to understand the politics of the future, the politics of a real united front, a real front of liberation that's quite different from a mere sect, a party, a fragment. That's what the future now demands." The gathering hunched craggy shoulders and nodded its agreement. Yet I doubt myself if those old revolutionaries were quite convinced. That came later.

Such was James's view. It was not widely shared. High above, where policy was made, it was not shared at all. But the dilemma still remained, and there had to be some answer to it. This answer, evolving through 1942, came in two parts. The first was to refuse all aid, or to give as little as might be consistent with the overall aim of helping resistance, to any movements that were not in favour of kings and governments in exile. Another aspect of this first answer was to boost the importance, or if necessary invent the importance, of any movements that were in favour.

The second part of the answer was "the doctrine of British control". This laid down that all resistance movements aided by us were assumed to be controlled by us. Right-wing resistance, if any, would of course obey our orders because these orders derived as much from kings and exile governments, most of whom were in London and living on British subsidies. As to left-wing resistance, once it became of such military value that help to it could no longer be refused, then left-wing resistance would simply have to follow suit and obey as well. The idea, not very difficult to penetrate, was that left-wing movements would have to keep in step with British policy or forfeit British aid; and only the British were in a position to give aid. It never had much chance of working; but when it completely failed, as it did in all crucial cases, the "doctrine of control" still retained a mythical value for British authorities seated on the horns of their dilemma. It made the posture a little less painful. They could always believe, or at least report, that we had the situation safely in hand.

Dramas soon developed: in southern Europe, first of all in Greece. During September 1942 a British team dropped into Greece and, in November, blew up the Gorgopotamos viaduct on the north-south railway vital to the Germans. This was a useful and daring operation, but was carried through with indispensable aid from Greek guerrillas already in the field. The Gorgopotamos success and subsequent operations now confirmed what was already pretty well known. There were strong resistance forces in Greece. They were an alliance of republican and revolutionary groupings for the great majority of whom the Greek king and his government in exile, and everything that this king and his ministers stood for, were not much less of an enemy, in the long run, than the occupying armies were now. They were, that is, left-wing.

This was found deplorable. The British government was pledged to restore the Greek king to his throne, along with a government of royalists; and Churchill in particular was attached to this restoration with all the fervour of an embattled nature. Efforts were thereupon unfolded to control or at least to split this Greek resistance so as to force it to accept the king, if not his exile government as well. The efforts failed. Even at the time, it was seen by British officers in the field that this was trying to make water run uphill. It was asking men to fight for a past which they detested, rather than for a possibly better future. But the advice of British officers in the field was rejected with anger and insult by crucially important members of the Foreign Office, and eventually by Churchill too. The efforts persisted, and fearful disasters followed on them.

That is not my story here, for it was very complex and I had no hand in it; but a little more may be said. When the efforts to control or split the main forces of the Greek resistance were seen to have failed, SOE turned its attention to creating or inventing or recruiting for pay in gold sovereigns a right-wing resistance which would do as it was told. There emerged from an earlier initiative of a different kind what Colonel Tamplin called "nat bands", it being strangely argued that nationalism was a monopoly of the right. Yet the concept of a "mercenary guerrilla" is a contradiction in terms, in so far as it is not a mere licence for banditry, and the "nat bands" were never any good at fighting the enemy. The part they played was a different one. With much waste and sorrow, as well as with plenty of political blunders and failings by the left-wing resistance leaders, especially the Greek communists, they were a prelude to the destruction of the Greek resistance movement and army by a British expeditionary force at the end of 1944.

The Jugoslav drama took a different course. Here we thought that we had a real and genuine right-wing resistance movement already on its legs. This consisted of the chetnik bands commanded by General Draža Mihajlović. Being raised by Serbian officers of the old Royal Jugoslav Army, these bands were entirely loyal to the exiled king and his government in London; and the latter duly named Mihajlović their minister of defence. No problem, then? On the contrary, for complications developed.

Back in the early days of Jugoslav resistance in the grim autumn of 1941, Mihajlović and his officers at first accepted Tito's proposals for an alliance in which the partisans, while retaining their own identity, were ready to take second place. It didn't work. Partly on secret orders received from their government in London by way of the two royalist officers who landed from *Triumph* in September 1941, the chetnik leaders scrapped this alliance, attacking the partisans at a moment when these were already under German assault. The main body of the partisans, with Tito in command, survived but had to move to other regions of the country. For their part, the chetnik officers and their bands retired to mountain tops, folded their arms, and sat down to await the end of the war. That would be their time to fight: against, of course, the partisans.

Tito and his movement saw things otherwise. They turned to their dual task of fighting for the renewed independence of Jugoslavia, and, at the same time, for the winning of mass support in favour of a new society after the war, a society in which old miseries and conflicts could be made to lose their power. So while the chetniks dwindled into nothing as a resistance movement, either on the sidelines of the fight or in alliance with the enemy, the partisans grew steadily in strength, fighting the enemy at every opportunity on a programme of wide patriotic and radical appeal. By the early months of 1942 the Jugoslav partisans had become by far the strongest and most combative resistance movement in any part of occupied Europe.

All this the British government and its agencies saw and marked with an understandable alarm. Yet perhaps something might still be done? Perhaps influence and material aid could still beg, bully, or build up Mihajlović and and his bearded bands into allies worth having? Nourished through many months of suave duplicity, such was the plan. Summing it up in July 1942, the chief of the Balkan section of SOE London, then Lord Glenconner, agreed in a note to the Foreign Office that: "As we know, any activities in Yugoslavia should really be attributed to the Partisans. But for public consumption we can see no harm in a certain amount of this going to the credit of Mihajlović."

Duly instructed, the BBC did its patriotic duty by improving on Lord Glenconner's advice, and told the world that all activities against the enemy in Jugoslavia were the work of the chetniks when, in truth, none of them was. The quiescent general of a non-existent army, Draža Mihajlović, was presented as Britain's number one hero in occupied Europe. In line with this, SOE missions and aid were sent only to the chetniks, and the partisans were studiously ignored all through that hard-fought year of 1942. When appointed G2 of the operational section for Jugoslavia in SOE Cairo, I was given not one word of advice or information about the partisans. So far as we were concerned, they were supposed not to exist.

But what certainly did not exist, and this we knew for sure, was any effective chetnik resistance. Stubborn efforts were now made to get the chetnik "nat bands" to fight. British missions were sent in to see what they could do about that. Orders to Mihajlović to fight the enemy, not the partisans, were painfully extracted from the exiled royal government in London. Nothing availed. On Christmas Eve 1942 we dropped in a senior British officer, fluent in Serbian, to reinforce these orders. It made not the slightest difference.

Drama again: for this was when the war turned over on itself. Great victories in Africa had opened the way for assault on the southern bastions of the Fortress. At this point, therefore, the British military chiefs called on SOE Cairo to secure a maximum effort in Greece and Jugoslavia, especially against enemy lines of supply to the Mediterranean theatre. Let the gallant army of General Mihajlović come forth from the heather and the ling and hurl itself against the enemy's railways.

But the number one hero and his men were unwilling to leave the heather and the ling. The duty of the Allies, they held, was to win the war against the Germans; then it would be the duty of the chetniks to win the war against the partisans. Messages to this effect came back from Mihajlović. Their tenor was straightforward: any fool could win the war against the Germans, winning the peace was what would call for men who were really men. Fighting the Germans would provoke reprisals, and only the dark forces of democratic chaos could benefit from that. The chetniks would not fight the Germans.

This again impaled SOE Cairo on the prongs of James's classical dilemma. Get your Jugs to blow up the railways, ordered general headquarters in Cairo. We've told them to and they won't, had to be SOE's lame answer. Then find other Jugs who will, retorted the military chiefs. We can't, said SOE, high policy won't let us. At which the military chiefs, aghast at the idea of running foul of high policy, subsided into muttering gloom and thought the whole irregular exercise still more useless, if that were possible, than before.

So it came about that the largest and most combative fighting resistance in all occupied Europe continued to be left unaided and ignored. Jugoslav partisan troops were holding down many enemy divisions; but not a word could be said about them. Their demolition teams were blowing up enemy communications wherever these existed; but their commanders could not even be contacted, let alone supplied with high explosive, arms, or medical supplies. The din and strife of partisan battle inside Jugoslavia were plain for all intelligence agencies to hear; but the BBC, which would never tell a lie, continued to inform the world that all was the work of chetniks who were now, in fact, no longer even on the sidelines but right inside the enemy camp.

Something had to give but it gave with huge reluctance, and in a bitter hour. Signs of British help would come, but only when this help risked coming too late.

Smarting from their losses, Hitler's command now gathered its troops in Jugoslavia for an all-out offensive against the main partisan forces. These fought their way southward into high mountains. But the enemy followed, and, moving in for the kill, encircled the partisans with a great superiority of German and Italian divisions. The German plan was to bottle up their enemy in these glens and gorges of Montenegro, and then, tightening their grip, leave nothing but the silence of the dead. To that end they called on General Mihajlović and his chetnik bands to help them by spying out the land, killing partisan couriers and sympathisers, and betraying partisan positions. And the chetnik bands, with enemy cash in their pockets, moved in to do all this.

Handed down from London, high policy had continued to forbid the slightest British gesture to the partisans, whether of aid or even recognition; and to order, on the contrary, more aid to the chetniks. Good men amongst us fumed and cursed; but the orders were there, and were obeyed. We were passing up a powerful ally in favour of a hero who would not fight. But pushing from below could get us nowhere. And who was there to push from above?

2

There was nobody to push from above. On the contrary, all those who made high policy pushed hard the other way. Hope of a change there could be none.

Though with some misgivings now, the Foreign Office in

London continued to stand firm for the chetniks. "We still feel," it confirmed to SOE London on 9 October 1942, "that we are bound to continue our support for Mihajlović because of his potential value, both military and political, at a later stage in the war." Given the desirability of ditching the partisans after the war, in other words, British support was to continue to go to Mihajlović "whether or nor he continues to refuse to take a more active part in resisting and attacking Axis forces in Yugoslavia." The term "Axis forces" meant Germans, Italians and their puppets.

SOE London had no misgivings. Though its chiefs had no brief to make Britain's foreign policy, but were in charge of a military organisation designed to help in winning the war, they continued to apply a political and not a military judgment. They remained unanimous, even frantically unanimous, in opposing any slightest British move towards aiding the partisans. This was not in the least because they were ignorant of partisan effectiveness, or of chetnik inactivity, but because, as one of them would tell the Foreign Office a little later, "the policy of the partisans does not suit us, nor would it ever be easy to bring them under our control." That was their policy, and they stuck to it.

With this situation present and prospective, the outlook for our doing anything useful in Jugoslavia, in the way of actually helping to win a war that was still far from nearing its final stages, seemed barely to exist. Only an angel from on high could make it otherwise.

No angel came; but something else did, and from the least expected quarter. This was the energy and will, and still more the stealth and cunning, of a small and rather bouncy man of the most conservative opinions: Colonel, and then Brigadier, C. M. Keble.

May he lie quietly in his distant grave. Much maligned, if with some reason, Keble was the man who really found the way to do the job. Not even Sleede could have imagined his methods. Not even the priest of Saint Rock could have rivalled his devious creativeness.

We move now into the Keble epic. It deserves no lesser name.

SIX

THE TONE MAY seem a little flippant here, considering the stakes in play by this time; and a touch of the 1930s did in fact add curious colour to the scenes and dramas of the Keble epic. The reader is asked to bear with this; I can only tell it how it was, and no one else will tell it.

As the true situation inside Jugoslavia came clear from various intelligence sources, two sides took shape in SOE Cairo: sketchily at first, and then with emotion as the facts were accepted or refused. Something like battle lines were drawn by the last weeks of 1942, and soon the opposing sides began to face each other with all the passion that set the Children of Light against the Children of Darkness. Fighting alliances were made, recruits were sought, morality wavered, truth lowered her head. Paper came into its own again. Squadrons of memoranda were loaded up and launched. As always in great confrontations, confusion seemed to reign; and commanders who came from SOE London to restore some order to the scene retired bleeding to their billets, regretting they had ever come at all.

The earliest visible engagement that I seem to recall took place, in what was to be a long fight, between Miss Flannery and the Warrant Officer, a senior sergeant whose name I cannot now recall. It concerned the management and control of those sinews of war most vital to any military establishment, the files. Miss Flannery and the Warrant Officer were divided by character as well as by sex; but this was more than a personality clash. It went to the heart of the business. An SOE veteran, Miss Flannery was a gentle wisplike lady, apparently pale and fragile, whose rage for smoking cigarettes outdid even James's. She had arrived in Cairo before the outbreak of war, and for reasons not known; but these were not, in any case, the kind of reasons that you would have asked her to explain. She was one of those British ladies of distinction who wander the world in perfect harmony with some mysterious objective or belief, and who succeed, no matter in what god-forsaken place they may decide to settle, in combining modest comfort with a discretion and good sense which only a character such as the Warrant Officer's would call in question.

Miss Flannery was frail but not feeble, and her air of being a waif blown by the wind's choosing was far from the truth. She was possessed of a fierce determination, and brought to its service a gift of tongues that any Celtic soothsayer might have envied. Having volunteered for the war effort, she had long found herself in charge of the files of the Jugoslav section of SOE Cairo. In that post she had seen countless majors, colonels and other ephemeral creatures come and go in London's annual purges of its hated dependant in the Middle East. But Miss Flannery stayed with what was permanent; and what was permanent was the files, growing fatter with every departmental skirmish and nourished unceasingly by the battles fought between London and Cairo.

Feeding and caring for her files, Miss Flannery had evolved her own system of arrangement. This was infallible upon one condition: that Miss Flannery should find the paper which you wanted. No one else could find it, for the secret of her system in this secret department was naturally hers alone. She kept her treasures in a disused bathroom at the end of my corridor. The first to arrive and the last to leave, she was thought to keep the bathroom key upon a chain about her person.

Yet the war turned over on itself, and the professional soldiers moved into increasing control of Rustem Building and its SOE amateurs. This was when the Warrant Officer arrived. Hostilities began without delay. Appointed chief clerk according to the immemorial procedures of the War Office, the Warrant Officer in addition was a Yorkshireman, a sturdy Saxon from Pocklington, and bound to know that he was always right. It was even said, perhaps maliciously, that his great-grandfather had done battle in the bitter War Office campaigns against the revolutionary zeal of Miss Florence Nighingale, after the Crimean War.

Moving in with the impact of a tank, the Warrant Officer drove through Miss Flannery's defences and installed the proper procedures. As Colonel Tamplin liked to repeat, there had to be an end to amateurish bungling, and Flannery's bathroom was condemned. From now onwards the files passed to the Warrant Officer, and became available, if at all, only upon presentation of duly signed and counter-signed *pro formas*. But Miss Flannery did not betray herself; she never gave in, and with an ingenuity that would have done credit to Brian Boru himself she mastered the *pro forma* business, and at several demonic points managed to keep even six or seven files in circulation at the same time. She attacked the Saxon from Pocklington in flank, and she attacked him in rear. She undermined his peace of mind with a wicked variety of devices, even rumoured to include the hinting at files taken home by error or left in a tram. And since the professional soldiers at this stage were thought to be passionately pro-chetnik, Miss Flannery became doggedly pro-partisan; and the Warrant Officer in turn was classed by her, in a suitably penetrating whisper, with the friends of that "silly old goat Mihadge-lo-vitch". His days creased with troubles such as Yorkshire should never know, the Warrant Officer was driven to call up reinforcements and obliged even to accept junior clerks from poor soft southern counties such as Surrey; but it really did no good. Files continued to circulate in defiance of his regulations. He put up notices, forbidding entry; but Flannery, presenting *pro formas*, entered all the same.

In that strange atmosphere of chetnik-partisan warfare, the game got nastier. It reached a point one day when the operational chief of the Jugoslav section, who was myself and now a well-marked partisan supporter and a great signer of Flannery's *pro formas*, was hailed before a court of inquiry on the perilous charge of having lost a secret file. With the Warrant Officer as the non-commissioned element on this inquiry, a verdict of guilty appeared certain. And proceedings for a court martial were averted only at the last moment, when the lost file was discovered at the back of Colonel Tamplin's cupboard. Miss Flannery never let fall a word on this feat of detection and recovery. She was not the kind of general to rat upon her frontline troops, nor could there be any question of my thanking her. The file was found in Colonel Tamplin's cupboard, not in the Warrant Officer's; but Colonel Tamplin, by this time, was regretting his choice of G2. The war, as you can see, continued.

Here I mention this obscure encounter because it was characteristic in its way of the wider warfare in Rustem Building. There was, for example, the singular battle that developed between two doughty fighters whom I will call Captain Aye and Major Bee. Geography and temperament again contributed to this partisan-chetnik clash. Captain Aye was a Geordie from the Tyne, where he had worked until the war in the tramways department, and was naturally a partisan. Major Bee was from somewhere in the south, Bournemouth I believe, where he was said to own a small hotel, or, rather, to live as a gentleman should on his father's profits thereof; he was just as naturally a chetnik. Captain Aye was commissioned from the ranks, but Major Bee from the officers' training corps of a school for the natural leaders of men: pretty much, it seemed, the Eton of Bournemouth. In Rustem Building they were both concerned with supply: Aye in the procurement of stores, Bee in their delivery by air or sea.

Captain Aye had never procured anything in his pre-war life, as I once heard him explain, save a neat little council house for Mrs Aye; but the war opened perspectives, and he saw beyond trams now. His ideas soared. Procurement became a pathway to the stars. He procured the impossible. He procured the non-existent. He bored and shoved his way into remote and secret dumps of stores, and there he made alliance with diverse decisive figures from Tyneside and the Cumberland Fells or even, at a pinch, from Lancashire, men with the flinty self-respect of those who die at their posts rather than surrender. But they surrendered to Aye, and they measured out for him a due allowance of the impossible and non-existent.

Aye procured the stores but Bee, it now appeared, could not deliver them. The chetniks, Bee informed Aye, were not fighting anyone at present, and there was no one else. Come off it, Aye would reply, there's the other blokes, send the stuff to them. Bee was bound to find this upsetting, given that the natural leaders of men had decided that the other blokes did not exist, but a proper upbringing reduced his range of verbal ammunition.

"We can do no such thing, Captain, even if the partisans do exist, which is highly doubtful."

"Balls to that, so what's the Jerries doing with seventeen blooming divisons in Jugoslavia, sunbathing?"

"There is no call for that kind of language."

But Aye had run the trams on Tyneside, vast blue and yellow monsters screaming through northern fog in streets wailing all the way to South Shields and back again; and what was running a pub in Bournemouth to compare with that?

"Look, I've got three fifteen-hundredweights outside this dump, loaded with stuff you can't find for love nor money, not between Port Said and Benghazi you can't, and what do you want me to do with it, throw it in the sea? You'll bloody well have to deliver it."

"The chetniks, I told you, Captain, are not at present fighting anyone."

"Sounds like sabotage to me," said Aye.

There should have been another court of inquiry into the captain's lack of a proper respect; but the fiasco of the missing file had just occurred, and Bee's advisers thought discretion the better course.

So it went, though; and with the British war now in its fourth year and all manner of assorted tram-conductors proceeding up the ranks and hierarchies in rivalry with the natural leaders of men, hostilities were bound to spread. It is the price that Britain always has to pay for her wars. James even developed a theory on the subject. He was talking one afternoon in the villa out by Mena House.

"We British," James mused, "can never expect to win campaigns in years one or two of any major war. We can only begin to win them in years three and four."

"Wavell licked Mussolini's lot in 1941."

"It wasn't decisive. Couldn't be. Because, if you look at the statistical averages, it's only in years three and four that the soldiers from Civvy Street begin to swamp out the natural leaders of men. That's when the shift comes. And by year five, of course, the men from Civvy Street have got the decisive jobs up the line of command. They go steadily to the top. Then we win."

If this subversive view had anything to it, Captain Aye would have risen far and high, and Mrs Aye, after the war, was going to have to polish up her own perspectives if she was ever to reclaim him for the use of trams. As it happened, the grey seas of the Mediterranean settled that problem one day late in 1944; whereupon no one, I have heard it said, was more upset than Major Bee. "The salt of the earth, old Aye," he was reputed to have said, "they don't come that way often." But this was long after the partisan-chetnik struggle in SOE had been resolved, and Major Bee, following the natural leaders of men, had changed his mind on that subject.

Yet all these hostilities paled before the onset of Brigadier Keble, briefly still a colonel when placed in charge of all the operational sections of SOE Cairo late in 1942. He was very unexpected, and it is not too much to say that he put all lesser figures and several greater ones, whether on the chetnik side or the other, entirely in the shade. This being so, you might assume him to be a tram-conductor: but not at all, Keble was a regular officer of an impeccable regiment, the cream of the cream of regular regiments on the exclusive list. Yet for sheerly ingenious military crime he soon showed us that all tram-conductors and their like were poor beginners: in this respect, at least, amateurish bungling did indeed come to an end, although in no way that Colonel Tamplin was able to foresee.

Shocks were felt on every floor. Even his physical appearance was alarming. Built to a squat and compact pattern, alongside which even the Warrant Officer's seemed weedy, Keble possessed a large round head mounted directly on broad sloping shoulders and capable, as was discovered, of butting through any obstacle that might present itself. Besides this advantage, he also possessed a long strong nose extremely well devised for the worrying of adversaries, along with a certainty that no one else could win the war such as made Miss Flannery's look like nothing. For months he had toiled at some secret desk in general headquarters, held obscurely down by the forces dominant in years one and two; but fortune's wheel had turned with the war itself, and Keble now was king. He intended to reign.

His manner of reigning combined the quick in-out of a commando raid with the onward drone of a brigade of tanks. He came down on us like the proverbial Assyrian, his round head burnished with the sweat of authority, and his sword arm bared from the habit of wearing only a vest and trousers and desert boots while he darted, in the Cairo heat, from one attack to another. His tactics looked strange, but they seemed to work. This was puzzling at the time. James, as usual, evolved a theory.

"You can't see it? Look at it this way. A king needs power, and how does a king in Keble's boots get that? He works the rules. You'd do the same."

This may sound all too ingenious or improbable. The fact remained that the rules of the army establishment provided for a man to become a major when he commanded three captains, a half-colonel when he commanded three majors, and so on up the scale. Keble had arrived at Rustem Building as a full colonel, but a little brisk assault work had soon raised him higher. Measuring his men, he had promoted Tamplin from half-colonel: there would be no trouble from him, poor fellow. Another promoted to the same rank of full colonel was the officer sent in to Mihajlović, on Christmas Eve 1942, with the latest set of orders to induce the number one hero to take the field. A third full colonel had been found advisable in Greece. Duly gazetted brigadier, Keble now faced the next upward challenge. But this was bound to be exacting because the Rule of Three grows harder to apply the higher you climb.

Like all sound principles of strategy this rule may look in theory as simple as the two-times table but it calls in application for cunning, ruthlessness, a keen appreciation of the enemy's intentions, and a fair bit of luck. All these would now be required. Not that I am saying, of course, that Bolo, as Keble was generally known in the army, placed the needs of his career above those of the war: on the contrary, the two went hand in hand for him, and who will throw the first stone? There is nothing wrong with a proper ambition, we are repeatedly told; and Keble's ambition, if that is what it was, really did help to win the war.

A captain himself by now, and afterwards to be a major, James reckoned up the odds. "Greece, that's one: we've more than enough missions there to rate a brigadier to command them in the field. Bulgaria? Not a hope, though maybe later. Hungary, did you say? Don't be silly. And Italy? We're not there yet. No, but wait—' and James's eyes gleamed hazel with discovery: "of course—Albania. A brigadier in Albania, why not? Small country, small brigadier, but size doesn't count. Then Bolo gets a third in Jugoslavia, and he's made it to major-general. After that it's all on the cards, Lieutenant-General Keble, Field-Marshal Keble, who knows?"

"But he can't get a brigadier in Jugoslavia if the chetniks won't fight," I demurred: "Not even Bolo can do that."

James looked at me with the patient disappointment of a teacher whose hopes of a dull pupil are dashed once more. But he only said, "Precisely."

Whatever Bolo may have really thought, this was in any case the time from which his divine madness can be said to date. Inwardly fired, he redoubled his commando raids about the building until the sight of his off-white vest, glimpsed along the corridors or bursting in on anxious file-consulters, completed the demoralisation of any remaining nests of opposition. There are those who have affirmed that he paid particular attention to the ladies of the secretarial staff, on the grounds that they generally had more information than the officers they worked for, and certainly about the officers they worked for. It was further claimed that he now acquired another nickname, at least among the ladies: Tim, being short for Touch-I-Must. But all this, I feel sure, was just another libel. Office gossip in wartime can become especially feverish, and the frustrated easily imagine what they fear or covet. There was much frustration, and of various kinds.

Still another claim was that his strange friendship for James began now, though personally I believe it came later. When it did come, and grew apparent, James's Egyptian friends wavered for a moment in their loyalty, it was said, and gave evidence of shock; but the central law of dialectics soon settled them. Others, not James's friends, were more than shocked. Security in the person of Major Warden-Baker, a department-store executive in civil life whose maiden-auntly bearing went together with a famous gift for sniffing out shoplifters and therefore subversives, was known to have protested. But Keble rode him down. Was Warden-Baker questioning his judgment? No, of course not, and indeed far from it, and yet and still . . . Rubbish, said Keble, we'll never beat the Russians if we don't beat the Germans first. It was the kind of utterance, a speciality of Bolo's tactics of aggression, that required in those days a little time to unravel, let alone answer; but Bolo never gave time for counter-attack. His vest flashing, he was gone long before.

Whether now or later, Keble befriended James. This was certainly for no reason of political sympathy, for Keble's own conservatism was of a forcefulness that put even Tamplin's in the shade. Approached for an explanation, James proved amiable but reserved. It was another case, one might gather, of the contradictions of history: a question of coinciding along the avenues at a moment likely to be crucial. Did Keble wish the avenues' topography to be explained to him: or, as James would have put it, the perspectives? It seemed unlikely, but it could be so.

"And he really thinks?"

James turned owlish and raised his right hand with the index and middle finger pressed together, pointing upward. This was his most episcopal gesture but I think that on this occasion it signalled, as nearly as James would ever signal any such thing, an impatience with fools.

"You don't see it? The objective factors oblige him."

"Oh, do they? Then what's become of your theory about soldiers and civilians?"

James lowered his hand and smiled forgivingly. "Doctrine is subject to interpretation, never forget that, it's another aspect of the central law."

I pressed no further on that holy ground.

Whatever the truth of all this, the New Year of 1943 appeared and with it came Keble's master move.

The factual position now was that we had two brigadiers in the field, one with armed resistance in Greece and another with a smaller resistance in Albania. The weak point was Jugoslavia. There, as was once more confirmed by our colonel with Mihajlović, the chetniks refused to fight anyone but the partisans; and many chetnik bands, if not most, were already in active and irreversible alliance with the enemy. At the same time, unmoved by wave after wave of documentary assault from below, high policy continued to forbid all contact with the partisans. The existence of these was beyond doubt, and their fighting effort now so great as to promise that any chief liaison officer sent to them should be at least a brigadier, if not a major-general. But high policy stayed firm for the chetniks. Stalemate.

Was there any means to shift it? Keble knew that the British high command wanted action in Jugoslavia. Only the partisans were providing this, and could provide more. What Keble needed, that being so, was the means to play a forcing bid. He had to show a hand so persuasive that even high policy could not reject it. And luck, as it happened, dealt him this hand. Some fortunate chance left him on the list of those rare intelligence officers at general headquarters to whom secret information, of a special nature derived from broken enemy codes, was most discreetly circulated.

It was dangerous to use this kind of information, for he might be accused of breaching confidence. But now it would be still more dangerous, he judged, not to use it. No kind of coward, Bolo made his forcing bid.

SEVEN

I

OBLIGED TO CONTINUE sending British liaison officers and men to useless or even hostile chetniks, I became aware of Keble's move soon after New Year's Day of 1943.

During a lunch hour, with the Warrant Officer off-guard elsewhere, I was consulting a precious file obtained on one of Flannery's *pro formas*, when the brigadier rushed in and locked the door behind him. With what seemed to be a more than usually hectic air, he advanced to my desk and put down several slips of paper.

Tensely, he said: "Enemy traffic. From now on you will receive them every few days. You will treat them as most secret. You will study them. You will await my orders."

Rapping out these instructions, Keble stood foursquare upon his desert boots, a stout perspiring figure with a strong nose pecking forward as though to nail each slip of paper to the desk. Only later did I understand his air of desperate decision.

This was when I studied the slips of paper. They were intercepts of German radio signals decoded by a British service devoted to that work. This was exciting in itself; but there was more. They were messages passed between different units of the German military security service, the SD, in Jugoslavia; and they told a remarkable story. Keble's bid was backed by the ace of spades.

For the intercepts gave, from the German side, details of continuous fighting between the partisans and Germans, as well as details of continuous chetnik help for the Germans. One SD unit advised another that a strong partisan force was concentrated on the Foča-Kalinovik road and chetniks were being called to reinforce a German operation against them. Another unit appealed for help against partisans who were preparing an offensive from the direction of the Glamoč planina. A third SD unit at Banja Luka warned of new partisan brigades in action against German units between Jajce and Kotor Varoš. A fourth indicated the location, as the SD thought, of partisan headquarters in Croatia. And so on and on, detail piling upon detail.

A few days passed, and Keble came again and locked the door

behind him. Had I understood the meaning of the traffic? Very well, then I was to prepare a map, a confidential map not otherwise explained to anybody, upon which all partisan positions thus revealed were to be plotted. The possible location of all partisan headquarter bases or positions was to be noted with especial care. Secondly, I was to make a running survey, noting numbers of partisan units as reported by the SD, with their strengths and armaments if mentioned, and probable lines of movement, together with all comparable information on chetnik collaboration with the enemy.

"You will show the traffic to Captain Deakin. Put him on to the detailed work. Otherwise, full secrecy."

From that moment I ceased to think of Keble as Bolo or as Tim, and acquired respect for this courageous man. He held the ace of spades and he meant to play it. Let the skies of high authority fall in on us, but he was going to play it.

I called in Captain Deakin, and this, although we knew it only in the outcome, was to be another stroke of fortune. Lately arrived from SOE service in North America, and now G3 or intelligence officer in my Jugoslav section, Deakin was unusually qualified. A former don at Oxford, he was accustomed to sifting information from quantities of paper. An historian in his own right, he saw the wider as well as the narrower perspective. He had great capacities of documentary judgment. He was wonderfully the man for this particular job. Not only that, he now revealed himself as belonging, like Churchill himself, among those conservatives who thought an alliance with the devil far preferable to allowing the nazis the least advantage. He had even worked for Churchill when the latter, abandoned in the political wilderness before the war began, was writing a history of his ancestor, the great Duke of Marlborough. He was in fact, I learned, a friend of the prime minister's.

Captain Deakin at once got down to the detail, and soon we had our confidential map. I kept it on my office wall, neatly marked with information taken from the intercepts, behind a mask of paper sheets. This and the running survey confirmed in detail, from confidential German sources, what we had long guessed in outline. The partisans were active in most regions of Jugoslavia. They were strong, effective, and aggressive. They were a formidable fighting force in constant use. Keble came in every day or so to study the map and the survey, and now one could see him at his proper stature. He was in full cry with the quarry in sight. He was a man who scented victory. But how was the evidence to be used? We blessed those distant British code-breakers, wherever they might be, and hoped they would receive every medal the army could bestow. Yet high policy, duly informed, showed no sign of budging an inch. The messages only confirmed, after all, what high policy had known for many months, even if the details had been missing. Never mind: "Mihajlović must be our choice." Loyalty to the exiled king and government in London could allow no less, not to speak of the perils of letting politics loose among unreliable Jugoslavs.

Then fortune dealt us another ace. Soon after New Year, with our map and running survey acquiring much substance, news came through that Mr Churchill would visit Cairo. And Mr Churchill's probable views on what to do in Jugoslavia were open to a fairly easy guess. In June 1941 he had moved at once to support Stalin and the Soviet Union when Hitler's invasion of the East began. He had made a great speech in the House of Commons, saying this was Britain's duty. Even before that, back in 1940 with France collapsing, he had called upon the French to form and launch a "gigantic guerrilla" such as would snap at the heels of the invading nazi juggernaut, rob its crews of sleep, spoil its parade of triumph, slip sand into its axle boxes, mine the roads before it and behind, bite at its flanks, kill off its outposts, and, with time, help even to breach the walls of the barricaded Fortress. Now, in Jugoslavia, he had this gigantic guerrilla. He would not let it go unaided. If, that is, he could be told that it existed.

If he could be told: the problem was exactly there.

Who would be able to spill the beans? Keble might be a brigadier; but brigadiers and even generals were two a penny at that altitude. How in any case would Keble get to Churchill? He would have to go through channels, and the channels were blocked with weed. He would also have to act extremely fast if the thing were to be done at all, for prime ministers in wartime do not wait around. The thing, in short, seemed beyond all doing. Yet done it was, and personally I think that it was thanks to the great Duke of Marlborough. At least his spirit fought a hidden battle on the plains of Cairo that was no less telling, in its way, than Blenheim's famous victory.

These have remained uncertain matters. Yet several facts appear. One is that Captain Deakin, who is now Sir William Deakin, was Mr Churchill's personal friend. A second is that

Captain Deakin knew, and was authorised to know, all the information in the intercepts. A third is that Captain Deakin was in favour of helping the partisans. A fourth is that his G2 discussed an idea with him. One cannot order one's junior to go to the prime minister over all the intervening hierarchy, but there is no law against encouraging two friends to meet; nor is there any limit, if one of them happens to be prime minister, upon what they may legitimately talk about.

Mr Churchill came and stayed a little while; and two other facts appeared. One was that on 30 January Mr Churchill sent for Brigadier Keble. Another was that Keble handed the prime minister a memorandum. This was not, as may be seen in FO 371/37579 at the Public Record Office near Kew Gardens, a very alarming document; but it was shrewdly composed. It said that we should go on supporting Mihajlović and the chetniks in Serbia. But it explained that there were other and evidently effective resistance forces in other parts of Jugoslavia, notably in Slovenia and Croatia. These deserved support, but were getting none. "If this situation continues, either the Russians or the Americans will, for different reasons, take a practical interest." We should therefore step in first. And this being desirable, more long-range aircraft should be allocated to us for the reinforcement of our four limping Liberators.

The effect was enormous and immediate. Almost within hours, as I recall, word filtered down that Mr Churchill had accepted the substance of this memorandum. We were to be given the green light for contacting these resistance forces in Slovenia and Croatia who were, as was soon confirmed, the partisans revealed in our SD intercepts. We were to receive an adequate number of Halifax bombers in support of our Liberators. Whatever might now come, one thing was sure. It exploded round the corridors of Rustem Building with the scattering effect of shrapnel. The Cairo "partisans" had won.

Tremendous rows still lay ahead, of course; and even now, long after, the dust has not quite settled on this critical event. But if mystery remains, the thing was certainly done.

SOE London blew its top and the Foreign Office wavered; even the chiefs of staff, hearing their cries of anger or their doubts, tried to limit the consequences. SOE Cairo continued to be divided, its "chetniks" fearing that contact with the partisan forces in Jugoslavia must soon lead to all-out support for those forces.

As late as 11 March 1943 Sir Charles Hambro of SOE London forwarded a long statement from SOE Cairo to Sir Orme Sargent at the Foreign Office, arguing all over again that "in spite of Mihajlović's drawbacks"—these being that Mihajlović and the chetniks would not fight the enemy—"he must be our choice". This was because "the policy of the partisans does not suit us, nor would it ever be easy for us to bring them under our control". At about the same time that March, and notwithstanding the prime minister's instructions to the contrary, the chiefs of staff declared that they could spare only four Halifax bombers, and this being so, were inclined to think that a partisan commitment should not be added to the existing chetnik commitment.

Yet the obstructers in London still had to reckon with the stern old man in Downing Street. No one could be more conservative and anti-left, let alone anti-communist, than Churchill, as his record over Greece or in the post-war years is enough to show. But he meant to win the war. Having that in mind, he had not sojourned in the political wilderness of the 1930s for nothing, nor had he campaigned for nothing against compromise with the nazis at the very time when leaders of his own party, the Conservative party, were making, in 1938, just such a compromise at Munich. He knew that "Munich gang" from the inside, and he disliked what he knew. In 1938 they had refused to heed his warnings, just as they had refused to clinch an alliance with the Soviet Union when that alliance was open to them; and war had followed on their Munich sell-out and that refusal as surely as night follows day. Then at the outset of 1942 they had actively intrigued to turn him out of office. But he was still prime minister, and he meant to win this war that they had blundered into.

He must have returned to London with some dark suspicions. Much, of course, had changed in the Conservative party since 1940. Lord Selborne, in fact, had never been a member of the "Munich gang", any more than had Eden, and was rewarded for his pro-Churchill attitude during the 1930s precisely by being given charge of SOE. Influential people, even so, liked to run their thought along traditional lines whenever they could or were allowed. In this matter of supporting non-chetnik guerrillas in Jugoslavia, Churchill evidently expected reticence which, if allowed, would amount to refusal. Selborne, for one, was known to be most strongly attached to the idea that Britain should support the chetniks in Jugoslavia or nobody at all. Churchill accordingly took his measures. As soon as he returned to Downing Street from his January visit to Cairo and other oversea commitments, the prime minister on 12 February gave orders to his private secretary, Major Desmond Morton, to show Keble's memorandum to the Foreign Office and to Lord Selborne with the comment that he, Mr Churchill, agreed with it in general terms, and considered it "a matter of the greatest importance to establish the desired closer contacts with the Yugoslav leaders": with, that is, the leaders of the partisans whose location we had fixed on the map we had assembled from SD intercepts.

All this sufficiently moved the Foreign Office, where the influential Sir Orme Sargent had for some time thought that contact with the partisans might have to become a wise move. But it failed to shake Lord Selborne and his fellow "chetniks" of SOE. With an astonishing tenacity they continued their cannonade of advice against the Keble memorandum and Churchill's decision. As late as 9 April Lord Selborne wrote to Sir Orme Sargent to argue against backing both sides; there being no question of our dropping the chetniks, this meant refusing to back the partisans. And on 12 April Colonel J. S. A. Pearson, flying in the face of the strongest military evidence to the contrary, felt able to inform the Foreign Office that the partisan movement had infinitely less potentialities than the chetnik movement. This statement was almost as foolish as it was untrue, and helped to defeat its own purpose, for the Foreign Office, not being staffed by fools, now began to suspect that SOE were not giving them the full story. Four days earlier, in any case, the Foreign Office had advised its minister of state in Cairo that they were considering contact with the partisans, while the chiefs of staff, for their part, had now come round to demanding a "tuning-up" of guerrilla war in the Balkans.

The Foreign Office might be "considering" a contact with the partisans, but Keble in Cairo was already doing a lot more than that. If guerrilla war in the Balkans needed "tuning-up" he knew how to do it. Besides, he possessed from the prime minister an authority to go ahead and do it that nothing could cancel so long as the order was not withdrawn. And it was not withdrawn.

Yet if the die was cast, a technical problem remained for the Jugoslav section of SOE Cairo. How should we stamp this die upon the map of the war? Once well and truly stamped there, as was clear, its mark would not be rubbed out: partisan effectiveness would see to that. As soon as we could secure contact, and then rush in further missions to confirm and broaden the contact, the dynamism and success of the partisan movement would ensure British support. So we set about using the die in good Churchillian fashion.

I was not present when James, duly instructed, gathered his flock in the villa out by Mena House and said that some of them would be asked to volunteer for missions with the partisans. But I should think that it was quite a field day, because the nicotined index finger, pointing down those avenues with all the assurance of the sacred law of dialectics, was now proved to have pointed right.

The chosen few, James told them, would have to take great risks. They would be dropped "blind" to map pin-points where they would probably find partisan concentrations. Probably: for partisan warfare is highly mobile, and where partisans stood yesterday the enemy might stand today. Having listened, all thirty or so of those Canadian Jugoslavs volunteered on the spot. When could they go? was all they wished to be told. Not quite yet, in any case, for every advance calls for consolidation: push on ahead but mind your rear is the right way of it. We did our best.

It was decided to risk two initial parties, each of two fighting men and one wireless operator. For the first party I recommended the wilds of central Bosnia, and for the second the Mala Kapela upland of western Croatia: in each case because the SD intercepts pointed to the presence of partisan commands there. Soon I was able to despatch Deakin to brief the chosen six in the villa out by Mena House, while, at the same time, we began to look around for British volunteers who could be sent on the follow-up missions.

London rampaged but Keble had the bit between his teeth and the political punch to carry us through. He kept on, his broad forehead bright with sweat, his short legs trotting in support. He had taken a mighty risk and had got away with it. But we "partisans" in the office, knowing that all might yet depend on broadening the breach and shoving men through it before fresh obstructions could be raised, gathered in support. The local "chetniks" also rallied, and bitter struggles flared among the documents. Nasty incidents occurred. This was about the time when the G2 Jugoslavia, judged by now a very dubious element, escaped court martial at Colonel Tamplin's instance for losing the file that was found, so disconcertingly, in Colonel Tamplin's cupboard. And about now, or not long after, Keble pushed James into a lavatory and said that security was after him, but that he, Keble, would protect him. It was a ragged running battle. But it was all in the grand tradition. Well might Uncle Toby have said of us, harking back to the days of the great duke himself, that "I wish you could have seen, brother, what prodigious armies we had in Flanders."

They were beautiful days. To the crash of falling barriers, we persevered. Fellow-workers became friends, and friends became companions. Captain Aye excelled himself. Even Major Bee proved his value. Good memories remain; but I find myself thinking chiefly of Miss Flannery, wraithlike as ever, a frail ghost of the truth that will prevail. Where are you now, Flannery, in all the years that we have lived, we the survivors? What good destiny has carried you beyond the hurrying pavement of Sharia el Nil, where you always hastened home among the modest galibiyahs, to the happiness you have deserved? The telly would never measure your worth. But I did and I salute you with respect, dear Flannery, wherever you may be.

Lord Selborne and his kind had to take defeat. Gravely, the chiefs of staff found that ten Halifaxes could be spared for us in spite of what they had said before: if not at once and altogether, then soon and several at a time. And on the night of 20 April, steering out above the desert, and then with the shores of Fortress Europe mirrored in the light of a small moon, two of these conveyed our chosen Canadian Jugoslavs to the pin-points we had specified, more than 1,500 kilometres away, and dropped them into the night. And some days later, upon the roof of Rustem Building where our wireless operators worked round the clock, Sergeant Stanley Brandreth picked up a call sign never heard before, the call sign of Sergeant Alexander Simitch of the "Fungus" mission dropped into the night of western Croatia. We were there.

Easily, in one sense, for the SD intercepts had done their job remarkably well: within hours, Simitch and his two companions were taken by partisan motor car to the headquarters of the partisans in Croatia. But narrowly, too. Finding that our men had two wireless sets but no credentials, the local partisan commander concluded they were enemy spies and decided to shoot them. Yet caution prevailed and on 28 April this commander, having informed Tito who was then far in the south, received from Tito some precise instructions. "Radio set must not be taken away from mission. You can ask them, if they do not need two sets, to lend us one. But I underline: only if they give it to you freely and without pressure. You can let them contact England."

They contacted Cairo, and Brandreth got the message. From this success others logically followed; and we scored them rapidly. Even the other three-man mission sent to central Bosnia came up safe and sound, if somewhat out of breath. Falling into an enemy offensive, they had joined partisan formations and had had to run for it. We were glad about their safety, and pressed on.

The next step was to send British officers. Would the Croat partisans accept them? Instructed by Tito, they agreed. Two British officers and a wireless operator and another Canadian Jugoslav dropped into Croatia on 18 May, this time to fire-signals on the ground; and from that success the rest all followed in due course.

For now it developed that direct contact should be established with Tito and the partisan high command itself. Whoever went would have a crucial rôle to play. He would have to be energetic; but above all he would have to be diplomatic and intelligent. A brigadier, no doubt: but where would a suitable one be found? Or a major-general? Of course, better still.

2

"Go down to the railway station tomorrow," came the order one day, specifying a time, "and meet Major-General Coppers, and bring him here." This was Keble's choice for chief liaison with the partisan high command: but would he do? Tapped on the terrace of Shepheards Hotel, the ever-clustered grapevine gave doubtful news. The major-general, it transpired, was known among his peers as Slogger Coppers, having gifts physical rather than intellectual. "Not intellectual at all, old boy," they said at Shepheards, "though you could call him mental." Further, it appeared that Slogger Coppers had just been sacked by Monty for messing up an operation in one of Monty's desert victories. They had returned him to base. They had made him available. Decent of them.

The presence was no more promising. Slogger Coppers emerged from his dusty railway carriage as a spreading figure with a scarlet complexion and a bad temper. No doubt he had been sorely tried; he at once proved sorely trying. Where was he being asked to go? Why couldn't I tell him? What was all the mystery about? He didn't like the sound of it. In any case, wherever he was going, he would have to take a batman. Could he take a batman? No, I thought, not a hope. Well, he'd see about that. His complexion deepened; and so did the G2's doubts.

Perhaps Keble would see that his choice was an obvious mistake? But then again, perhaps not. The Slogger was certainly a major-general, and a brigadier cannot be expected to remain below the rank of the man whom he commands. Then the Slogger was a regular, and so of course was Keble: probably the two had messed together, some time on Salisbury Plain or up among the hills of India. I delivered the Slogger to his immediate destination, and went away to ponder on his future. He would have to be stopped; but for that, it seemed, cunning would be wise, a little of Keble's own brand.

The Slogger was received and briefed broadly on his mission; but he asked for more detail before making up his mind. Where exactly was this fellow Tito? Who was he, anyway? And where was the enemy? At this point, perhaps distracted by the sheer glory of success, Bolo lowered his guard. He agreed that the Slogger's questions should be answered. He ordered a map briefing.

A pathetic scene ensued. Keble of course was present, and so was Tamplin and his dignity, and one or two others of senior rank with the Slogger in the midst of them. Across one wall of the room, mounted for the occasion, I had spread a map of southern Jugoslavia and the menacing mountain contours of Montenegro, blue and deep blue and eventually, for snow, white.

"Show where Tito and his chaps are," Keble said.

Using a chalk pencil on the transparent mica sheet that covered the map, I drew a small red circle in the middle of the mountains. This was fairly accurate, for now we had a lot of information.

"Show the enemy," Keble continued recklessly.

Using blue chalk, and again with accuracy, I drew fat arrows pointing into the red circle from east and north-east and north. These were German divisions, some of whose identities we knew. The Slogger leaned forward and seemed to understand. It was hard to be sure, but in any case the chalk pencils were only beginning their work. Other arrows, yellow now for Italian divisions, struck in from north-west and west and south-west. Only the south remained, and on the south there was the Adriatic sea and the minefields off Albania. Minor purple arrows for chetnik units helping the Italians, less accurate than the others but also less important, rounded the whole thing off in a quite artistic way.

The Slogger stared for a while at this design, which had all the hopelessness of a collapsed rugger scrum, and said that he would think it over. He went away and was seen no more.

Now time pressed, for Tito's situation was really as presented on the map: in fact, as we found out later, it was even worse. Someone must go at once, or else we should risk losing contact for an indeterminate time ahead. I naturally urged my own claim, but this was rejected in favour of a much stronger one, that of Captain Deakin, who was certainly, as it proved, a better choice than any other could have been. Early in the small hours of 26 May on a night of fearful wind, he and a wireless operator, Walter Wroughton, dropped into the mountains in the middle of the red circle.

The circle was smaller now, and the blue German arrows were already tearing into it. Early signals from Deakin described heavy fighting. Next he told us that enemy bombing had killed his companion, Captain Stewart, and slightly wounded Tito and himself. Then followed a terrible silence.

But on 13 June, after four days of that radio silence, we received another signal from Bill Deakin. It said: "Have broken through the German ring north across Foča-Kalinovik road near Jelec last night. Tito has extricated over ten thousand men. Bitterest fighting witnessed." It was, we learned afterwards, a modest statement. The Fortress, here, was well and truly breached.

3

With Deakin's exploit warmly approved by the prime minister and mentioned by him in the House of Commons, our own little fight was over. The "chetniks" were silenced, though they put in one last kidney punch. High policy had agreed that Deakin should go, for nobody but Churchill could stop him, but stipulated that he should carry with him no manner of material aid. We argued back that Tito and his troops were fighting for their lives and desperately in need of bandages and medicines: for Deakin to arrive with completely empty hands would be a poor start to his mission. Thus pressured, high policy consented to his taking 1,500 kilograms of medical stores. But at the last moment somebody in Cairo sent through an order to cancel these supplies. On the desert airfield where Deakin was ready to embark, these supplies were loaded; and they were then unloaded. Deakin had to arrive with empty hands.

A worse sadness occurred, and this continued. Against all the evidence of chetnik complicity with the enemy, high policy insisted on sending more British missions to chetnik groups; and no fewer than nine such missions were despatched from April 1943 onward through the summer. All of these tried to make the chetniks fight; none of them succeeded. Each suffered sore frustration and was lucky to survive. Not all survived: one of their officers, Major Neil Selby, was betrayed to the enemy and shot down while trying, very bravely, to escape from German prison guards.

Meanwhile we piled in missions to the partisans in Slovenia and Slavonia and other parts of Jugoslavia. Each reported continuous action against the enemy, including the widespread destruction of enemy lines of communication. This "gigantic guerrilla" was no phantom and our work expanded, becoming really useful for the first time. Yet for me it was also a miserable time, if only because the fruitless sending of missions to the chetniks had to continue; and besides, the action called.

Nagged and badgered, an already harassed Tamplin said no; and he continued to say it. In this, of course, he was in line with good SOE practice; Lord Selborne, had he known of so remote a matter, could only have approved. If you are really obliged to sup with the devil, use a safely long spoon and no other. Tamplin no longer thought me a long spoon: on the contrary, there could be no question of allowing me to join the partisans. Very well: but was not SOE and specifically Colonel Tamplin supposed to promote resistance in countries north of Jugoslavia? In Hungary, for example: what was Tamplin doing about Hungary? Nothing, it appeared. And so a plan began to shape itself in my mind. Taught cunning in this Keble epoch, the G2 Jugoslavia asked to be returned to his original mission. I would go to Hungary by way of Jugoslavia. With Jugoslav partisans operating inside Hungarian-occupied Jugoslavia, that should be possible now. And if possible, it should be done.

To this argument Tamplin eventually yielded. No doubt he was glad enough to lose so continuous a source of trouble, while the plan in any case must have looked singularly fragile. And so on 15 August after one or two unavoidable delays, I dropped into the hills of Bosnia. In this way, lately landed on the fortunate shores of love and married most happily, D's man for Hungary set out with his wife's brave blessing to return there. It is better to travel than to arrive. Perhaps that may be so; but on this occasion I was happy because I knew that, whatever might now befall, I really had arrived.

EIGHT

I

THANKS TO BOLO KEBLE, a British fighting partnership with the strongest armed resistance inside Fortress Europe was at last able to be made: at least twelve months later than it should have been on any military consideration but never mind, better late than never. Once made, it prospered greatly. Yet a footnote may be needful here, for where, you may reasonably wish to know before going further, is the man who launched that fortunate alliance? Where is Field-Marshal Keble now? Surely the laurels lie soft upon his brow as he pens a memoir for the Sunday papers in some quaint old mill beside the waters of the Windrush? And as surely are the salons of Buck House saluted by his sturdy feet whenever the Queen gives honour to her foremost warriors? No, nothing like that.

Bolo was still a brigadier when the war took him late in 1944, and lucky not to be lower in the ranks. For Bolo grew dizzy with success, Bolo over-reached himself. There are those who consider that he went entirely round the bend. Others are less unkind. All are unjust, for much must be forgiven to the man who got the intercepts and used them. Yet the story of his last period was very strange, and I offer it here in warning to all tram-conductors who may contemplate a military career.

The story is so extraordinary, even excessive, that it long remained untold. Only thirty years later did it come to light when a group of survivors gathered in one of Her Majesty's grace-and-favour mansions, situated in the pleasant meadows of Windsor Great Park. Cumberland Lodge dates chiefly from the reign of Queen Anne but now has plumbing and other comforts, and is generously given for the use of discreet meetings connected with Her Majesty's service. Over a weekend in 1973 we talked through a morning and reassembled in a sunny drawing-room, after lunch, to hear a contribution to history from one of the most distinguished of our number, Sir Fitzroy Maclean. What Maclean had to say provoked a silence.

In the period of this book, now the middle of 1943, Fitzroy Maclean was a captain in the Special Air Service; and he it was who became the third brigadier. Yet this was not at Keble's instance, nor was he Keble's choice. On the contrary, Keble had managed by this time to achieve the apparently impossible, and commission a brigadier with the chetniks, less than useless though these remained. He was of course happy to have a fourth brigadier in the field, and the partisans certainly rated that; but for reasons that will now become clear he wanted no one less than Maclean. He fought a desperate battle to prevent Maclean from going at all. He lost, and never in fact had any chance of winning. But his lone stand, continued when his ammunition was spent, his reinforcements gone, and his positions shot to pieces, must have its place in any record of recklessness. It may have been deplorable, but it was war.

He was really fighting a long way over his weight. A decently ruthless ambition will carry the right man up the ladder once a war breaks out and happily continues; and it carried Keble all the way from lieutenant to brigadier. But the going gets rougher all the time, and roughest of all for those who do not come out of the right drawer, which is the top drawer. In spite of his exclusive regiment, Keble was out of a rather middle drawer: even, malice whispered, lower-middle. No ancestors of his had ruled a numerous tenantry or ruled anyone, so far as can be known, save a couple of slaveys from the Durham coalfields. No Keble of that ilk, the records indicate, had as yet bestowed talent and vigour on the upper classes. This particular Keble meant to do all that, and more.

Now he measured himself against a rival without ambition, or without any that could be properly recognised as such. Maclean was only a captain, and a much younger man than Keble; but Maclean was a laird of the clan of that name, a scion of innumerable generations of his kind, a long-boned Highland aristocrat for whom the notion of having to make a career could only be absurd vulgarity. Some upstart in the Middle Ages may have defied his ancestors' right to rule; nobody in their right mind had done it since.

He was also an aristocrat of courage and intelligence. Disgusted with the compromise at Munich, he had resigned from the Foreign Office in 1939, and when the then unavoidable war duly followed, had enlisted as a private in the Cameron Highlanders. But for troops in Britain there was little to do save wait for Hitler's invasion and, when that did not come, there was still less to do.

In 1941, accordingly, a newly-commissioned Lieutenant Maclean was elected to Parliament in the Conservative interest. Yet Parliament saw nothing of him, for the war was still there. Transferred to the Middle East, Maclean looked around for relief from footslogging boredom. When the call came in 1943, Captain Maclean was in command of a small but picked unit built for difficult raids behind the enemy lines. This kind of raid on German aircraft based in Crete was his next operation; but the Germans moved their planes away, and it was cancelled. Perhaps it would be better to give up hit-and-run raiding, and get himself permanently inside the Fortress?

Happening to be in Cairo during that June, which, you will recall, was a week or so after Deakin's landing in the middle of the besieged red circle, Captain Maclean pushed the word around, as such words are pushed by such persons, and thought that he might drop into Greece. But the man who happened to get the word was a senior British diplomat called Rex Leeper, and Leeper sent it to the Foreign Office in London; and Sir Orme Sargent saw at once what the answer ought to be. Sargent explained this to the prime minister, and Churchill saw it too. They were looking for an officer with a good diplomatic record, and with political credentials of the most staunchly conservative sort but not stupidly so. This was the man they would send to Tito in Jugoslavia so as to tell them all about it. Who better than Maclean, whom Sargent happened to know from before the war?

Hailed down from Palestine, where his raiding unit was based, Maclean was told that he would go to Jugoslavia. Flying back to London for interview with the prime minister, he expected to be sent to Mihajlović and the chetniks, because, not yet being in the know, he had heard nothing of chetnik inactivity or of the partisans. He learned better in Downing Street. He was to find out, Mr Churchill told him, who was killing most Germans in Jugoslavia, and how Britain could help whoever that was to kill more of them. The likely party seemed to be Tito and the partisans. They were communists, but politics had to be a secondary consideration.

"Have you," asked Maclean, for whom asking questions of prime ministers held no terror, "thought out the implications of backing a communist-inspired movement bound to be responsible to the Russians?"

"Yes," replied the prime minister, "we have."

Maclean repeated the same question in another form several months later. He was now sure, from personal experience, that Tito would win. He was also sure, he told Churchill, that Tito's Jugoslavia would be communist.

"Are you going to live there?" asked the prime minister.

"No."

"Neither am I, so had we not better leave the Jugoslavs themselves to work out what sort of system they are going to have?"

And so the "classic dilemma" was solved for Jugoslavia; and, thanks to partisan strength there, it was solved in favour of backing resistance, and therefore backing the people in that country who wanted a fresh start after the war. If James could have hovered above that room in Downing Street he would surely have raised his right hand in blessing by the sacred law. Lecturing his flock in the villa out by Mena House, he had got it right. All the sadder to relate, then, that it was evidently for the last time. After the war he got it wrong, and even much worse than wrong: which no doubt goes to show, among other things, that you have to be very careful when you dabble with sacred laws.

Maclean was to be promoted brigadier, Churchill continued, and go to Tito as the prime minister's personal representative. He could have his pick of the whole army in choosing a second-in-command, and SOE had been given all the necessary orders. Speed was of the essence.

Thus empowered, Maclean set about fulfilling his orders. This proved less easy than you might think, or than he thought. Lord Selborne at one end, and Keble at the other, had different ideas. However previously opposed to each other, they were now drawn together by a common sense of outrage. They at once made common cause against this dastardly attempt to remove the prospective link with Tito from their direct control, and consign it to the Foreign Office or, worse still, the prime minister himself. Selborne evidently saw that if this should happen his own policy of backing the inactive Mihajlović would go irretrievably down the drain, while Keble's certainty was that he would be cast upon the sidelines and forgotten. So it must have been: for Keble's rage, like Othello's, certainly swept on to bloody thoughts and capable revenge.

Leaving Downing Street, Maclean went round to Baker Street and asked for air transport to Cairo. They told him there was none to be had. He waited, and asked again. Nothing doing: the weather was simply not fit for flying. Instead, he was bidden again to Downing Street. There the grand old man in the siren suit showed Maclean a signal from General Sir Henry Maitland Wilson, commander-in-chief in the Middle East. General Wilson, the signal said, considered Maclean totally unsuitable for the job. This surprised Maclean because General Wilson—and what could be more natural?—happened to be his personal friend. But he need not have worried, for the prime minister understood the game in play. He showed Maclean the reply that he had sent to General Wilson over his personal radio link. This told Wilson to do as he was told, and send Maclean.

The Selbornes and Kebles should have known their England better; and, come to that, their Scotland too. Leaving Number 10 Maclean walked across the Horseguards Parade where he happened to meet a friend who happened to reveal that he was flying to Cairo the next day. They went to this friend's office of authority and phoned the air ministry. No planes flying? Yes, of course there were planes flying. Then didn't they know that Maclean urgently required a passage to Cairo? Yes, they'd heard about that, but SOE had told them that Maclean did not really want to go. He did? Then tomorrow of course.

Maclean went back to Baker Street, where, with suitably long faces, they told him that the weather still prevented flying. He informed them that he had his passage in his pocket. Ah well, they said, pausing, then you had better see Lord Selborne. Lord Selborne was all smiles, but suggested that he should take an oath of loyalty to SOE. Captain Maclean demurred: and why indeed should a British officer take an oath of loyalty to any save the monarch? At this Lord Selborne pointed to two little leather cases embossed in gold with the letters DSO, for Distinguished Service Order, a prestigious medal then and since. "That," he said, "is what we do for those who serve us loyally." Now I doubt if even Bolo would have tried this one; and James would certainly have looked peculiarly owlish.

Arrived with no more delay in Cairo, Maclean was received by General Wilson. Why had the general advised Churchill that he was totally unsuitable? The general had done no such thing. Somebody had sent the signal in his name. Somebody was going to pay for it. Maclean was to get himself gazetted brigadier forthwith, and return for help if further trouble loomed.

There followed a meeting between Keble and Maclean at

Rustem Building. It was not friendly. Why, demanded Keble, was Maclean dressed as a brigadier? Because, Maclean replied, the commander-in-chief had so bidden him. Why had he gone to see the commander-in-chief? Same reply. Then, said Keble, he was not to go again, not even if ordered by the commander-in-chief. Further, he was not going to be sent to Jugoslavia: SOE would see to that. And meanwhile Keble had forbidden anyone to show him any files, signals, or other useful information whatsoever. End of meeting.

This is where one sees the force of the argument of those who held that Keble had actually gone mad. He must otherwise have understood that the flashing vest and burnished brow could not help him here. Bullying Tamplin and his kind was one thing: bullying the scion of innumerable Highland ancestors was another. He raged and threatened; but he might as well have hit the wind. For Maclean was not only a man of impeccable good manners, of unfailing generosity to all who depended on him, and modest to a fault in the general run of things. He was also a man who expected to be taken for what he was, and who, if not so taken, possessed a steely will to trample on offenders. Those who would not take him for what he was found him stiff, cold, insulting and ambitious: they mistook for ambition, that is, what was nothing more than the natural assumption of a place at the top. After the war Maclean returned to Parliament and just as naturally failed to reach high office there, for he failed still more in the art of scrumming that any success must depend on in that competitive arena. He was the last man to go in for scrumming.

Keble's madness continued. Returning to General Wilson after his interview at Rustem Building, Maclean found the commander-in-chief in conversation with Colonel Vellacott. A distinguished academic in private life, Colonel Vellacott's special duty was to disseminate lies. In the Middle East command, let me explain, he was the centre for spreading those "whispers" which so delighted the priest of Saint Rock.

"Tell Fitzroy," said General Wilson to Vellacott, "what you just told me." Whereupon Vellacott explained that SOE had asked him to spread a new "whisper" round the best bars and army grapevines. This was to confide in all useful ears that Maclean was a hopeless drunk, an active homosexual, and a consistent coward. Vellacott said that he was sure that SOE must have excellent reasons for wishing this impression of Maclean to get around, but even so had felt it wise to secure confirmation from the commander-in-chief.

And that was pretty well the end of Keble. A top-level meeting called by General Wilson launched yet another purge of SOE Cairo, and all obstacles were removed. But well forewarned now, Maclean took another step to win the war. Happening to have the right connexions, he provided himself with a separate and secret radio link, by wavelength and code, between himself in Jugoslavia and General Wilson in Cairo, as well as with the prime minister in London. So that later on, as he told us thirty years later, "when I found that Churchill was not receiving signals from me [at Tito's headquarters] that had been duly despatched [via SOE Cairo] and acknowledged, I was fortunately able to repeat them to him in full by another [radio] channel."

This was really the last that was heard of the man who got the intercepts and used them, and a few months later he was dead. Which only goes to show, no doubt, that if you are going to reach the stars from somewhere far below you had better take a firm hold on James Klugmann's sacred law; and a lot more besides.

Maclean departed to join us in the hills of Jugoslavia, though careful, as he recalled at Cumberland Lodge, not to take the first parachute offered to him. There he fulfilled his mission with a steadfast authority and courage, tact and talent, such as no one could have bettered; and both sides, the British and the Jugoslavs, had the strongest reasons to be grateful for his work. He never got one of Lord Selborne's DSOs, you wouldn't expect it; but afterwards he was made a baronet, which many of us thought the very least that he deserved, and lives happily ever after.

2

Maclean arrived in the hills of Jugoslavia and our war began to get somewhere. Greater events had also just occurred. Two weeks earlier, Badoglio's Italian government surrendered to the Allies. Now the Italian walls of the Fortress were strongly cracked and broken into, and our troops poured through. But they were unable to pour very far: across the waist of Italy, the Germans put down powerful defences. It would have to be a slogging match, and a costly one.

Italy became the chief theatre of war in the south.

Following the armies, our SOE base command and supply

establishment were able to move in the spring of 1944 from Cairo to the Italian town of Bari, near the foot of the Adriatic. Here they were much better placed for operations into the Balkans; and they were close to the scene of action in Italy itself.

Having moved from Cairo, SOE hived off an Italian operational unit, and here I shift the story to Italy for a while.

This Italian operational unit was labelled Number One Special Force, but its future seemed doubtful. Was it going to have a simple run, helping Italian patriots fighting north of the enemy lines, or was SOE's chetnik-partisan conflict, repeated in various forms in Greece and Jugoslavia and Albania, going to be renewed in Italy as well?

The answer, when it eventually came, was to be a rather strange one. But before that, towards the end of 1943 and while SOE headquarters were still in Cairo, other questions had to be settled first; and SOE had nothing at all to do with these. Were there going to be any Italian patriots fighting north of the enemy lines? If so, were there going to be enough of them to make much difference? And to these questions, asked after Badoglio's generals had sunk their army without trace, and as the long and painful slogging match for Italy began and continued, and as the Germans closed their grip ever more firmly on the Italian provinces they occupied, the answers seemed both blank and negative.

PART IV

ONE

EARLY IN THAT winter of 1943–44, while the events just recorded were unfolding in Jugoslavia, the ex-prisoner of the Essaillon had continued for a while in the peasant house at Ramaceto far up the hillside above the gorge of Favale, waiting for his first volunteers; and gradually the house had filled with men. Maria cooked for them the food the peasants gave, and Enrica ran among their feet and tripped over their rifles: whenever, that is, they had any rifles, which was seldom.

Bad news, more bad news, accompanied the coming of the winter, as well as a wind from the alpine north. It became known that the spearheads of the Allied armies, shoving up southern Italy from landings in Sicily and Salerno, had slowed and then stopped. Down there in the south, far away, the frontlines were said to have grasped each other in a clinch that could not shift until the spring; and the spring was on the other side of winter, and the winter had only just begun.

Many left the band of Cichero, and other bands too. Discouraged or despairing, they went home or to anywhere else they could hide. For these, perhaps, there might be some middle ground on which to survive and wait? They watched the well-fed German hunting teams motor past into the mountains on the search for any who might remain of the band of Cichero and its like. They dodged the spies and torturers of Mussolini's *bande nere*, Blackshirt units, as these "national front-ers" went about their work of sniffing out resisters or any who might sympathise with resistance. But the middle ground grew hard to survive on, and narrower day by day.

The first snows fell. Not gently with a muffled warning of worse to come, but overnight and for days on end till the tawny land was lost beneath a freezing blanket. With this the door of the year was shut fast and the key turned, while against it the snow went on piling a tall and sodden tumult. Vanishing into that snow and ice, Marzo's band of Cichero was down to six men and one woman by New Year's day of 1944. Other bands fared no better.

The face of the rockbound land changed, and now was bare and public to the view. From the Favale gorge to the slopes of Cichero, and on towards the peaks above Santo Stefano and across the valley of the Trebbia and up again beside the cliffs of Antola, where hamlets clung with hidden roofs against the rockface, the paths they used were trodden into telltale trails upon the glitter. Their sentries posted at the entry of the hamlets where they lived could stare at these trails that came across the hills; and then again, after another day's snowfall, the same sentries could see men moving at the head of new trails that crept towards them like the scrawling of a pencil on a white page. These men came in hours later, dragging their feet, their heads down; and you could see their effort as they sank through the crust at every step. They reached the sentries and told the news. The news, invariably, was bad.

It got hard to say much against the ones who lost heart and went home. On Monte Penna five partisans froze to death. Others lost a foot or an ear. And the spring was a world away.

Even so, there were those like Marzo who did not go home. They had glimpsed the vision of a new companionship, of a new start for Italy after the donkey's bray of Mussolini's decades. That was their programme, and they were ready to stay with it. Answering its call, men began to join them again. Trying to find out what best to do in a situation that none of them had known before, these few dozen traipsed about their mountains round Cichero or crouched in huts pinned to the rockface, nursing hunger, chased.

Had anyone else an idea of what should be done? In Genoa, somewhere deep in secrecy, there was the Ligurian committee of liberation. Bini took the road down Fontanabuona to Chiavari, now again under Blackshirt rule, and slipped along the riviera into the city. He was gone for some days.

"Well?" they asked him when he came back.

"There are other groups formed later than ours. They are doing more."

"But we have begun to give a lead, to form the people needed for tomorrow."

"The people needed for tomorrow are not formed by talk. They are formed by action."

What kind of action could advance their programme, extend the politics of liberation into war, responsibly, wisely? It was much discussed.

They made their first attack against a fascist post on the bend of the Fricciallo. There were said to be fifteen Blackshirts with automatics. And food supplies, and even blankets.

Falling snow covered their approach. It also froze their feet and hands while they waited till the small hours. Silence inside: but give them another quarter of an hour. Then shoot out the lock and in through the door. Bini and Marzo first: leaders should lead. A room full of everyone firing at everyone else. So get out quick, and with luck. No casualties. Some fascists hit, but no weapons captured. *Un bel pasticcio*: a mess up, really. Try again.

They lost Severino on the next attempt: one of the three Sicilians who had come up first, the best of the three. They attacked the "national front-ers" in the little town of Borzonasca, and these captured Severino. The houses of Borzonasca fell then, as they do now, into a steep valley where they jumble around a little square. That is where the Blackshirts killed Severino. They tied him to a chair which they took from the church, and shot him first in the feet and legs, then higher, at last in the head. After which the local fascist boss, a grocer with the national flag of Italy sewn across his chest, his name Spiotta, shouldered his automatic and the grocer's men clapped their hands: nice work, and you were even paid for doing it. They left Severino's body on the square for three days, and then people were allowed to bury what remained.

But the band of Cichero continued stubbornly to grow in numbers as the middle ground narrowed. After Severino's death they were able to form a new unit, a new *distaccamento*, and the men of this unit followed the practice now beginning to take shape. They chose the unit name they wanted. They called it the Severino. They elected their commander and political commissar, with deputies for these, and brought the names for approval by their leaders, Marzo and Bisagno and Bini. And the units of Cichero tried a third time: against a fascist garrison at Ferriere where the road from the east rears up towards the great pass of the Scoffera and then, north-westward, plunges down to Genoa. Quite an important post for the Germans, this: Ferriere gave them protection on one of a dozen routes radiating from their stronghold in the city itself. The Germans had confided Ferriere, as other such posts, to Blackshirts under veteran fascist command.

Better planning this time. Arrival by truck, rapid encirclement of barracks, calculated covering fire: good surprise. And Bisagno. Who leaps the fence of metal posts, lobs a grenade through a window, clambers inside and lights the fuse of a suitcase of explosive that he has carried with him: and gets out again. But no explosion, nothing. So Bisagno, while everyone is firing back and forth, goes calmly back inside and relights the fuse. He jumps clear just in time. And they are into their truck, heading for the mountains, before the din of the explosion has entirely lifted from their ears; and this time they have also captured weapons. It is very much Bisagno's victory. Bisagno needs no such reassurance, but for those who do, this is probably the moment when the band of Cichero takes off into its future, which will be several of the best partisan divisions in all northern Italy. More volunteers begin to flow up from the towns, for now there is another side that will fight, and this side has shown that it knows how.

Besides, the middle ground is vanishing fast. In November 1943 the Republic of Salo, Hitler's puppet state in German-occupied Italy, has issued an order for the mobilisation of all men of the classes of 1922, 1923, and 1924: of all those, that is, who are aged between nineteen and twenty-one. Mussolini's police and Blackshirts set about rounding up these conscripts. Other kinds of pressure are applied across the gamut of society. So the choice becomes ever harder to avoid: join the fascists or fight them. For parents, too, the choice becomes a pointed one: deliver your sons to the fascists or take the consequences: fines, loss of property, beating up, prison, or less and less rarely the firing squad.

The band of Cichero and its like are still few in number, but now they can see some light at the end of that winter's tunnel. What they see is small and dim and far away, but down in the towns the rumour begins to run. They are not a few dozen up there, or even a hundred and very hungry; they are thousands, well armed, well fed. There is another side to join, and it is possible that this other side will win. Even Radio Londra urges the patriots of occupied Italy to rise in war against the Germans and the fascists, so it's clear that the Allies are backing the partisans. There is another side to join, and it will govern Italy tomorrow. The ex-prisoner of the Essaillon, hearing all this as it filters up the valleys and using his forty-seven-year-old legs as though they were young again, gets into trouble with his doubts. It is all too good to be true. But it may happen.

Or it may not. Angered by the attack on Ferriere and other such attacks, the Germans hit back. They put confident columns into all the valleys radiating up from Trebbia and Aveto, and Marzo has to be everywhere at once, moving units, shepherding, shoving, hiding them as best he can, and the best is still bad. Bisagno does the same; so do others. There are disasters, enemy reprisals, the shooting of hostages, the burning of hamlets; and the units of Cichero become a cluster of fugitives. The problem is to stay alive.

Allied aircraft fly over at night, and the gossip from the towns speaks of arms dropped by parachute to the units of Cichero.

"People will believe anything."

"But it can be true. You haven't heard?"

Bini has received an instruction from the Genoa committee who have got it from God knows where. Radio Londra will broadcast a signal during the news. Then fires must be ready at the appointed place; and Bini has chosen a plateau high on the Forca. *Gatta ci cova* are the words of the promised signal.

"It'll never come."

But the words do come, crisp and clear, and men climb to the icy plateau of the Forca and stand beside unlit fires for hours, even for whole nights, thin figures etched upon the starlit snow.

Only the words come. All the same the Allies are there, and the Allies are with them. Hold on: get through to the spring, somehow, anyhow: and then. The avenues of time may run crooked, but they run.

They run for others now: still for very few, but not so few as months before. In the woods of Piedmont spread above the vineyards of Cuneo and Cavour, Barbato shows the way; and there are more to follow him. Further north again, where alpine valleys open to the smoking plains of Lombardy, Moscatelli does the same; and so it develops all round the tall arena of the southern Alps and across the rice fields of the Po, and south again into the hills of Liguria and Tuscany and the plains of Romagna and Emilia. The lost few of the start of that winter of 1943–44 have become legendary; but they are legends who are alive.

Those who come through to the spring of 1944 are units with tried leaders, weapons taken from the enemy, dependable morale. Ahead of them now there are the months of spring and summer, clothing the woods with cover, warming the huts that hide in mountain gulleys, offering food. In their mountains above the sea mists of the long riviera, the band of Cichero becomes one among a profusion of bands reaching east beyond the pass of Cisa above the bay of Lerici, and west behind Genoa into the hills of Savona and as far as Imperia and the frontier with France. Croce and Moro shoot up the fascists in the valley of Trebbia, attack municipal offices, burn records that could serve recruiting officers of the "national front", recapture food taken from the peasants and restore it to them; and Gino, who commands the Severino, and other leaders and their units do the same.

Down in the towns the word goes round. Perhaps these men possess the future. Perhaps they do.

TWO

THE WORD WENT round, but not with any certain consequences. Politics were getting loose among Italians, but politics after twenty years of nothing but the donkey's bray and visits from the police had small attractive power. Pondering on the future of the world, Prime Minister Smuts might look out from South Africa and fear the worst, but for a while confusion seemed the only real result.

When the Germans occupied Rome in the wake of the armistice of September 1943, the King of Italy and his new prime minister, Marshal Badoglio, stayed to lead no resistance but commandeered a coach and took themselves in headlong flight to the south. There they set up their government under Allied protection. There, too, the leaders of the anti-fascist parties surfaced in a new legality but found themselves barred from entering Badoglio's government. There were reasons for this. They were liberals, republicans, Christian-democrats, Action party, socialists and communists, but it was far from clear, as yet, what mass of people they might severally or collectively represent. Most of them thought that a democratic future could have no place for a king who had sold out blatantly to fascism, but they seemed for a while to agree on little else. The Allies kept them at arm's length. Their day might come, but not yet.

Formed to make a revolution against fascism, the more radical of these democratic leaders now discovered that fascism was overthrown without them, and were much divided on what to do next. With men of the radical-liberal Action party here and there, the communists generally took the lead in supporting armed resistance north of the German lines, an area that still included the whole of central as well as northern Italy: but what should be the aim of this resistance? Was it not to open the way for that general process of "bolshevisation" so vividly anticipated by Smuts and his eminent friends? Anti-fascist unity for the time being might be an obvious necessity but after that, at any rate for the communists, there should be revolution; or at any rate, for them, Moscow would point the way. Not surprisingly, the other democratic leaders found it easy to believe that this was how the communists saw the future. And most of the communist leaders then in the south probably did see it like this. The old tradition held powerful sway among them.

Yet the message that now began to come down from the German-occupied provinces, where Marzo and his like were beginning their fight, proved to be a different one. Most of the early partisan units that survived and grew in strength were led by communists, but the great majority of all the men and women whom they led were non-communist or anti-communist: their war aims were to chase out the Germans, make a final end of fascism, and afterwards go home and live in peace. The necessary revolution, for them, was some kind of democracy free from police spies and repression. If the communists were to preach other objectives, then the communists would be left in isolation; and in isolation they would perish.

Genoa showed this. Its reputation all through the fascist years was "red", but the real number of communists remained insignificantly small. At the great Ansaldo shipyard, in 1943, only about 50 men out of some 4,000 were members of the communist party; in the Elletromeccanica no more than 30 out of 2,900; while the highest rate of membership, at the San Giorgio yards, was 204 out of 5,000. Not all these party members were by any means active; and any knowledge even of their membership, reaching the police, guaranteed a long prison sentence.

Aside from this sparsity of numbers, the experience of resistance was one that made increasing nonsense of any kind of sectarian politics. For what were you going to say to a devout Christian like Bisagno who blows up the fascist barracks at Ferriere? If you were going to wait for his conversion to communism, you were going to wait until you were dead. But if you were not going to wait for that, on what basis would you fight alongside him? Relearning their politics, the communists in the occupied zones came to find that anti-fascist unity possessed a value in itself, an essential value, even a permanent value, and was no mere tactical necessity. Revolution should remain the long-term aim, but a revolution which could be made to develop from the broad unity of democratic action.

This process of rethinking was to command the future. Yet for many communists it long remained partial and painful, and not only in Italy. I remember chatting with Sasha around this time, with the winter drawing to a close in the plains of the Vojvodina, about the years of the war before Hitler attacked Russia.

"But they don't count," said Sasha, "that was an imperialist war."

"They damn well do count, and it wasn't."

"Well, who cares? We're all in this together now."

Sasha happened to be my friend as well as our unit commissar, a tough and true partisan but also a man of Sombor where, as they explain in a song of those parts, folk are so enlightened that even women drink wine. Not everyone was of Sasha's enlightenment, and least of all our regional commander, old Slobodan Grulović, filled even in 1944 with the fury of sectarian bile.

Not everyone, in northern Italy, was like Marzo. Yet those communists who had begun to rethink their politics were nonetheless among the ones who mattered most, and they included Luigi Longo, the leading communist in Milan, the leading city. The crucial military figure in the Milan committee of national liberation, the committee for northern Italy that soon exercised authority over all the other six-party liberation committees in the German-occupied zones, Longo saw the vision that Marzo had seen, and he saw it from the same point of view. To follow one dictatorship by another, however differently motivated, would be to kill that vision. The unity of anti-fascists necessary to winning this war must be the same unity that could launch a democratic society in Italy. This was the rethinking that would long afterwards develop, across all the obstacles of loyalty to Stalinist ideas and practices, into what the 1970s were going to call "eurocommunism".

This rethinking emerged from the needs of the time: it began, that is, with a companionship in arms. It crystallised around an idea of democratic unity that was in fact—and the post-war years were going to prove this time and again—completely at odds with the orthodox tradition of communism, the tradition that had become "Stalinist"; and it met with corresponding doubts, hesitations, or sheer refusals. Yet it continued to make its way, for that was what the times demanded; and it developed further as the committees of liberation began to endow the fighting units with an effective and unified organisation. This was the organisation, emerging at the "grass roots" in village and town, that was conceived and used as the groundwork for a democratic future.

In November 1943, with the snow already falling in the high hills, the underground network of the communists in the German-occupied zones sent round orders for an effort to fuse neighbouring bands into larger units with better discipline and a capacity for combined action. These orders were long in taking effect because of the winter that followed. But larger units did emerge in course of time, and these were given an orderly structure. Each had its elected commander and commissar, communist or not (although the senior commissars, it was hoped, would be veteran party members), together with a set of rules binding on behaviour and a clear political line. The rules varied. Now and then they were a bit utopian: as when the new Parma brigades were instructed to form and carry round "a small library of good books of varied literature", an order which the bands of Cichero, at any rate, would have found hard to carry out. But the political line did not vary, and was not in the least utopian. This line was to create and maintain a trend of increasing unity of thought about a democratic future, and about the means to achieve and guard it.

Taking early shape in the winter of 1943–44, these brigades could wear any clothing their members were able to get hold of, mostly from the enemy, and they could also wear a red scarf. But the redness of the scarf was not only the redness of the workers' flag. It was as much the redness of the tradition of Garibaldi and the fight for Italian unity and progress against other dictators and oppressors a hundred years before.

"Here we make Italy, or we die," Garibaldi had told his thousand ragged volunteers, many of them with guns that would not shoot, before they beat the army of the Bourbons in the first of Garibaldi's decisive battles long ago. Afterwards it would sound like high romance in the best Italian manner: at the time, the choice for those volunteers was crudely as Garibaldi put it. And the choice was just as crude for the volunteers of 1943–44: either they fought and won and opened the way for a new Italy, or certainly they died. The lesson was read to them every day by the circumstances of their resistance. If later volunteers came with a tendency to swagger, the casualties soon stopped that. There were many casualties, for these units were formed as assault brigades and their duty was offensive. They were called the brigades of Garibaldi. Their fighters called themselves Garibaldini.

The next most active party in the German-occupied provinces was the *Partito d'Azione*, the Action party, formed some years earlier as a rallying point for anti-fascists who were neither socialist nor communist. Their chief man in the north was a notable patriot called Ferruccio Parri. Under Parri's lead the Action party followed the communists, in February 1944, with the formation of their fighting units into brigades; these were called *Giustizia e Libertà*, Justice and Liberty. They never achieved more than a fraction of the strength of the Garibaldini. But they had much the same structure; and they placed a similar emphasis on political commissars whose special task was to promote and reinforce a unity of thought and action.

Other brigades appeared as the spring grew into fine weather. Some of these were socialist, others liberal, others again republican. Together with the Garibaldini brigades and those of Justice and Liberty, they were given the same political line and came under the general control of the six-party committees of national liberation hidden in the towns. Not all of these brigades were of much use, and some were of no use at all. A few bands of self-respecting brigands also appeared, and, not self-respecting, several groups of mountain-topists who made local treaties with the enemy: treaties that left the roads free for enemy use while the mountain-topists ate in safety off the peasants whom they "controlled", just like the chetniks in Jugoslavia. Later on, the brigands and the mountain-topists were hunted down by the genuine brigades and their leaders forced into disbandment or, if recalcitrant, shot.

With a due and human stumbling, all this effort marched with the wider movement of opinion. More and more ordinary people were carried into sympathy with resistance by their own feelings about what the future ought to be like. Various pressures also pushed them. The nazis pushed them with their deportations and persecutions. The fascist "national front-ers" pushed them with their aping of the nazis. Trying to regain a base in popular support, this "national front" now began talking left, just as the nazis had done when their future was still uncertain. They left off denouncing the socialists and communists (but went on destroying these whenever they could), and spoke against millionaires and plutocrats, the lords of high finance, and of course the Jews. They even spoke of socialism. None of it took, for the donkey's bray had no more credit.

Big demonstrations became possible. In March 1944, with the snow in early thaw beneath the feet of new brigades, half a million workers struck for a week in Milan, Turin and several other cities. Local demands were made, but the strike was an avowedly political action under a communist lead, and called above all for an end to the war and its miseries. Let the partisans come down from the hills and take over the factories, and the workers would see to it that the factories worked. So it was talked in those exciting days: and were there not by now, this March of 1944, 300,000 partisans in Lombardy alone? Really, there were as yet only a few hundred in that province; but the strike was the largest ever known in Fortress Europe, and foretold a flood of volunteers for the partisan brigades.

All this was in the German-occupied northern provinces. Down in the Allied-occupied south, an odd situation meanwhile persisted. Badoglio's royal government was in power, backed by the Allies, but possessed no popular authority or support. The six democratic parties that did possess such authority and support, or at least could claim it, were not in the government and therefore not in power. Once again, something had to give: either the hope of democratising Italy, or else, given Allied policy, the anti-king dogma of the democratic parties.

The dogma gave, denied from an unexpected quarter.

On 27 March a man from Moscow disembarked from a steamer in Naples harbour. He was Palmiro Togliatti, secretary-general of the Italian communist party and a long and lucky resident in Stalin's capital. He was expected to take a very stiff anti-king line. He took the reverse. Our policy, he announced, is one of unity in the fight for liberation and the resurrection of Italy. The communists, he said, are in favour of any measure which will advance that unity, even joining the royal government. Sensation: and not least among the communist leaders in the south, who hurried off a coded message to their colleagues in German-occupied Rome. "Madrid and Stockholm"—Togliatti and his fellow-arrival Ruggero Grieco—"advise us to participate in the government," said this message. "Act on this, and agree it with Pietro": with Nenni, the socialist leader, who was also in Rome. They didn't find it easy, and they didn't all like it; but they obeyed.

This switch upset the other democratic party leaders even more. Weren't the communists supposed to be the tough ones, so dour and difficult as conveniently to exclude themselves from the practical politics of power-sharing? Now Togliatti had jumped over all their heads, and the communists were suddenly the party of sweet reason.

Unprincipled opportunism, said some; others thought it the merest trick. In fact, as gradually emerged, it was a new formulation of the politics of democratic unity: wrapped inside this formulation was the "new communist party" that Togliatti soon called for, a party that should no longer be a sect, but a mass party capable of leading a whole nation. Wrapped inside it, too, were all those developments within Italian communism that would afterwards turn against the lies and tyrannies of Stalinism. Meanwhile Togliatti exercised his authority according to the practice of the "old party", the sect, and insisted on his orders. Democratising this party would be another process for the future, and no doubt a long one. What Togliatti was doing at the moment was to get his party in the south into line with his party in the north, and thereby enable it to play a key part in national politics. And this proved decisive. With the king question shelved till peace came, the democratic parties went into the government soon after.

Yet these parties could never hope to function without a strong movement in favour of democracy. This was the historic rôle of the Italian resistance. For it was the resistance which produced this movement among multitudes of people in whom the miseries of fascism had previously stifled the hope or understanding of honest politics. Now, in the enemy-occupied zones where committees of liberation were at work and partisans fought, there came a decisive groundswell of democratic action. By May of 1944 both resistance and groundswell were growing fast.

In that month the Milan command put the total figure of partisans at 100,000, but this was optimistic. A month later Mussolini's chief of staff, the Marshal Graziani who had bombed Libyans and Ethiopians into silence and then taken a beating in Africa himself, told the Germans that the partisans totalled 80,000. But Graziani also had an interest in swelling the figure. He was anxious for the Germans to hurry up in sending him the conscripted fascist divisions then being trained in Germany. Perhaps the true total in May of 1944 was upward of 50,000 organised and effective fighters, most of whom were Garibaldini, with another 50,000 volunteers available if arms could be found for them.

This total of fighting men was already ten times' larger than the total at the end of 1943, and considerably better able to fight. Letting politics loose among the people was ripening its fruits.

THREE

I

ALL THE EVIDENCE assembled later was going to confirm it: the politics of armed resistance had become the politics of a radical democracy. The politics, very much, of youth: for the vast majority of all partisans everywhere were under thirty. This was the politics they argued over round countless campfires or in shivering cold, and what they fought for in a multitude of engagements large and small, and what, more or less consistently, they very often died for.

The avenues there behind us show this very well. Yet it may be a truth still worth insisting on: because, to see it now, you have to push back past and through the distortions and suppressions of the long "cold war" which followed on this one. And this again is because the beneficiaries of that "cold war"—identify them as you wish—have shrunk the armed resistance to mere personal adventurers, to depoliticised media serials about this or that individual, and to sentimental loyalties such as would never have withstood the actual test. Such adventures and loyalties had their place. Of course: but they were not the substance of the great uprisings against nazi-fascism that inspired the youth of those days, they were not the epic of those years. The true epic of those years lay in the courage and determination with which countless men and women followed the hope and vision of a radical democracy. Vaguely perceived, perhaps: sometimes utopian, this too: and yet so real and so worthwhile, in the grim conditions of that time, as to be worth everything you had to give.

No doubt people joined the great uprising from a multitude of motives, just as you would expect. But the politics of that resistance then took them into its companionship and joined them, when they could stand the pace, in a wider purpose, the purpose that saved this occupied Europe from utter misery and despair, the purpose that stood for any worthwhile future.

This companionship asked much of them, sometimes everything; all the same, most did stand the pace. For it gave them in exchange a penetrating sense of worth and value, so that very ordinary people, and most of us were very ordinary people, could and did begin to feel that they were good and useful builders of a different and decent world. Very consciously, or less so: I don't say it was always like that. But it was often like that.

The same truths were measured by the makers of Allied policy, and found difficult to accept. Most of these makers of Allied policy, as all the records have since confirmed, were very conservative persons, even far more conservative than is easily imagined now. They had their own vision of a future freed of nazism, and it was perfectly sincere: British conservatives fought and died no less gallantly than British radicals, and had their full part in the victory over nazism. But their vision had no place for far-reaching social change. They had begun by distrusting the armed resistance in occupied Europe, and soon they were deploring it.

There came a moment, even, when these conservatives seriously considered abandoning the whole Greek resistance movement on the grounds that it was hopelessly, and therefore dangerously, democratic. They went so far as to recommend this to London; and even that very conservative Foreign Secretary, Sir Anthony Eden, was provoked to comment that it could not be done, "for the war has to be carried on". Jugoslavia provided another warning of the damage that the politics of armed resistance could do to cherished conservative aims. And now Italy seemed to be threatening to compound the damage. Yet with Churchill still clamouring for "gigantic guerrillas", even with reservations as to Greece, these rudely popular resistances could not be thrust aside. Somehow or other, they had to be supported.

That was bad enough. But there was more. We were in year four now in our forces at home and overseas, and assorted tram-conductors were moving up the ranks: and, as they moved, so did the corrosions of democracy.

It was natural enough, after all. Out in these war theatres there were great armies of our people, citizen volunteers and conscripts with their own vivid memory or tradition of democratic struggles; and these were the armies that really mattered in the military balance, the armies that fought and won the bloodiest battles and gave the greatest sacrifice of life. Did they ever suppose they were doing all this for the sake of kings abroad and conservatism at home, for some kind of return to the misery of the 1930s and the "men of Munich"?

It seems that they did not. On the contrary, in this matter of the great uprisings against nazi-fascism, it seems that what they heard about the partisans they greatly liked. They were fighting against the same enemy: even, possibly, they were fighting for the same objectives when the war was over. All that, now, began to be in the atmosphere of thought, whenever anyone had time to think of it.

Coming out of Jugoslavia with dysentery, I was hospitalised in Bari for some days. Lying in the next bed was a captain of British infantry about my own age which, by now, was rising thirty. We chatted about our lives.

"We've got some partisans too," he said, "up on 8 Army front."

I asked him about them a bit patronisingly, I fear, from a conviction that no partisans could rival those I knew. But he would not have it. He talked about the "Eye-tie" *partigiani* fighting beyond the German line, threading that line with useful information or to carry back ammunition, the kind of people they were; and he talked with admiration. He spoke of them as equals, and with respect. He thought a lot of them. And he wasn't the only one.

The historian Edward Thompson was a lieutenant of tanks on the same front. He told me later how his most orthodox ex-lancer regiment gave birth to a "huge wall newspaper" in the days before tackling Monte Cassino, and how "the first and major item was about Tito's partisans". Waiting for that ferocious battle to begin, "men got their feet under peasant tables" and then came back and said what they had heard "about tiny partisan operations and immense nazi revenges". Did they draw further conclusions? It may be hard to be sure, but again it seems that they did.

Plenty of privates and corporals as well as officers, it further appears, were now beginning to draw conclusions about what they might be fighting for. And far more privates and corporals than officers. As, for example, in the extraordinary affair that developed in Cairo towards the end of 1943, and was called the "Forces' Parliament".

Even with the war far in the desert to the west, there were still many British troops in and around Cairo at the end of 1943, and many more returned there on leave from the desert. There was little to distract them in that lonely and often hostile city. The army education authority conceived the idea of encouraging lectures and debates in a well-appointed concert hall given over usually to a programme of "music for all". Applied to for permission, the natural leaders of men, now chiefly represented in

Cairo by the general officer commanding, the GOC, Brigadier Chrystal, gave their approval.

Then someone had a better idea. Why not turn these debates into a mock parliament? A large number of privates and corporals seemed to like the idea of that. The "Forces' Parliament" was billed for its first session on 1 November 1943.

Paying an entrance fee of seven piastres (about 2 p today) some 400 "members" rolled up for the opening session. Nobody had much idea about how a parliament was supposed to operate, but then it was discovered that a South African lieutenant among them had made a study of the science of British parliamentary procedure. Then he'd better be "Speaker", hadn't he?; and so he was voted into office. As will be seen in a moment, he proved a valiant choice.

What would the "parliament" discuss? Well, politics of course, what else? But wouldn't that be a breach of King's Regulations, of Article 541 in fact, forbidding servicemen to take any active part in the affairs of a political party? Obviously not, this was a mock parliament with mock parties. All the same, just to make sure, the "members" agreed that proceedings would be supposed to be taking place in the future, after the war was over. There could be nothing wrong with that. Weren't they, after all, fighting for democracy, and didn't democracy mean debate?

Thus fortified, the "members" cheerfully divided themselves into "government" and "opposition" sides, and moved for business. That was about all they did in the first session, but things took shape a little more in the second, that of December, when "parliament" debated a Bill to nationalise the distributive trades, and passed it by a large majority.

A month later another large majority passed a Bill for "Inheritance Restriction". But at this session, the third, it was noticed that the area education officer was beginning to look worried. Yet the "parliament" was growing popular, was widely talked about, people were enjoying it: so never mind the area education officer, but press on. Even a mock parliament ought to have an elected government, as democracy also insisted, and so they decided to organise a "general election".

Every "member" coming to the February session was handed a ballot paper containing the names of the four parties in presence: conservative, liberal, commonwealth, and labour. Nearly half of the approximately 500 "members" present—some of them, newly back from the desert, hadn't yet caught on—cast their votes in due and proper form, and the results were very clear.

Labour romped home with 119 votes, commonwealth (close to labour) got 55, the liberals 38, and the conservatives came last with 17. And with this it was very soon understood that persons far more important than the area education officer were more than worried, were positively alarmed.

In the March session a labour "government" duly took office under the prime ministership of Private Harry Solomons of the Pay Corps, a former East London councillor and the future Member for Hull, while commonwealth was led by an aircraftsman, the liberals by a flight lieutenant, and the conservatives by a corporal in the Royal Air Force. A King's Speech was then read according to the best procedure, and the next session was announced for 5 April, when "parliament" would debate a Bill to nationalise the banks of Britain. Well, you can see it coming: the next session, that of April, was going to be the last. Six hundred "members", many again on leave from the desert, attended this last session and took their seats on "government" and "opposition" benches; but so did the GOC, Brigadier Chrystal. He was clearly a lot more than upset: first there had been those subversive voting figures, and all these attacks on sacred property, and now they were going to nationalise the banks. The whole thing would have to be stopped; and at once. The GOC's sense of humour, it further appeared, was not well developed, for he was additionally moved to wrath by an item on a German radio broadcasting in English. Based on press reports and suitably aimed to annoy, this item had affirmed that British troops in Egypt had taken over the country and set up Councils of Soldiers and Airmen. Red revolution was obviously on the way.

Chrystal came with military police, just in case, and began by ordering out the press, which had greatly enjoyed and reported the proceedings of the "parliament". Then he announced that the whole enterprise was dissolved, forbidden, and suppressed. All cables and letters referring to it, press or private, would be forthwith stopped by censorship. Moreover, its proceedings were held in contravention of Article 541 of Regulations. As a wit remarked at the time, this was like indicting an actress for murder because she had played Lady Macbeth; but it made no difference. Each of the party leaders spoke in protest, the strongest of these speeches being made, as it happened, by the conservative spokesman,

Corporal Bob Tambling. And at this point "Speaker" Arthur Lewin came into his own, not having studied British procedure for nothing. Neatly outflanking a now sorely troubled GOC, whose own understanding of that procedure was evidently no more advanced than his sense of humour, "Speaker" Lewin put the protest to a vote of the "House", and the "House" voted for this protest by exactly 600 to 1, the GOC's vote being the only one against.

Though without benefit of wig, "Speaker" Lewin then announced that the GOC's ban could apply only to the following session, and called on the chancellor of the exchequer to move the order of the day. Aircraftsman Leo Absе, who was chancellor, at once got on with it and introduced a Bill "to make provision for the Establishment of a National Banking Corporation"; and this Bill, after an enthusiastic debate, duly became "law" by another large majority.

And that was the end of the Cairo parliament, which was never able to meet again. Some of its leading "members" were hotly posted to distant places, but a special fate was reserved for Aircraftsman Absе. In after years he became the popular and distinguished Member for Pontypool, a seat which he continues to adorn today. In the meantime, he was at once placed under arrest and sent off for eventual disposal on an island in the Persian Gulf. Under arrest: but good heavens, hadn't the man undertaken to nationalise the banks? Only pressure in London availed to rescue him before they had shipped him out of Suez, but military police then lost little time in placing him aboard a troopship for England. It may be hard to believe today, but that is what they did to him.

So it emerged, in any case, that "the troops" had begun to have a fair idea of what they might be fighting for: not only to smash the nazis but also to build an England that would be different from the squalor of the 1930s. It was not only among the peoples of occupied Europe, by all the signs, that politics were getting loose. And other scenes to the same effect confirmed the fact. Here I can offer the sketch of only one of them.

During February 1946, two ships of the Royal Indian Navy (still of course a branch of the British Navy) mutinied in Bombay harbour, and their Indian crews took control. The immediate grounds for mutiny were grievances over food and such, but another clear ground, unquestioned at the time, was that the mutineers backed Indian Congress demands for an end to British imperial rule. Carrying this anti-colonial demonstration further, Bombay trades unions declared a general strike in sympathy with the sailors. Both strike and mutiny were settled in the end by mediation through Indian Congress spokesmen. But in the end no few of the strikers were dead.

Another well-known British writer, Mervyn Jones, then a lieutenant of infantry, told me about it long afterwards. He happened by chance to be there at the time, as were many other British service personnel. Curious to know what was afoot, he went to the mill district of Bombay while the strike was on. "While I was standing with a crowd in the street," he wrote to me in later years, "Bren carriers manned by white soldiers drove through, firing on the move. (I was nearer being killed than any time in the war.) Altogether over 200 people were killed in this way in three days."

Now it happened, too, that some 150 kilometres from Bombay, at a place called Deolali, there was a big depot of British troops. Not having a great deal to do, they had formed a Forces' Parliament on the Cairo model. It became just as popular, with average attendances of several hundred.

To this numerous gathering Lieutenant Jones gave a coolly factual account of what he had seen in Bombay, and moved the adjournment in protest against it. This was carried by a large majority. "Parliament" was then closed down by the army authorities. And again no wonder: for the anti-nazi war, logically enough, had here developed its anti-colonial dimension.

We had no such scenes in our remote neck of the woods, where there were next to no British personnel and the enemy was always on our backs. Even so, the politics of armed resistance to nazi-fascism had their various effects. They worked much less directly than on the partisans. All the same, they worked at a number of levels, and even in no political way at all. As may be seen, or so it appears to me, from the sympathetic case of Corporal William and Colonel Peter.

2

Jumping ahead in this story, into 1945 from 1944, I first saw William on the muletrack from Monte Antola that leads into Fascia and then—but nowadays there is a road—goes wandering down the hills to the valley of the Trebbia.

This was early in 1945 when Colonel Peter was our chief liaison officer in Liguria, and when for a while we had our base in Fascia, another of those hamlets whose roofs cling to the slope of a mountain that is really a cliff. It was also shortly after Peter had sent round orders for all British ex-prisoners to report for duty. Several, we had heard, were still living in peasant homesteads where they had sheltered since escaping from prisoner-of-war camps at the time of the Italian armistice. All of them should have gone south long before, back across the lines to their units; and many had succeeded in doing this. Now the lingerers came in over several weeks, alone and liable to be nervous; and at Fascia they were duly braced by Peter and despatched, in varying mood, southward on their way.

William came in too, and William was the only one who shook his head and would not go. He came down the track into Fascia from somewhere up beyond Carrega, a meagre figure in the rags of a battledress somewhat assisted by other ancient garments. And he said in mournful tones that he was reporting for duty, but back through the lines he would not go. Now Peter, though a man of human feeling, was strong on discipline and duty.

"Of course you'll go."

"Sorry, sir, I can't do it."

"Nonsense, you'll go."

"It wouldn't be right, sir."

An escort through the lines? A mighty risk of court martial with a stiff sentence? William took it all and continued to say no, somehow allowing it to be understood that no escort would ever get him there. He would stay with us and do his duty, but back through the lines he would not go. He was very small and thin, ill fed, a child of the hungry 1920s and the hungrier 1930s, a wisp of an Englishman with puzzled eyes to whom the world had clearly done no good. But not even Peter's gruffest barking could shift him. He too had seen his vision, and he was going to stay with it.

It came out gradually. William had nothing against the war, as such: the war was part of the general run of life, along with unemployment, barrackroom bloodiness, blizzards, hunger, and other forms of customary hopelessness. No possible prospect of an alternative pay-roll had taken him into the nearest recruiting depot, I think it was in Portsmouth, somewhere around the middle '30s when he was still a lad. And just as one bit of bad luck naturally followed another, the army had taken him into the war. And

William had fought in the war like all reliable infantrymen, doing whatever was required of him, taking his chances with the rest, miles away from ever thinking it sensible, and, sovereign necessity in all reliable infantrymen, studying his officers. And the war, in due course, had taken him into the bag along with the remaining survivors of his unit.

"Bloody Rommel, and our officer had lost the transport."

And the Germans had handed him over, with all the others, to the Eye-ties. And the Eye-ties, poor buggers, had shipped him across the Med to a prison camp beside a river called the Po. With all the others. Until the armistice.

"Hopped it then, sir," said William, and allowed himself a slow and cautious cracking open of his lips and a wrinkling upward of his bone-thin cheeks, and a glimmer of amazement at the frailties of mankind. The rest he would confide, at first, only to Peter. He had walked up into the hills, moving southward through that autumn, and worked on farms for peasants glad of an extra pair of arms in exchange for a sack on the floor and food with the family. He had meant to go on southward through the lines, but the lines were enormously far away in that autumn of 1943, and then the snow began to fall, and William stayed. The spring of 1944 came, and he continued to stay. The summer passed, and William became a peasant himself. He also found Isabella.

"She's a good girl, sir, and she's my girl, I'm going to marry her." And that was that.

William stayed with us and did his duty; and gradually he told his story. It took him into various judgments. For the Germans he had a certain professional respect, as all our fighting soldiers did; besides, it appeared that they did not lose their transport. Of course we should beat them in the end. Why only in the end? Well, he'd studied officers but he didn't say it, and at this point you had to press him a little.

"You really think we'll beat them, William?"

I remember that he looked up at me, from down among the boots that he was scraping clear of mud, with a disapproval more in sorrow than belief.

"You're having me on, sir." He always called me "sir" out of respect for useful procedure: besides, he believed in equal treatment and in any case had more important matters on his mind. Mussolini's armies he considered to be the victims of misery and an awful quartermasters' commissariat: they had little to begin with and always lost even what they had, not to speak of their transport. He looked away over the grey roofs of Fascia when speaking of Mussolini's armies, and sadly spat into the mud. But for Mussolini's Blackshirts he had a particular and vivid hatred. This reached back before the war, when he had run into Mosley's British Blackshirts. "Proper shower," he said of Mosley's Blackshirts: "Give 'em a flag and they'd shake their fannies off." But Mussolini's Blackshirts were even worse. "Scum they are, they'd lick their fannies off. If they could."

Isabella's brother, it further came out, had been taken by Blackshirts from a farm where no Jerry would have found him. Isabella's cousin on her mother's side had been taken too. Isabella's father had been hauled into Parma for nothing at all, some trumpery question of taxes, and beaten for days on end. And Isabella had narrowly escaped a mauling at their hands. "That Mosley lot," said William, for whom the finer political distinctions were of no interest, "I'd shoot that lot."

But perhaps he could have joined the partisans with this in mind? William put down the boot he was cleaning and gathered himself more or less upright and turned his head slowly to the left where I was standing by him, and gazed at me with the weariness of a wisdom teased by a case of adolescence. "That," he said. "That's a load of politics, isn't it?"

He had nothing against the partisans, and even in a quiet way approved of them. Let them run round with red scarves if they wanted to. They were all right: they didn't steal, they didn't demand taxes, they didn't lick Jerry's arse or anyone else's come to that, and they'd never try it on with Isabella. Now Colonel Peter had come to help them, and so it must be all right: he hoped they'd win, they'd sort out Mosley's mob.

A bit of a contradiction here? Not really. William's vision had nothing to do with saving his own skin: if, that is, his own skin should be in question. But there was something serious in question. It came out gradually, and Peter explained it to me. It came out that nobody had ever depended on William or even, as it seemed, ever so much as thought William capable of being depended on. But Isabella did. Isabella depended on him. And whatever Isabella's depending on him might require William was going to provide, or else bust himself in trying. He had seen the pearly gates and he had seen them welcome him: the rest was kid's stuff. Letting you get a good firm grip of this, his face assumed an expression of bleak and devious but unshakable defiance. From England's endless list of outcast human cyphers, names on someone's nominal roll or no one's, William had got himself into reality, warm and living and loving, and nobody was going to shut him out again.

"You have to understand that," Peter explained to me, barking for William to bring his boots. "It's a human question, not some ridiculous politics. *Boots*, William!" And William brought the boots and they were clean, for William had gathered Colonel Peter into his world, and ranged him truly in the circle of his household gods. The war swung its battering paw about the place, and now and then it even did a little good. I suppose this was where the real contradiction lay.

William was permitted to stay, and Peter, another embodiment of ancestral authority rather on the model of an English version of Fitzroy Maclean's, took William to his heart. James would have called it individualism, another of those clashing European symbols that he liked to punctuate his lectures with; but for my part I think that Colonel Peter and Corporal William, being irreducibly English after their time and different fashion, were in the grand tradition of Tristram Shandy's Uncle Toby and his Corporal Trim. They were absolutely at home with the rights and wrongs of any personal enterprise or problem that might present itself. But the rest was useless complication, and usually peculiar to foreigners. They called it politics. Human relations being their strong point in common, they became in a sense inseparable because they understood each other and approved of what they understood. Great gains came from this. Determined that William should do his duty by Isabella, whose family was duly produced by William in witness of his truth, Peter put him in charge of our little commissariat and we lived better than before. With money from the mission purse, but more from William's standing among the peasants, who all knew his story and naturally applauded it, chickens appeared where none was known to survive, eggs were laid by non-existent flocks of fowls, and goats yielded cheese after weeks of shy reluctance. And William, giving due account according to a scale of commerce that would have baffled the Warrant Officer, shuffled himself into a reliable infantryman's attitude of speaking to authority, sucked hard on his pencil, and reported to Peter on the funds.

"Eggs double last week's, William?"

"She needs the money, sir, her old man's got a bit on the side, don't feed her proper."

"Chickens down, William, that can't be right?"

"Don't warrant more, sir, takes rent off three families, she does."

"There'll be trouble, you can't go fixing prices as you like."

But it turned out that William was doing no such thing, but fixing prices by consensus, and after what you might call an assembly of authorised persons. He was seen in the midst of such assemblies, his cap on the back of his head, his pencil behind his ear, in close and clustered session with other parties whose peasant caps were on the back of their heads but whose faces had the flintiness of stone. There was no trouble. Democratic justice was being seen to be done.

A further fact was that these two essential but extraordinarily different Englishmen, each in his own way, became immensely popular. Old ladies would arrive, families would arrive, even young persons would arrive; and William would receive them and listen to them and question and consider and consult with Peter and advise, giving judgment from a seat on someone's porch with a straw judiciously between his teeth. Who will dare to say the English are unloved? But others may sing their history as it should be sung; we shall not do it here, although we could. All this, in any case, is running ahead a little. By May of 1944 the Italian partisans had won a strength and identity of their own. They had survived the winter. Now they had the task of growing strong.

FOUR

IN THAT SPRING of 1944, around the time when William was landing on his happy shores and entering the pearly gates, Marzo and Bisagno and their commanders were beginning to think that the worst might be over for the units of Cichero. They were premature.

Early in May, while the high snows were thawing even on the Forca and the tops of Antola, the enemy put in another *rastrellamento*, again with the intention of isolating each partisan unit and killing it by a system of co-ordinated probes in strength. By this time the units of Cichero numbered several hundred fighters, but they were still far too few to stand and fight.

Marzo took some twenty men, with Bisagno and other commanders leading other groups elsewhere, and marched them inland over the peak of Cichero. A few days of hiding might be enough, but the hiding would have to be complete. Behind them, as they climbed, advance details of the probe aimed at Cichero got out of their trucks and began loosing off into the hillsides. News came up from peasant informants as they made a halt to eat: the probe against Cichero seemed to be a large one, it would move again at dawn.

They marched through the night and were finally halted by Marzo against what seemed to be the side of a low cliff. This was a blue-grey landscape strewn with boulders and paved with lumps of rock, and in the last half-hour before dawn the going had been difficult. Lucio had a lantern and vanished with it into the side of the cliff. When they saw him again, he said, "It's all right, in you go." Beyond the entrance of the cavern, Lucio's lantern flickered about the walls and roof of a cavity that might have been a small cathedral. It was the quarry at Orero.

This was complete hiding, but it was not enjoyed. To begin with, the cavern was bitingly cold as well as dark, and no fire could be lit for fear of tell-tale smoke. Worse, stones thumped down from the roof every half-hour or so, little stones but sounding like the onset of an avalanche. What need prevent the roof from falling in? Nobody had worked this quarry for decades, and its timbering was long since gone.

Marzo said: "It's just like I found it years ago when I was a kid, I don't see why the roof should fall in. We'll stay here and then we'll see, we can go out one by one at night. Better not to shit inside, you'll foul the air."

They sat it out for two days and nights, pretty well, and then it was the general opinion that they would rather take their chance outside. They came out before dawn and went a little way and met a peasant informant, Romeo from Crocetta d'Orero, who had walked up to give them news. Bad news. Further along the same hillside, not far off the mule-track, they found a dense clump of gorse and crept through its spines into the midst of it. Next day Romeo dropped a pitch-forked ball of hay at the edge of the gorse, and there was bread and cheese packed inside it. Next day the same, and the third day too. On the fourth day, Romeo stopped and shoved his way through to them without bothering to whisper when he spoke. The fascists had gone back to the riviera towns. Had they found anyone? Romeo thought not, or not around here, but last night two fascist units had shot into each other by mistake. Three killed and five wounded. Perhaps.

Marzo took his group back to Cichero, collecting news along the way. Other bands had suffered worse conditions of concealment but none was lost. Further, on the way back Bini heard another signal from Radio Londra on his radio receiver: there was going to be a drop this very night. In the midst of a *rastrellamento*? Yes, but what could Radio Londra know about that? Never mind, it might be true. Bini and three others marched their legs off to the agreed dropping point on a plateau north of Cichero. They reached it before midnight. Nothing would come, of course: they were all sure of that. Yet they might as well gather fuel for the signal fires, nine little stacks in a cross. Bini beat his hands together and addressed the other three upon their virtues, severally and collectively, as responsible persons and pioneers of a happy future. Then they stood beside their little stacks with the blue-cold night of the northern Apennines biting into their bones; and even Bini's voice was made small and distant by the canopy of stars. They stood there till nearly dawn, and their words, whenever anyone spoke, clattered like pebbles on a frozen pool. But incredibly, when the dawn was faint on the skyline, they heard the drone of aircraft, and then it was a struggle to get the stacks alight, so that Bini had to sacrifice the last of his shit paper, treasured fragments of the *Giornale d'Italia,* as the drone came nearer. Was it coming from the south? It was indeed: and it continued to the north. Of course.

After that they walked over the edge of their plateau and saw the hamlet of Cichero far below. At this altitude light comes strangely and plays tricks. The hamlet of Cichero seemed out of focus, oddly blurred. They began to hurry. Running down, they saw that its roofs were wrecked and its walls blackened with smoke. They continued down the hillside to the place that had been their home. Even the dogs were dead.

But the May *rastrellamento* petered out with little more than wrecked villages and young men, trying still to survive on the middle ground, found and taken for the fascist army. Civilians died, peasants mostly. The mood of the Cichero bands changed and stiffened: with bitterness, but also with determination. They had thought there was no choice but fight: now they knew it.

The bands of Cichero set about recovering the ground they had lost. Attacking wherever they could, they cleared the enemy from a zone on either side of the Trebbia valley; and they multiplied in numbers. Once again it was proved, for any who might still require the lesson, that in this kind of warfare there was one sure way to lose and die; and that way was to stand aside and wait.

As for the underground quarry at Orero, it fulfilled their fears. Marzo told me, long afterwards, of passing that way in the autumn of 1944 and finding the cavern blocked by fallen stone and the rockface split with gaping faults. Had there been anyone inside? "I shudder still," he said, "we could have been."

Then, in June, Miro came.

Miro came as the larch woods on the southern slopes of Antola were a glimmer of enamelled promise and summer breathed upon their threshold. He came tramping up the mule-track from Pareto where the road from Genoa ends and the track into the mountain zone begins: a man from nowhere who was also a man from everywhere, a citizen of their world of companionship. That was his reputation, and much was spoken of him. He had fought for the Republic in Spain. Slipping away from that defeat, he had gone to Ethiopia with Barontini and organised Ethiopian guerrillas against Mussolini's army of occupation during 1938 and 1939. Who knows how he had done that? But he had done it. Then he had reappeared during 1941 in Vichy France and helped to organise an early *maquis* in the Bouches du Rhône, and later, with the war engulfing new countries, he had vanished again and emerged as a Jugoslav partisan in the hills to the east of Trieste. He was that kind of person, changing his scene of action as often as people on the middle ground changed their hiding place. And now the military command in Milan had sent him to Liguria to give a hand to the units of Cichero.

You may be thinking Miro's reputation a trifle overdone: one of those agitprop inventions of adjectival heroism? I thought so myself at first, but I was wrong. It was all true, and more. And you believed it was true almost as soon as you got to know him or even saw him, a large comfortable figure with innocent blue eyes and the disarming smile of a man who feels no slightest need to justify himself. I never knew any other outstanding person who bothered less about the impression he might make, unless it was Marzo; Miro, in fact, bothered not at all. He was convincing in himself, and even our Colonel Peter was convinced, a conviction all the more striking because Peter, on principle, was bound to disapprove of Miro in every point of politics. But he said approvingly: "That man makes sense. Doesn't talk." Which was not necessarily the case, for Miro loved talking: it was rather that he possessed what you might call a sense of natural cover. Besides, I think he found it boring and therefore wrong to talk about himself; and there was even a large sense, as least as he projected it, in which this massive figure could be said to admit to no personal existence.

Perhaps this came from his moving around in a world of companionship, for at times he seemed to merge into a cloud of witnesses; or perhaps it came as well from long-practised habits of clandestinity. Ask him how he had passed all those frontiers, how escaped arrest, and he would smile and shrug his wide shoulders and look at you in wonder at your finding any interest in all that. Technical details: what could they matter? The only adventure that I ever persuaded him to talk about, and largely I think because it appealed to his sense of fun, was a trip to Corsica at some time in 1942. In the Bouches du Rhône they had received a message from that island, asking for military advice. Obviously Miro would go. He went on a puffing little steamer in the disguise of an interpreter to an absent officer of the SD, and the food and drink were excellent. Miro was never a man to despise minor pleasures or to put his trust, save prudently, in anyone who did. Was there a lady in the case as well? A German secretary on the way to Corsica to whom he referred with a large enclosing gesture as though she, too, were reasonably human, even if a nazi? "No, no," he protested, laughing at himself, "she wasn't a nazi, only confused."

It was after returning from Corsica that Miro left France and joined the partisans in northern Jugoslavia. Nothing more logical: by trade he was a railway worker of Trieste, his mother an Italian and his father a Jugoslav. And again it was all true, his real name being Antonio Ukmar. Miro has remained averse to writing letters, but Marzo had a visit from him only the other day.

In that June of 1944 he came into Liguria from nowhere in particular, and by means of transport as far as the upland hamlet of Pareto that were perfectly mysterious; and from there he walked up into the mountains of Cichero. Here they held a solemn meeting, Marzo and Bisagno and Croce and the others, and reported at length to their new commander, and asked for his opinion and his orders. Pushing blond hair from his eyes and thrusting an arm through difficulties and leaning on the table as though it might as well crack beneath his weight if that was the kind of table it meant to be, Miro told them. He told them as though it were completely clear, merely logical, and what they might just as well have thought for themselves. He swam into their companionship as he had swum in other such assemblies these dozen years and more. There were going to be many arguments with Miro, but not about himself.

"The bands of Cichero," Miro told them, "are no longer bands, Bisagno's band, Marzo's, Croce's, the others you have formed. The time for bands is over. Bands are irregular formations. Now you are the units of a regular formation, the units of a brigade, the third brigade of Garibaldini." There might be other bands who would disagree? "You'll absorb them. If they won't accept discipline, you'll disarm them."

That applied to others than Garibaldini? "No, the Justice and Liberty bands form their own brigade." And so on down the line. Over and finished, too, he said, was the time of traipsing round the mountains. "Now we shall control the roads, seize motor transport, occupy zones, enlarge these zones, attack outwards."

And so began, in this Ligurian zone as in other zones under enemy occupation, what became known later on as the great summer of the partisans. And it was no exaggeration. In that summer the Cichero brigade expanded continuously in strength and offensive action until it grew into two brigades and then into three, when it became a partisan division, the first Ligurian division of Garibaldini. And still the volunteers continued to arrive at the sanatorium of Rovegno, where the command had fixed its point of reception in the valley of the Trebbia.

Coming in June, Miro also affirmed that the Allies were in favour. The Allies would even send arms. They listened and thought of fruitless nights of waiting in blue ice and snow; and they let him go on about this in mere politeness, for there are limits even to a disciplined belief. But it turned out that Miro could be right even about this. On 25 June the Allied radio broadcast an appeal by Field Marshal Alexander, the Allied commander-in-chief, calling on all fighting patriots to redouble their efforts, and to hit at enemy lines of communication while Alexander's armies resumed their northward drive from Rome. And shortly afterwards, while they were responding to this appeal, the new Ligurian division received its first drop of many parachuted stores that were to come: Sten sub-machine guns and ammunition, Mills grenades, Chesterfield cigarettes. In that first drop there were enough Chesterfields to allow two cigarettes for each fighter: except for commanders, each of whom received one.

By the end of July they had cleared a large zone on either side of the Trebbia, and set up within this a new administration governed by local committees on the six-party basis, or at least on the basis of representatives from any of the six parties who happened to exist there. In Bobbio Bini began to bring out a newspaper for this liberated zone, the sixth zone of Liguria, called *Il Partigiano*. It was nicely printed across four pages; and a little later there came another innovation. Newly-formed women's defence groups, *Gruppi di Difesa della Donna*, began to use the Bobbio printing house for a paper called *Noi Donne, We Women*, since, as they explained, the liberation of half a people would be a poor sort of liberation. And this may be the place to mention that some 35,000 Italian women served in partisan ranks, in all parts of Italy from first to last; and that of these 623 died in combat or in front of enemy firing squads, while 4,635 were imprisoned or sent to the death camps in Germany.

With Marzo as their chief of staff, the Cichero units set up military headquarters in the valley town of Gorreto with its bridge across the Trebbia; and this became the capital of a little partisan republic. They had more successes, and fresh volunteers flowed in; among these some now came from the enemy's Italian conscripts, not least a brigade of Alpini with their good equipment and veteran training. Altogether they became a force to be reckoned with.

Reacting, the Germans now gave Mussolini's commander,

Graziani, the two conscripted fascist divisions trained in Germany, the Monterosa and the Littorio, and both were sent to the northern Apennines. These reinforcements enabled the Germans to mount another major *rastrellamento*, and for several weeks the republic of the Sixth Zone vanished into its sheltering hills. But the little republic more than survived, and its troops by September numbered as many as 3,500: not counting other brigades elsewhere in Liguria or, of course, the many brigades and divisions in other regions of German-occupied Italy.

Their experience became wider, their blunders fewer. Hot arguments continued, not least with Marzo, often with Bisagno, sometimes with Attilio, and Miro would argue with innocent eyes and a gesture of astonishment. He was imprecise? But so was war: whoever fought a war save by fighting in confusion? He was averse to planning on paper? But whoever won a war with paper? There might be archives growing at Gorreto, but Miro kept his own in the pocket of his windjacket, a crumple of papers that was produced and prodded, though not often, with a stump of blue pencil. Pressed, he would take these papers out of his pocket and wave a fistful as though they were magic spells. But he preferred to argue from the facts on the ground. With these he was perfectly at home.

He must have walked a huge distance that summer. Even the most remote units saw him, plodding down towards them as they manned their positions on the outskirts of the zone where enemy-held territory began. Here they might be six men or ten or a dozen if lucky, raiding by night, watching the enemy, reporting information to the brigade commands in the peaks above them, opening the route to brigade-strength attack on selected targets. Often these most advanced units were severed from regular contact with the main forces in their rear. But Miro came, swimming into their companionship, and listened and explained and told them what to do. They were not alone; and no one thought they were.

FIVE

THERE WERE OTHERS who were very much alone, and who died alone.

The hangmen of Hitler's Hungarian fascist puppet, Szálasi, came for Prince Niki Odescalchi in his Budapest prison early in the morning as was usual in their work. Otherwise it could matter little when they came, for they had tortured Niki to the point that he mostly lay unconscious in his cell. He would as little notice if he died soon or late.

So they probably thought: but when they came for him they found him naked, his clothes beside him torn and cut to shreds. "He said to me that he would not let those thugs have the benefit even of his clothes," the warder of his cell afterwards explained to a Soviet newspaperman who reported it on Moscow Radio under the heading of "Prince and Patriot", and whose report was repeated by the BBC.

The hangmen carried the naked prince on a stretcher to the scaffold and propped him upright there for long enough to be hanged.

Odescalchi had joined an abortive military coup against the Szálasi fascist Hungarian régime installed by Hitler in March 1944. Its leader was a small landowner called Bajcsy-Zsilinszky; he and other of his friends were also taken and hanged. Others again, then or later, were deported to the death camps. George Pallavicini managed to survive Dachau, only to die later in Soviet internment.

All this came out; but afterwards.

SIX

I MUST ADMIT that it would be easier for you, at this point, if you were reading a regular history of the anti-nazi war. Instead of having to zigzag through the local news and *faits divers*, you could relax with the front page and satisfactory headlines: Their Finest Hour, The Grand Alliance, that sort of thing. Armies could be moved around the map and emotions disciplined in rank of respectability and dressing from the right. Odescalchi was certainly a prince, but his death achieved no headlines, and nor did that of countless others in his degree of solitude.

A regular history of the anti-nazi war would reveal this summer of 1944 as more remarkable for the decisive victories of great armies than any other in the records of warfare. What earlier summer ever shook and trembled with the stamp and dust of troops as this one did? The gods of battle came steel-visored over the crest of a thousand hills.

On 11 May our armies in southern Italy began their drive on Rome. On 18 May, scattering their dead, they stormed the heights of Monte Cassino. On 4 June they entered the Eternal City, now a very hungry one where the next day seemed far enough, let alone eternity. On the night of 5 June an armada of 4,000 ships crossed the English Channel and landed powerful British and American forces on the Normandy beaches of Hitler's Fortress; and these had good success. On 10 June, chiming with this invasion of north-western Europe, the armies of the Soviet Union opened an offensive on a wide front that was to be long and victorious, pushing the Germans far back towards Berlin.

There were other events. On 13 June the first of the V1 buzz-bombs launched from the neighbourhood of Calais landed on the people of London. In succeeding weeks nearly 2,400 V1s out of a launched total of 8,564 got through the defences of London; and on 8 September they were followed by the V2s, which were heavier, buzzless, and harder to stop. None of these roused more than sorrow and anger, and London could rightly say that its people had won another victory. On 14 August British and American armies in the Mediterranean crossed the sea and landed near St Tropez in southern France, and from there drove northwards to join with General Eisenhower's forces in northern France.

Nowhere near the front page or indeed any page, the story of these months of 1944 in Jugoslavia had much the same pattern. Tito's army of liberation shook off new enemy offensives and became a still stronger ally in the anti-nazi fight. Theirs in large degree was no longer partisan warfare; much less was it "resistance" in any usual sense applied to the word. Now it was regular warfare by large military formations. These drove the enemy out of his defences and ensured the safety of wide liberated zones within which new administrations were brought into being by elected committees and executives. Thanks to Brigadier Maclean, all this was faithfully made plain to Mr Churchill so that he, grimly content with this "gigantic guerrilla" and not yet worrying much about what might come after, received Tito in friendship and got along with him, on the whole, remarkably well.

Better supply aircraft came to hand, now that American factories were fully into gear: above all the twin-engined Dakota or DC 3 whose war-winning virtues included an ability to land on short strips of rough grass and take off from the same. With these Dakotas, more stores could be delivered than by parachute, and severely wounded casualties evacuated to hospitals in southern Italy. Then we went to Tito's aid in another way. After his mainland headquarters had escaped disaster in a German paratroop raid, he and his command were re-established in the security of the Jugoslav island of Vis, where they were additionally guarded by British naval and marine units.

Yet even in 1944, when Tito's army numbered various army corps and many divisions, there were still partisans in Jugoslavia. They were not many, and they were difficult to find even by their friends. Only their couriers or peasant guides could take you to them, and the route imposed a tricky minuet around enemy ambush-points, garrisons, blockhouses and the rest. Far out on the ultimate fringes of liberated territory, and often beyond those fringes altogether, these partisan units were called *odreds*, and existed for purposes that were specific.

They had duties both military and political, but they could be decisive in neither, for they were far too small. The central purpose of these *odreds* was to help the whole liberation movement to go on growing from the grass roots of Jugoslav society, feed its big fighting formations and executives with nourishment "from the base", and generally ensure that peripheral areas stayed in organic attachment to the liberated areas.

Such *odreds* were small and they had to be, for the enemy they lived among was seldom more than a few miles away and sometimes a good deal closer. So these *odreds* could survive only by an intimate and continuous reliance on popular support, in food, shelter, information or other needs. All this meant that nowhere else could an outsider so thoroughly sink himself, through the layers of the merely military, to the real groundwork of ideas and aspirations which explained the morality and mentality of this partisan movement.

Time was needed to understand all that, a lot of time: partly for the outsider to become accepted as one of themselves, or something near it, and partly because partisans are usually on the move and movement is distracting to such studies. But SOE's man for Hungary had plenty of time, and in inventing a mission for myself I had invented better than I knew. What really is a liberation movement, and how does it come into being? What must it do, and not do, in order to succeed? The course of instruction was to be energetic, but the education of the best.

This not being a tale about myself, we will cut quickly through the personal undergrowth. I cut through it slowly at the time, largely because there was everything to learn as well as the language. Yet in time I could speak well enough to pass for a Jugoslav from another region, and even the riding of bone-backed and most unwilling horses, for I foolishly left old Mirko behind in Bosnia, lost its terror. There were harder lessons; but time, as I said before, was not in short supply.

I went down from the hills of Bosnia on the mission I had invented for myself, and joined the *odreds* of the plains of the Vojvodina, in and beyond the fringes of liberated territory. Thus removed, the former G2 was left generously to himself. As far as I remember, no new order from base in Egypt or Italy, of any kind or import concerning what I was supposed to do, ever reached me between the time that I arrived in Jugoslavia in August 1943 until the time I left in November 1944. Far away the dramas of Bolo Keble's final bid for power and glory might blast and thunder; not even their smallest echo sounded on these shores of Central Europe. The good works of Brigadier Maclean might go from level to level, but precious little could be learned of them here. Even the legendary Sleede, holed up in the caves of Crete and meditating upon ink, had no freedom to compare with mine.

Base did whatever it could to help, often very patiently; and I tried to carry out the mission to Hungary and link up with armed resistance there. In due course I went over the midnight Danube and sojourned in enemy-held towns and listened for a sign from the north. But no sign ever came.

At my request base thoughtfully provided me with a fake Italian passport in the name of Giovanni Bandini of Turin, entered into which were splendidly exact Hungarian visa and frontier stamps. Using this passport and speaking tolerable Italian, certainly better Italian than any I was likely to meet on the way, I might get into Budapest in some assumed legality. Yet this presumed the existence of good contact there: contact I could use to good purpose, and be hidden by. But there was no contact, none of any kind; and, besides, official Hungary was no longer Italy's friend. There could be no sense in using my fake passport. A proper hero would perhaps have risked a blind journey into Budapest, but let me say again that we did not have the telly for a guide. We were living in reality.

Not that I was particularly scared of using that passport, even without a contact in Budapest. This was no great credit to me: it was simply a reflection of the state of mind that we had reached. We had ceased being scared, even if we were often afraid—the two, oddly, are not at all the same thing; and as for me, I had altogether stopped worrying about myself or bothering about the question of where I belonged. Except in thinking about Marion and wondering if we would ever meet again and make the life we had planned, I had even stopped thinking about myself. Well, most of the time. The fact remained that there was no resistance in Hungary to link up with. Having many civilian links with Budapest, the Jugoslav partisans of the Vojvodina had tried hard to find some. They had stationed a clandestine delegate in Budapest for many weeks; but even he had found none. We know now that there was a little. Bajcsy-Zsilinszky and Odescalchi and some others went to the scaffold, and Pallavicini to Dachau, but their brave gestures had little sequel. Here and there, but late in 1944, small groups of Hungarian resisters took the field. One such group was led by an admirable man whom I got to know, long afterwards, during the Budapest rising of 1956 which he helped to lead against a Stalinist dictatorship. Paul Malatér was still wearing his red star of 1944 when he went, in that November of 1956, to parley with the Soviet commanders whose tanks ringed the city; and when, breaking their promise of truce, these commanders seized him and sent him to his death. But in 1944 we knew nothing of Malatér and his comrades.

The mission proving impossible, whether for me or for a staunch Hungarian Canadian who had joined me from base and who was ready to take whatever risks might need to be taken, what else was there to do? The answer was obvious. I joined the Jugoslav partisans so far as they would let me. After all, I was growing up. The 1930s were already far behind.

SEVEN

I

IN THOSE DAYS you came out into the plains of the Vojvodina by riding or walking down a long slope from Bosnia rather as if, though on a smaller scale, you were to walk down the Welsh hills into the plains of the Severn valley. Once on the flat, you nipped through a broad meadowland controlled usually by chetniks in enemy service, and then, if all went well, you crossed the river Sava by a ferry if it was in service or a fishing punt if it was not. Beyond the muddy bosom of the Sava, a surging flood in winter, you were at once within shelter of the woods of Bosut. These spread a broad covering of oak forest very desirable to partisans, not least because of its edible population of wild domestic pigs; and there, in the plains of Srem, you found their partisan command.

I had come that way myself in the autumn of 1943 and found them there. They were a group of proven veterans of the great Srem insurrection of 1941–42, and were commanded by a man of oak-like character and courage whose name was Aćim Grulović or Slobodan by partisan usage. I got to know him well, and to admire his stores of stubborn persistence. Nothing deterred him, so far as I could tell, and nothing could sway him from what he thought already. This came out unluckily for me, for what he thought already was that no British officer could have come here for any good purpose. He carried out Tito's orders to help me but with the sore suspicion, or so it seemed to me, that a grave error was being made; and James, alas, was not on hand to instruct him in the workings of the sacred law.

But we got on well enough as the weeks passed, if not without some hard words said on either side; and in any case, besides Slobodan, there was the ever courteous General Orović, an elderly Montenegrin patriot and a man of parts with whom, as with the fighting commanders and their men, I soon found firm friendship. Slobodan and Orović were quite exceptional in being old, even beyond fifty; otherwise this was a very young army, and it had to be to stand the pace. The deputy commander, Kolja Sreta Savić, was twenty-nine, while Dule Petar Matić, commanding the *odred* in the Fruška Gora, was younger still; but even they were old when compared with the men and women in their ranks.

These commanders and their companions had all come through the fearful tests of 1941–42 and had somehow survived, often by the merest chance; and they had stayed here in the Vojvodina, rather than going to the big units in the mountains, so as to carry on the war in these difficult plains. They were exceptional persons by any standards, as was their local political senior in the communist party, Jovan Veselinov; and it seems to me now, as indeed it did then, that the adjective heroic could be used of them without romance or exaggeration. But they had patience with this unexpected arrival and gradually, as the months passed, they took me into their company and taught me the elements of the astonishing war they fought and won.

All were local men. Operating between the rivers Sava and Danube, they moved around in their long and narrow plain according to the shove and shift of military pressure. For cover here they and their units had only the woods of Bosut on the south side, and the small hills of the Fruška Gora on the north side; with a night march between the two, across the middle of the plain, of about thirty kilometres.

This plain and its woodland fringes are called Srem, the Sirmium of Roman times; and here in Srem they fought a partisan war such as nobody had previously thought possible in such open terrain. With two *odreds* totalling about 400 fighters, sometimes more and sometimes fewer, they were strongly supported by the bulk of the local population from which all of them had come as volunteers; and they were immensely successful. Since Srem was inside Hitler's puppet state of "independent Croatia", this was war to the knife; but as well as *Ustaša* (Croat fascist) garrisons the Germans were also thick on the ground. This was partly because a major strategic line of rail ran through the middle of Srem, linking Germany with Greece, and partly because Belgrade, the Jugoslav capital city, stood at the eastern end of Srem. Yet in most hours of every night and often in the daytime the Srem *odreds* made themselves the masters of their homeland.

They had three objectives. One was to harass the enemy in the neighbourhood of Belgrade and blow up the line of rail. A second was to collect volunteers from the far-out plains north of the Danube, the plains of the Bačka and the Banat, and convoy these southward over the Sava so that they could join the big fighting units in the mountains of Bosnia. A third objective, but of primary importance, was to promote and support a network of committees of national liberation throughout all these plains, openly where possible and clandestinely where not, and to carry on the work of political organisation.

2

Onwards from late in 1943 these *odreds* acted with a rising level of achievement. They fought offensively. They collected thousands of volunteers. They set up and sustained a web of committees and supporting organisations. Nimble feet were needed, a skilful use of darkness, a peasant knowledge of the terrain, and a high morale; but they applied all these. Casualties were high among the peasants, German and puppet terror being as merciless as ever, while partisans caught in hiding holes, dug for them by peasants in their farmyards or among the woods of the Fruška Gora, died at once if they were lucky or after torture if they were not. But the *odreds* held on.

Advanced patrols skirmished to the suburbs of Belgrade itself, and their demolition crews, become skilled to a point of recklessness, blew up that main line week after week or several times in the same week. No traffic could move on it at any time in 1944, save at snail's pace and preceded by a foot patrol looking for partisan mines; and frequently no traffic moved at all. Sometimes the demolition crews called for peasant volunteers with long staves and led them down to the line on a moonless night, where they levered up and overturned the track for a hundred metres or more so that you saw it, if the stars were bright enough, bend up and over in a brief long flash of useless steel.

By this time, too, our British base in southern Italy was dropping in supplies to this remote Vojvodina, and now, with Dakotas available, the nights of waiting were not in vain. My surviving notes record one aircraft on 9 January dropping to us some 28,000 rounds of small-arms ammunition, 120 rifles and two Bren machine-guns, and sundry other useful stores. These supply aircraft came more frequently as the weather improved; and on one extraordinary night in the woods of Fruška Gora along the Danube, the night of 8 May, twelve Dakotas dropped arms, ammunition, and medical stores on 244 parachutes as well as many freefall sacks of boots and clothing. It was a memorable occasion for us and it must have been for the enemy as well, for the circling Dakotas and even our dropping ground on the knoll of Glavica were well within sight of a large enemy garrison, not far away at Mitrovica, through that cloudless night of stars and moon. But all the stores were collected safely and distributed, and, at least on this occasion, none of us was hit by a sack of boots. Between mid-April and early May my notes show that we also received five tons of explosives for use against the railway line, and they were fully used.

Enormously more difficult was the position north of Srem. Here beyond the Danube were the endless plains of the Bačka, of old Pannonia, that run on again northward into Hungary. Occupied by the Hungarian Army and police since 1941, these Bačka plains were completely without woods or forest cover; and they seemed to be an impossible terrain even for the toughest of partisans. But they possessed large populations and could not be left beyond reach of the liberation movement. If little fighting might be feasible there, they could still yield a rich harvest of volunteers. But to reap that harvest there would have to be exemplary action on the spot. In August 1943 the Vojvodina command decided to have a go.

They called on partisans of Bačka origin to volunteer for a new *odred* that would carry the liberation war into the plains north of the Danube. Twenty-nine men and one woman were chosen, and Sveta Veličković was appointed their commander. A rare survivor of early partisan fighting north of the Danube during late 1941, Sveta was a little older than the others, I think about twenty-five, and of well-reputed courage and initiative. With his twenty-eight men and one woman, who was Leposava Andrić or Baba by her partisan name, Sveta completed his plans in the riverside woods of the Fruška Gora. Early in that September of 1943 they went north over the Danube by punt, crossing its starlit breadth a little way to the east of the Bačka town of Palanka, and landing midway between two Hungarian blockhouses on the river's brink. This crossing place became much used; and nowadays there is a little monument to mark the spot.

They got across the main road on the other side without incident, and vanished into the tall maize of late summer. There they found a welcome in friendly farms and were able to eat and shelter through the hours of daylight. They began attacking enemy posts and communications with some success. But the maize withered in early winter or was burned on the stalk by the enemy, and they were sorely chased. They suffered bad losses, and so did the families who sheltered them. After a while they wisely withdrew south of the river into the relative safety of the Fruška Gora; and here at last I found them near the end of 1943, living very privately in a corner of the woods and considering how soon they could go back again where they belonged.

This proved impossible until the spring of 1944 and the pushing of a new harvest of maize up through the good black soil of the Bačka plains. Anticipating this, Baba and some others of their number slipped back north of the river in March 1944 and found the necessary friends on the other side, and, with the help of these, reopened a line of contact and concealment for the rest of the *odred*. These followed and now, with the summer ahead, they stayed in their plains north of the river and fought their way through to the end of the war in these parts. This came when the Soviet front line, shoving westward from its latest victories in Russia and Roumania, reached them in November 1944. After that the members of the Bačka *odred* were absorbed into the regular Jugoslav Army and joined in the fighting pursuit of the Germans.

Those final battles, in which Sveta and his second-in-command were to be killed in action, still lay far ahead when I joined them over the Danube in April 1944. Provided with civilian garments for use in towns, and a fake Hungarian paper of identity by which from time to time I ceased to be the partisan called Nikola and became Rudolf Dolinek of Maribor in Slovenia, "because you don't speak badly, but you've still got an accent, and here they'll easily think it Slovene," I went on with my education. This was where the lessons became stiffer, and still more political. They were hard to learn but necessary; and in after years, met by the same kind of lessons in Africa, especially in Angola, Guinea-Bissau and Mozambique, I was going to be grateful for having learnt them here.

3

Wrestling for credibility in these bare lands north of the Danube, Sveta and his group faced problems special to the region. Yet these problems were also general to Jugoslavia; and Jugoslav history shows why. The end of the first world war, in 1918, had brought the collapse of the old Austro-Hungarian empire. This had decolonised the Austrian-ruled regions of Slovenia and Bosnia and the Hungarian-ruled region of Croatia; and these had joined with Serbia, already independent, to form the Triune Kingdom of the Serbs, Croats, and Slovenes: in short Jugoslavia, the country of the southern Slavs. But early enthusiasm for this new freedom and independence did not last.

Triune Jugoslavia fell under the domination of the king who had been King of Serbia and now was king of the whole country, together with his generals of a Jugoslav Army commanded chiefly by Serbs. These formed a ruling group, or élite if one may call it that, and went into partnership with merchant and bureaucratic allies, again predominantly Serbian. They ruled the country "from the top down", and soon were much disliked by most non-Serbs and by many Serbs as well. All this helped to split Triune Jugoslavia with regional and social dissensions, and the king lost little time in declaring an outright dictatorship as his only effective means of staying in power. Already the principal beneficiaries of the country's independence, the king's generals and bureaucrats now ruled ever more strictly "from the top". Reformers were silenced. Revolutionaries were sent to prison.

Governed by this small and often corrupt circle of persons whose general idea was to get rich quick no matter at whose expense, Jugoslavia lost the little economic independence that it had, and declined into an economic satellite of strong outside powers, chiefly France and Germany. Foreign capital came into Jugoslav mining and other enterprises concerned with the export of raw materials, and the statistical total of annual output grew larger. But this growth was evidently not the same as any kind of all-round national development: for most Jugoslavs there was no development. So that Jugoslavia, by the end of the 1930s, remained a very backward or "under-developed" country riven with disputes; and these disputes became increasingly violent. When the nazis and their allies invaded in 1941 the country at once fell apart, with one nationality or "tribe" against another; and old hatreds flared into bloody conflicts.

The picture, in short, becomes familiar. Like many new states of the 1960s, especially in Africa, Triune Jugoslavia between 1919 and 1941 became a typical "neo-colony". We didn't have the term then, but it fits exactly.

This was why the Jugoslav movement of liberation, like any other genuine movement of its kind, had two inseparable tasks. The obvious first task was to get rid of the nazi occupying power and its local puppets. But this was a fight that had to accept great self-sacrifice, given the nature and intensity of nazi and puppet terror. And who was going to provoke and withstand that terror unless the prospect for the future could be very different from the "neo-colonial" miseries of the past? A handful might; many never would. And the point was doubly proved in Jugoslavia by the chetniks: they were well enough content to go back to the past, but they still refused to fight for it.

So the second but parallel task of this liberation movement, without which there could be no military success, was to win political success. Nothing useful could be done without that. The pioneers and leaders of the movement had to work out and put across a political programme for a Jugoslavia that could expect good government and an end to violent strife. This meant introducing the ideas and practices of an egalitarian democracy: letting politics loose among the people became the only road to salvation.

Locked in strife, the peoples of Jugoslavia had gone to the devil in 1941, and the devil had taken a savage price. Then it was the genius of the partisan leaders, and above all of Tito himself, that found the key to the lock, and, using it, developed a political programme capable of winning a unity of mass support, no matter what terror this had to meet and accept.

The basis of their programme was an apparently simple one. They looked for the common interests that could unite the warring "national minorities" or "tribes" of their country. They saw that each of these nationalities, Serb, Croat, Slovene, Macedonian and the rest, suffered in fact from the same miseries, and could be won for a common struggle against those miseries: against poverty, a profound fear and experience of injustice, police dictatorship, poor schools, few doctors, an arrogant bureaucracy. Only the chetniks and their kind, who represented the old Serbian domination of Triune Jugoslavia and hoped to dominate again after the war, were ready to go back to those miseries. The majority of all the rest knew that society must greatly change, or the end of the war could bring them nothing but more evil.

Knowing this, they responded massively to the partisan call. It asked them to fight together for their common interests against all those interests which had previously divided them and made them wretched. A federal Jugoslavia, after the war, should combine all the nationalities in a common effort to build a happier society and heal the country's gaping wounds. This effort, in turn, should open the way for large changes in political and economic structure. The "national problem", in other words, was to be solved by solving the "social problem", and this solving of the social problem was to provide a unity that the Triune Kingdom could not know. As Amilcar Cabral in Africa was to say much later, but in comparable circumstances, any genuine liberation had to mean a revolution.

Such was the essence of the matter, as we saw it at the time: and such was the programme, allowing for human frailty in due measure, that won the partisan war.

Now all this "background" was present in the plains to the north of the Danube, where Sveta and his *odred* lived and fought and argued for their cause; but it was present in an exaggerated form. Here there were at least five nationalities jumbled up together, with each living in its own villages or homesteads, each locked within its own national history and culture, each loyal to its own "motherland". The Hungarian occupation of 1941 and after was fascist and therefore harsh, and could generally count on local German peasants as well as on local Hungarian peasants and townsmen, and on some of the Croats. Only the Serbs and Slovaks were solid for the partisans, though for a variety of reasons we need not enter here. This was the unpromising ground on which Sveta and his comrades had somehow to build the beginnings of a unity of thought and action.

They set about it with an admirable courage and optimism, and found that the nature of the enemy helped them. For the nature of fascism and racism was essentially divisive, no matter what its claims might sometimes be; and their local "national fronts" were no more than smaller tyrannies aping their masters. They divided people into categories of political or racist virtue, and sowed rivalry or hatred between them. But the message and the practice of the partisan movement was one of unity across all such divisions, and people saw this because the partisans came from all nationalities and religions. This message and practice of unity, of reconciliation, told weightily on the partisan side. For in all the bloody horrors and confusions of that time, one certainty stood clearly out: the puppet "national fronts" of the enemy might prate of patriotism and the "national interest", but were in fact, as everyone could see, the instruments of hatred and subjection. Blocking the future, facing only the past, the "national fronts" were brainless Frankensteins. Clubs in hand, they beat down every argument of reason. Violence was the only argument they knew.

That was not of course what they said. In their propaganda the nazis and their "national fronts" said they offered something new. They too talked of revolution and of uniting Europe across all its old frontiers of strife; sometimes, though rather seldom in 1944, they even talked of socialism. They also spoke of friendship. In photographs across the glossy pages of *Das Reich*, a finely printed magazine that you could buy at a kiosk near the main square of Novi Sad, the chief town of the Bačka where Rudolf Dolinek had some business, flaxen-haired maidens in folklore outfits danced with strong young heroes back from the front, while Hitler hovered gently over little girls who gave him flowers, and all was love and happiness.

Nobody in the Vojvodina thought it was love and happiness, for there is no exaggeration in saying that violent death and the fear of it were everywhere in this place. What the nazis and their puppets actually did was the opposite of what they preached in their propaganda. Today this may seem so obvious as barely to be worth mentioning; but in those days we were less well instructed. They killed senselessly; and somehow one had to find out why. What became clear to those who were obliged to find out why, and many were, was that this thing called nazism or fascism or their equivalents had not simply flowered in any man's mind, Hitler's or Mussolini's or whoever's, but on old and deep roots: whether among the Germans or Hungarians or anyone else. These roots drew their food from old quarrels, hatreds, fears, suspicions, superstitions long present beneath the surface of everyday life. What the nazis did, the nazis and their kind, was to make these roots yield fruit.

It was often said in the 1930s, whenever a note of hope misjangled with the jokes of public farce, that you can't change human nature: meaning that you can't make it better. But what the nazis proved, the nazis and their kind, is that you can certainly make it worse. This was one of their lessons. They taught it convincingly. Early in March 1944, being at that moment in the woods of Bosut, we were driven out of the little Srem village of Rača by units of 13 SS Division. Rača was a solidly partisan village and had long harboured the Vojvodina command. Departing, we therefore took with us all save the very young and the very old and mothers with babies; they, it was thought, would at least be safe. The units of 13 SS came in and stayed for some days. When they too departed, a few of us went back into

Rača on their heels. What we found was death. I made careful notes.

The provisional total of peasants killed was 194: of these 83 were women, 50 were old or oldish men, and the remainder babies, infants or small children. "Slaughtered in the most fearful conditions," say my notes taken on that day of our return: "throats cut, bodies thrown into the woods or burnt . . . some cases of corpses being so mutilated and shot through that it's impossible to say how they were murdered." In one place there were ten female corpses cut in pieces; in another we came upon a pile of ashes, and old men who had escaped death affirmed that nine women and three children had been immolated there. Our political commissar, Lala Beljansky, stirred those ashes with a careful hand. I remember that he fished out a baby's shoe, the flat disk of an infant skull and other charred fragments which he, who had studied medicine in pre-war political imprisonment, could identify as human. Afterwards, other corpses were found: altogether, in Rača, 370; in the neighbouring village of Bosut, 212; and 109 in Morović.

Not all died who had been left for dead. At Grk, another village along the line of woods, we found a little girl whose name was Slavica Crnić. The peasants were coaxing her back to sanity. Hit with a blow from a hatchet or something like it, Slavica had escaped death because her mother had fallen on top of her. And Slavica had stayed quiet beneath her mother's body while the killer hacked her mother to death, and in the evening she had pushed out from under her mother's body and run into the woods.

The men who had done this were commanded by Germans who were nazis. Yet they themselves were neither German nor nazi: for the most part, they also were peasants, Bosnian Muslims whom the nazis had pressed into their service, or who had taken service willingly out of hatred for Croat fascists who had persecuted them. Once in that service, these Muslim peasants had degenerated like others in their situation until they were just like their masters. Yet the Jugoslavs whom they hated might be also on the German side? Never mind: contradictions of this kind were precisely those the nazis used. They took the fears and hatreds of these various communities, and combined them to their purpose. They worked on the worst elements in human nature, and made these worse again. Racism, religious bigotry, personal obsession: they took all these and danced them on puppet strings.

Those who opposed them they simply killed. As among their descendants today, they had no slightest capacity for working through the contradictions of society that history must always produce, and for aiming at the resolution of these contradictions in a creative synthesis. They could only wield their clubs and kill. That was as true of the "national fronts" of those days as of the "national fronts" of today. The words may speak of happiness, of the decency of old traditions, of the patriotic love of country: the results are death.

And in the plains north of the Danube, far within the Fortress where the nazis and their kind generally felt safe, and therefore free to do as they wished, death was literally everywhere. You could find this puzzling, seeing no sense in it, but the facts were thrust beneath your nose.

4

In the town of Novi Sad, late that summer, I spent some days as Rudolf Dolinek in the study of *Wehrmacht* transport, then flooding back westward from the Soviet advance out of Roumania. At this time I was living in a sympathiser's house with my wireless operator, Sergeant George Armstrong, whom no trivial circumstance such as transmitting in morse from an enemy town ever caused to turn a hair. A useful place to sit for the purpose of studying German transport was a café on the main street, then known as the Café Stolz after its owner, and nowadays as the Vojvodina. It was a peaceful occupation, and very comfortable after living in the maize, but one day there occurred an interruption.

A column of civilians came walking up the street. They were a strange crowd. In rags and tatters, they stumbled rather than walked, men and women who looked old and dying, shadows, shifting skeletons. On either side of this column there came brisk and cheerful German soldiers who raised their automatics to the sky every now and then, and let off a short burst or two to prove their eager health, and gave a helpful kick to one or other of the disgusting creatures stumbling along beside them, or a shove to keep some scarecrow moving and in line.

Who were these? I whispered to Rile Gavrilović, leader of the newly-founded Novi Sad *odred*, whose skill and nerve had brought us into the town. He said in my ear: "They are Jews from the camps in Serbia. They are going to the camp in Szeged."

It was known in the Vojvodina what the camp in Szeged meant. Those who went to the camp in Szeged did not return. They died there: or, it was rumoured, they died in other camps still further into the Fortress. In any case they died.

But the full facts were not known: not yet. When they were, it was known that the nazis murdered several million Jews, not counting another huge total of non-Jews, gypsies, liberals, socialists, communists, and a still further huge total of persons who were simply of Slav origin. In 1950 Mr Churchill wrote that the killing of the Jews of Hungary alone, a mere fraction of the totals that were murdered, was "probably the greatest and most horrible crime ever committed in the history of the world". Yet it took time, even when all these facts were established by direct evidence, including evidence from the murderers themselves, for the crime to be believed in countries where the nazis had not ruled. The equivalence between nazism and death proved hard to understand.

On that day in Novi Sad the equivalence was singularly clear. All this *Wehrmacht* traffic going west and north-west was the transport of an irreversible retreat: the Germans knew, as we knew, that they would never come back. These Jews taken from nazi camps in Serbia might have been left behind; and the partisans, who were their own countrymen, would have set them free. They had no military potential. They had no potential of any kind: they were dying on their feet. But they were not left behind. Troops were detached to take them from their camps and drive them further into the Fortress so that they could be killed according to the rules: for the rules prescribed that they should be killed in gas chambers, and the Serbian camps had no such apparatus.

Perhaps one had to be there in order to grasp the nazi-death equivalence for what it fully was. Some weeks before Rile and I were sitting in that Novi Sad café, watching from behind the happy pages of *Signal* and *Das Reich* while the Jews from Serbia stumbled to their death according to the rules, one of Britain's most distinguished war correspondents on the Eastern front entered a place called Maidenek. This was not in Hungary but in nazi-occupied Poland further to the north. Reached by the advancing Russians on 23 July, Maidenek was the first of the camps to be found where death was administered according to the rules. Auschwitz was reached a little later, and then Dachau, Buchenwald and all the other death camps.

Alexander Werth entered Maidenek a few days after the first

Russian troops had pushed on beyond it to the west. Working for the BBC, he reported what he saw. First, within the wire, there was the bathhouse where the convoys were delivered: *Bad und Desinfektion.* Here the victims, whether men, women, or children, were told to undress and wash, piling their clothes for later collection. Next, uninformed on their fate, they were ushered naked into the gas chambers: first the men, then the women, and the children in the last round; "and at this point," reported Werth, "even the most unsuspecting must have begun to wonder." For the next rooms, or rather series of six rooms, were windowless square concrete structures without light. The victims were given a little time to wonder. Each room had to be crammed with at least 200 persons, according to the rules, before the door was clamped shut. At this point the air was pumped in by an SS guard outside who turned a switch, and then a shower of pale-blue Cyclon crystals. After that, "in anything from two to ten minutes everybody was dead".

Werth next saw the crematorium with its large furnaces and piles of coke and tall chimney.

> The place stank, not violently, but it stank of decomposition. I looked down. My shoes were white with human dust, and the concrete floor around the ovens was strewn with parts of charred human bones. Here was a whole chest with its ribs, here a piece of skull, here a lower jaw with a molar on either side, and nothing but sockets in between. Where had the false teeth gone? To the side of the furnaces was a large high concrete slab, shaped like an operating table. Here a specialist—a medical man, perhaps?—examined every corpse before it went into the oven, and extracted any gold fillings, which were then sent to Dr Walter Funk of the Reichsbank.

> Records were recovered, for the rules imposed method, and the nazis were methodical. It seems that in Maidenek a total of some 1,500,000 persons were gassed and cremated according to the rules.

But what Werth reported to the BBC was not broadcast: or not then. The BBC refused to publish Werth's story. "They thought," he wrote after the war, "that it was a Russian propaganda stunt." And the BBC was not alone among responsible media in thinking, as the *New York Herald-Tribune* concluded of the Maidenek story, that "even on top of all we have been taught of maniacal nazi ruthlessness, this example sounds inconceivable". Only later was the truth accepted. Yet nazi ruthlessness was not in fact "maniacal". The men who ordered and organised these holocausts, much less the men who did the menial tasks of gassing, cremating, collecting gold teeth and the rest, were not mad: at least in any clinical sense. They were simply carrying the necessary equivalence between nazism and death to its logical conclusion.

Scepticism about nazi horror might be generous to a defeated enemy; but it was a generosity hard to take for those of us who came back afterwards from inside the Fortress. In London, after the war, sometimes people wanted to know what life had been like there. But when you told them they grew liable to impatience. "We've knocked down the nazis," they would say: "do you want us to stamp on them now they're down?" And so the multitude of middle and minor nazis escaped with their disease intact. We should have stamped on their disease. But we didn't; and now the same disease spreads among us once again, though under the name of other "national fronts": a small snarling misery as yet, just like the nazis were when they began.

Sveta and his comrades of the Bačka plains could not stamp on the disease, for it raged on every side and they were few. Their idea was a different one. Military only in the second place, this was to produce and use an antidote to reinforce the decency of ordinary people and keep the blood of moral health in circulation. They could not kill the disease. Only a new and different social order could begin to do that. But they could show that a new and different social order was possible, equivalent with life not death; and they could promise that this future would happen.

Who would believe the promise? Their antidote had to be themselves: the example of their own behaviour, their own courage and belief. It was much to ask of them, for they too were ordinary people. It remains that this is what they asked of themselves. This, really, is what their struggle was about. Perhaps you cannot change the nature of other people for the better. But you can change your own.

EIGHT

I

SVETA AND HIS *odred* were a cheerful crowd, which was just as well, because every day north of the Danube was a struggle for survival, let alone a struggle for anything else. They had to live on their nerves, but their nerves were sound. Now and then one or two of them went over the Danube to the woods on the southern side for some organisational duty, usually to convoy volunteers; but when they had done it they came back again.

They crossed back north in a rubber boat the first time that I went with them, and it should have been a solemn occasion, what with the enemy and his machine guns on the northern bank and the breadth of the river. But the boat had sprung a leak: a good Royal Air Force product dropped into Bosnia months before, it had suffered on its journey, and Djuritsa Vadaski had to use the handpump. And while the pump snored and the boat ballooned around in pain, Djuritsa began to chuckle and then to laugh, and so did Djordje and Milovan, and the echoes of their laughter skimmed across the ripples to the other side.

Nudged at last into the northern bank, the boat was hidden under brushwood and reeds while Djuritsa went ahead to look for signs of ambush on the main road. He would take a bullet through the shoulder a few weeks later here, but tonight there was nothing. Beyond the road lay the soft fields of late winter.

"Nikola, you'll have to take your boots off."

Of course: the rest are wearing peasant sandals, anybody's sandals, but boots are easily tracked.

"And you'll have to run."

It is another lesson and too difficult: bootless city feet on shortcut stubble cannot run, they can barely walk.

"Put them on again, it can't be helped." And Djuritsa, whose talent is for laughter, strikes a gendarme's pose and begins tracking boots. "Why not walk backwards?" he says. "That's been known."

Stalingrad next, according to its partisan name: the first safe farm on the northern bank, a two-roomed *sallash* of the Bačka plains with a barn beside it and a pig sty, near a line of poplars that signal the hamlet of Chib. Its roof-ridge cuts the flat of the horizon but its buildings hug the ground.

There is a silence in these plains at night so deep and dense that it could be waiting for the world to begin: providing the dogs don't bark. But the *sallash* dogs do bark, from *sallash* to *sallash* for miles and miles, one after the other, right away into Palanka where the enemy notes the suspicious fact and will come out next morning to find out why. Opening her door with a rush, Mama Matsa curses her dogs to silence and shoos us in.

Inside there is candlelight and warmth and talk. She is a tall thin lady with a very straight look in her blue eyes, untouched by age or, so far as I can see, the least anxiety. She is one of those extraordinary peasant wives of the older generation, often more courageous than their peasant husbands, who give the movement here so much of its anchorage and base. They hide the fighters whenever these ask to be hidden, and then they face the searching enemy with dogged denials.

Now she brings food and asks questions. "We're in the movement now," she argues, "we've got to know things." From far away in the grey hills of Bosnia the movement thrusts its promise and its meaning even as far as this, and brings its companionship, its vivid life, its need for putting questions never asked before. And now the movement has even brought an Englishman to her widow's holding with its narrow acres and an unknown world beyond.

Her bright eyes measure this phenomenon. But everything is possible now, and he hasn't fallen from the moon. Does he have a wife, this Nikola? And has he got a picture? He has, and the photo is passed round. And how many children have they made? Well, no time, you see. Mama Matsa shakes her head: you don't need time for that. Never mind, they'll make some after, and meanwhile there's Radovan in trouble, Radovan, that's her third: in trouble for fighting with a neighbour, a Shvab, a German: can Radovan go over the river to the partisans? Yes, he can.

And there's Mara, that's her fourth, Mara's got it into her head that she wants to go. Here present in some eighteen years of daughterhood, Mara stands up and looks serious.

"Do you agree?" Djordje asks her mother. Djordje Stojaković commands our party and is Sveta's second-in-command.

"Well, I don't know."

"She agrees," says daughter, fresh from battle.

"Well, if it has to be," says mother. "But how will she go?"

Baba will tell her. Ah well, if it's Baba: when will Baba come? But of course she shouldn't ask; and Mama Matsa, embarrassed, stands up and goes to get us bread and bacon.

For the remains of the night we lie in the loft of the barn, with bread and milk before dawn. Mara brings it and lingers, wanting to talk, but we're half asleep. A long day's waiting follows, and after nightfall a walk through ploughland to the Palanka road, and across the mud road stepping backwards, and half a mile or so along an irrigation ditch, slopping through the water, and at last in the small hours there is Baba at the rendezvous outside the town.

There is something else as well, the noise of an aircraft above our whispering and suddenly the sweep and roar of a four-engined bomber, a giant in silhouette against the sky. Not for dropping stores, this one, but for dropping mines in the Danube, British mines to catch the laden steamers paddling from Roumania with cargoes for the Reich. We push back our heads and watch it go, a black and lovely shape among the stars, a message of support from immensely far away: but also with respectful caution, for a party of ours, rowing over the river, missed a burst of misdirected machine-gun fire from one of these mine-layers the other night.

On into Palanka now, but first a field of winter wheat tellingly soft even in its rigour before the spring, and then an outline of low-storeyed houses and a silent street between. A big village really, this Palanka, but with thousands of inhabitants and a sizeable enemy garrison. Djordje leads in and there is more trouble with boots.

"My god, Nikola, they thump."

"He's an army, they'll run when they hear him coming."

Nothing to be done; and we follow Djordje in file, moving along the side of the street from one tree trunk to the next. Somewhere above, now, another mine-layer. The warm message of its engines reaches down into Palanka and finds us waiting while Djordje, across the street, is tapping on a window pane. Inside, then, the four of us. A woman bravely frightened, welcoming: and within minutes, thumping by outside, the boots of another army.

"You've missed them." And abruptly the woman is laughing.

"They've missed us," says Djuritsa. "They always do, you know."

Such visits into the middle of towns are usually concerned with problems, with resolving problems. On this occasion there is the problem of the *illegaltsi*: a highly political problem, and Baba's business. The *illegaltsi*, for the most part, are the volunteers: thirty-five of them just now, and all requiring to be hidden, encouraged, instructed and generally kept happy while awaiting the next convoy over the river into Srem and on to the hills of Bosnia. They are peasants and townsmen from these plains, often from far away, and this time, as it happens, several deserters from the Hungarian Army who want to join the community of the partisans.

All the aspects of this problem are Baba's business in the case of Palanka, for she is the *terrainats* of the zone, the partisan detached for political work in a particular place and expected to stay in that place no matter what may happen, and represent the movement, and organise what can be organised, as well as looking after the *illegaltsi* in the various houses of Palanka where they are hidden. Looking after the *illegaltsi* is no easier a task than other tasks; often, it's more difficult. Their nerves are not sound, not yet, and their politics are elementary. Baba has to see to all that. Many dozens of *illegaltsi* have passed through her hands; hundreds more will follow.

Baba lives at present with an old Slovak lady on the main street, and the house is reasonably safe, but for a reason that Baba does not like. Last year, in 1943, the old lady's son died in action as a partisan. Ways have been found of telling this to the police of the occupying power, Hungarian gendarmes here, so that, knowing of his absence, they will think it not worthwhile watching the house. But the old lady hasn't learned of her son's death, though she knows he joined the partisans, and Baba believes that she dare not tell the old lady. For the old lady would greatly sorrow, and the sorrow would become public, and the enemy would investigate. Her "safe house" would be lost to us, and very likely the old lady would be lost as well. Yet this not telling is a sore affliction, a dishonesty, and all the more because the old lady, as is clear from the days I lived in that same house, loves Baba and trusts her absolutely. Yet the old lady's life is also in the balance. "Borci ginu ako moraju," Baba says to me on this point, "ali i ostali?" Soldiers may have to die, but the others?

Baba's own husband died in 1942 from wounds received in a clash with Hungarian gendarmes who had arrived in this Jugoslav region in the wake of the invading Hungarian Army of 1941. Then a village girl of twenty with no more notion of politics and war than to follow her man, she quit her village alone and at night in a mood of rage and despair, and went across the river and joined herself to the companionship of the partisans.

Brown-eyed and round of cheek, bundled in a shawl and woollen dress, Baba in 1944 still looked like a village girl, but the appearance was misleading. "The movement's been a school to me, yes and a university," she explained to me. "Two years ago I was a peasant girl with no ideas but the price of bacon and how to fool the tax collector. I could read and write, because we Bačka peasants can go to school, and we live well. But I didn't read books, and I didn't write anything but shop accounts, and my husband was about the same. He was a good man, but he didn't understand, what did any of us understand? He went with the partisans because we were Serbs and those others were Hungarians and gendarmes, and they hated us, and we hated them. We didn't see beyond that. We didn't know what unity means, what unity has to do. And we women, we thought we were there to serve the men, and that was all of life. We were even proud of it. The movement has changed that, I've changed myself." And Baba, saying this, looked at me with her serious brown eyes, and probably wondered what remote chance there might be that I would change myself.

The immediate problem of the *illegaltsi* was a question of preparing for the next convoy and took some days to settle, but meanwhile Baba could help the bootwearer. Contacts with Hungarians? None of a political kind, no: only the odd Hungarian *illegalats* on the run. Then the identity of enemy troops: paybooks, personal documents, anything to add to our knowledge of the enemy's order of battle? More possible, but why? Given once, the explanation is not asked a second time. Here is another new thing to be understood and pushed along; and the bootwearer's credentials, by this time, are beyond question.

The old lady's daughter, a slip of a girl in a canary yellow dress, has a Slovak boyfriend in the fascist army, a nice young chap in the trim uniform of the frontier troops. He sits with his canary yellow admirer on the sofa in the front room, holding hands and swinging them in time to the ticking of the old lady's cuckoo clock of polished pine, while the bootwearer has the use of his paybook in the back room. Második Határvadász Zászlo Aly, second frontier battalion: signals section. Bolo Keble would sniff, and rightly, for who the devil can possibly care what troops may sit along this distant Danube? But the bootwearer is only doing his duty.

2

All that was quite peripheral. Yet aside from the need to get such information, for those were the orders, the getting of it also helped to reveal the nature of this partisan movement. Here, very surely, its nature drew most largely on two sources. These were not what have usually gone into the books under the heading of "partisans"; and they had nothing in the least to do with romantic adventure or gun-toting terrorism.

Moral integrity was one of the sources; political wisdom was the other. The wisdom had been hard to come by—perhaps it always is. Moral integrity at the degree of stiffness required here—required by any success, that is, but also by any survival—can never be easy to come by. They had it, Baba and her comrades had it, I think, from a number of formative experiences. From fear and overcoming fear; from confusion of mind and finding a way through that; from the anger of despair and the turning of it into hope. Yet hope is too soft a word. What they had come to feel, it seemed to me, was the conviction of having got firm hold on a future that could liberate the decencies of life.

Does this sound rather little as an aim worth dying for? The decencies of life? Yet in that time and place it was very much, and it was also very precise. The circumstances of nazi-fascist occupation were immeasurably sordid, and when not sordid they were desperate, and when not desperate they were death. To stay sane and stand firm required more than any vague hope: it asked for a hope, however vaguely expressed, that was hard and clear in what it meant and promised.

Towards the middle of November 1943, ten of the Bačka *odred* then operating in the vicinity of the Danube-side townlet of Palanka were driven from the open country. With the harvest gathered and the winter coming there was no more shelter to be found except in occasional farms like Mama Matsa's; and repeated use of these farms would betray them to a searching enemy. Commanding this group, Djordje took them into hiding inside Palanka as a temporary solution. Six of them, Djordje being one, went to the house of Djordje's parents where two hiding holes had been dug beneath the floor months earlier; and the others in their group took the same kind of shelter in neighbouring houses.

They sat in that house and considered what to do. In case of need they would sink into the two holes and Djordje's parents would close the "doors" above them and mask these with carpet and furniture. Four or five feet down, they would wait while the enemy stamped around overhead and questioned Djordje's parents. I have sat in such holes myself, and the experience was not pleasant. The farmer and his wife would not betray you, even with rifles pointed at their chests, but the stamping of enemy boots or the thumping of enemy poles might strike hollow, and this would. Some of those innumerable *bazas*, concealment holes, were simple in construction; others were ingenious. At Koja Rumić's in the village of Jazak, where I hid for some time that winter with enemy patrols passing along the road outside on most days of the week, the *baza* was excavated under the outside privy; and this was considered very safe, since stamping around above it would naturally give back a hollow sound, but without being suspicious. Another in my own experience was in the bank of a stream, and this was not so good, although constructed with a baffle-wall inside it to take the impact of grenades thrown in. We had to abandon it because the entrance to the hole could not be properly concealed. But the *bazas* in Djordje's parents' house were considered to be safe.

The question for Djordje and his group was a painful one. Should they cross over the Danube to the Fruška Gora woods, which could be regarded as admitting defeat: or should they "stay on the terrain" where their duty was, and, if so, how? Unwilling to resolve this question for themselves, they had put it to the Vojvodina command and asked for a decision. The answer would have to come from far away, and by a difficult journey for the courier in question; and now they waited for it.

The courier in question was Klara Feješ, aged twenty-two and, as her name shows, of Hungarian stock. A surviving photo taken when she was twenty shows a pretty girl in a sailor suit; the courage that she had would be hard to guess from it. After a long and dangerous journey from the eastern Vojvodina, where the relevant command then was, she came into Bačka Palanka on 12 November and, so far as she then knew, all was safe. She reached the house without incident. With her she brought orders from the command that the whole group was to make a temporary withdrawal across the Danube to the woods of the Fruška Gora.

If all went well, they could go that same night. But all did not go well. By whatever misfortune, Klara reached the house with the enemy hard behind her. Driving up in cars and trucks,

Hungarian troops blockaded the house and prepared to search it.

Of the seven partisans hiding there, three took cover in one hole and four in the other hole. But the three were spotted before they could properly hide. They shot it out for as long as they were able. One was quickly killed outside the hole; the other two, one of whom was Klara Feješ, died in the end from their own grenades, taking two and possibly three of the enemy with them.

The remaining four partisans passed dreadful hours. Struggling for breath in their hole, understanding the worst, waiting to be found themselves, they heard the shouting and the shooting and the final crash of grenades. But they were not found, no doubt because the enemy expected no second hole in the same house.

That night the four shoved open the "door" of their hole and climbed out to a scene of devastation. The dead were still where they had died. Djordje's parents and younger brothers had vanished. The four went out of the town to the open fields. Later again, with other survivors of their group, they found a Danube skiff, stuffed its leaks with their shirts, and went back over the river to the Fruška Gora woods. There, a little after, they learned that Djordje's parents and younger brothers had been taken by the enemy, and probably were dead. This was when I found them in the Fruška Gora, three weeks after, still numbed by their experience but waiting to go back again.

In that desolation it required more than mere bravery, or any longing for revenge, if those who survived were to stay sane and stand firm. It required a belief that resistance, and only resistance, could make life possible again. The shooting of prisoners, of women and children along with the men, was only one enemy proof among many. In Srem that winter the ruins of a score of villages were still clothed with the stink of fired houses, a stench that no one will forget who has ever breathed it; and tank tracks stiff in the mud were reminders of as many massacres. The decencies of life, in this partisan ethos, were what stood against all that and what could overcome all that.

But it is true that they asked for more than the decencies of life. How they expressed this further and larger aim would depend upon the speaker. It might go into the slogans of the communists who led and organised this movement; and it did so all the more easily because peasants (and most were peasants, including many communists) prefer in any case the language of familiar symbols. It might sometimes be defined historically, philosophically, if there was time for that kind of conversation. Or it might, more often, not be defined at all: it might be taken for granted. This was because participation in the companionship of resistance to evil became, of itself and out of its own nature, more than a mere joining of wills. It became the shaper of a new state of mind. It became a mental and moral commitment to the good that opposes evil.

And this was why, among other attitudes, they could and did set the vision of a world without violence against the violence of those times. In the measure that these men and women were able to meet the demands of their participation and of what these demands implied, they used the minimum of violence; and in spite of all the death and suffering they still used it selectively, distrusting it, while week by week the enemy showed them what violence could do if it were not distrusted. In June 1943 Dule Matić and his units in the Fruška Gora ambushed an enemy company of 108 men in a clearing of the woods. Twenty-eight of that company survived the ambush. But they were not killed. They were held prisoner. It didn't always happen that way; but it happened, at least to my knowledge through many months, wherever circumstances allowed it to happen.

In such attitudes, the partisans were altogether different in their ideas and motivations from the senseless banditry of terrorism. They did not believe for a moment that any power worth having came only or even initially from the barrel of a gun. They believed that the power worth having came from moral force: even if the moral force was powerless without a gun. I am not saying that they were saints, nor even extraordinary people in the general run of events, nor that fearful things were not done. I am only saying that such were their guiding convictions, and that, as ordinary human beings answering an enormously difficult challenge, they set themselves to act by these convictions. This was what they meant when they talked of liberation; and this was all the central content of their politics.

And this was what they meant when they acted out their politics. The difficulty of describing them is great because they had to act within a drama played outside all normal experience. The case of Klara Feješ, who took a fearful series of risks that ended in death, and accepted them all, was not particularly rare. There was for instance Dragutin, a Slovak fighter whom I knew in one of the *odreds* south of the river. Pale and thin, but everyone was thin, Dragutin had joined with the unsureness of some twenty years in confusion. Yet he was encouraged to persevere, and early in 1944 he was entrusted with responsibility. This was to maintain liaison with a number of *bazas*, each unknown to the occupants of the others, where wounded were in shelter.

For this purpose and others linked to his assignment, Dragutin lived in the skirts of the enemy, because wounded had generally to be "based" in villages, and villages were occupied by the enemy or liable to such occupation at the shortest notice. He was often obliged to hide in a *baza*; but it happened once too often. On this occasion the stamping overhead was what gave him away. Now in such cases there was really no way out, and everyone knew this. The troops overhead would find the "door" and would open it, and then they would shout down to you to come out. If you came out you would be tortured for the information you might have, and then you would be shot. The right procedure was to shoot yourself. But it is one thing to know the right procedure, and another to carry it out, especially if you are twenty, as Dragutin was, and, as it happened, quite alone in your hole. What Dragutin thought about the matter, after the door was found and opened from outside, was never known. But he had a lot of information, and he acted out his politics. He carried out the right procedure.

3

The everyday drama was not at that intensity, but the intensity was always there, lurking after every dawn of every day. Baba with others lived for many months, even for years, in that situation. But what she was required to do, save for moments of intense danger, was not dramatic: on the contrary, her success depended upon her being able to reduce the daily drama to the level of calm sense and reason. Her job as a *terrainats* was to wrestle with panic and unreason, with old fears, with ancient superstitions, with ingrained perversities, with habits of mind that were against the meaning of liberation; and to struggle for a future, a collective but also personal future, that would be altogether different. I remember a conversation, through one long day of waiting for the dusk, with a new volunteer from Belgrade whose nerve and understanding, it was thought, required some help.

Baba had been explaining to the peasant woman of the *sallash* what later years would call the woman question. The peasant woman had wished to know whether partisan women slept with partisan men? Baba explained that they did not; which, allowing for the frailties of human nature, was generally true, and certainly true of Baba. Women were in the movement, she explained, on a basis of equality and respect between women and men; and their not sleeping with men, all reasons of discipline and security aside, was a necessary guarantee of that relationship. She developed the theme at some length when the volunteer from Belgrade came into the talk.

"That's right," he said, "we respect our women because they are brave and help us."

"No, Momo, you haven't understood. We don't help the men. We fight and work alongside them, we're equal with them. That's what liberation means. What progress would there be if we simply helped you? We might as well have done with it and sleep with you. I daresay you would call that helping you?"

"Well, you might," put in Djuritsa, enjoying himself.

Djordje said: "Don't talk so loud."

Baba said: "You shut up, Djuritsa. No, we're in the movement because society's got to change. It can't if we women don't."

Momo grinned, a large townsman with a sleepy face who knew a trick worth two of that. "That's right," he said. "Like when I was a clerk before the war. We got around, you know, we clerks. And you wouldn't believe how easy it was to get a woman. They did it for money, they didn't do it for love and human feeling."

Baba was looking at him in that pale attic light, and I saw that she was considering the problem. Persuasion or attack? It was the nice point of tactics. But Baba was for attack: perhaps it was the man's complacent eyes.

"That's corruption, Momo, that's nothing to do with us. The trouble with you is that you're proud of all that. You'll have to change your ideas if you stay with us."

"Baba, don't talk so loud." Djordje had lifted a tile in the attic roof to see across the fields, for the dogs had barked all last night and hours must pass before the dusk.

"I'm not talking loud, I'm telling him."

Momo chose to be offended. Those Belgrade girls might be a bit easy, but they were nice girls. "Nice girls," he repeated, blinking. "They didn't preach and prate, they understood life. They didn't have to nag about it."

The talk continued, making little progress, and even Djuritsa buried himself in the hay beside me. In that good warmth their voices dwindled, and only the small cold feet of mice, making their own inquiries, disturbed a dream of distant comfort. Djordje kept watch at the tile, a catlike man, caring for nothing but the value of his little group, the means of conserving it, the actions that he had in mind. Momo turned to complaint: he'd expected something different from the partisans, not this running and hiding in holes. He didn't like it here. It wasn't what they'd promised him.

Djordje turned suddenly, his patience giving. "All right, we'll send you back. Over the river, if that's what you want. We don't force people to stay here."

"No," said Momo, yet not meaning it, "you're under-estimating me. You're putting me down." But in Belgrade they'd talked to him of a fine and free life with the partisans, not this skulking in corners. And all this politics. And all this nagging.

They let him be in the end. They would send him over the river to the relative safety of Srem, and the *odreds* in Srem would pass him on to Bosnia, and there the army would absorb him. He wasn't a bad man; but he wasn't any good for here.

Around six we came down from the attic and the fields were grey and welcoming, hidden in the gloom beyond the *sallash* fence, and the night was ours. We crowded into the kitchen for some food, and later on set out across the friendly fields.

Shortly after, convoying volunteers, a few of us moved to the Danube bank, and Baba brought a new contingent for the crossing into Srem. Djordje gave them his usual talk, his black eyes gleaming in the pallor of a moon half-full, acting out his orders, decisive but appealing: no talk, no cigarettes, above all no panic. They listened anxiously, and were not blamed for their anxiety. It was the point at which, if anything went wrong, then everything must. Djordje led off across the fields to the brink of the water, and the *illegaltsi* followed in line ahead, with Djuritsa out on one flank and me on the other.

At the brink the moon was higher, with the brink itself a black line against the silver Danube; and this was where, with the volunteers crowding up, delay would be unfortunate. But Kara and Stanko, rowing in from the southern bank some 500 metres distant, brought in their punt on time, a big village vessel broad enough for thirty people. All crowded in save Djordje and Baba, and then I got in, having business on the other side; and then Djuritsa, coming with me as a gesture of friendship by Sveta's *odred*. A belt of water widened till the figures of Djordje and Baba, waiting to see us clear, vanished in the night.

NINE

1

NOTHING FAILED ON that particular crossing. Beyond, through the woods of the Fruška Gora, a short march led up to Proka's camp in Janok Dol where the shelters were new-made in beech branches and thatched till waterproof. Proka was sitting beside a small fire, drying his socks.

"Take off your boots, Nikola," said Proka, making space. The small heat of his fire steamed our clothes that were wet from the river, and comfort came with the warmth. Djuritsa and Proka swapped their news and found on either side, amazingly, that all was well.

A cumbrous mighty figure much older than the rest of us, Proka Popović was the elected peasant responsible for civil administration in this neighbourhood. A veteran guide and counsellor, he was one of those who gave the partisan ethos its strong and very human mixture of peasant shrewdness, tolerance, severity and sheer competitive physical strength which somehow matched the demands of survival. He would talk wonderfully if you drew him out. Poaching deer in his youth, back before the first world war, had taught him the paths and tracks of the Fruška Gora: for all these woods, he said, had belonged in former times to Prince Odescalchi, a great landowner in the days of the Austro-Hungarian Emperor Franz. We did not know it then, but that same prince was the father of the Niki Odescalchi whom the nazis, a few months earlier in this year of 1944, had killed for defying them. The war by now was really one of startling contradictions.

Proka was also a magnet for useful information; the local news appeared to reach him without the slightest effort on his part. Now he swayed forward in the firelight and gave the local news, his beaky nose and round red face alive with the assurance of a man who tells because he knows.

I said: "You wouldn't have slivovica, Proka?"

Proka sat with his knees huddled by the embers of the fire, a figure like a small mountain in a sheepskin covering, and above it a round head and matted gleaming hair. Now he turned, his eyes blinking.

"What's that you say?"

Others stirred. A woman's voice put in: "What's that he said, that Nikola?"

"See if there's slivovica," Proka replied.

"Did you say slivovica?"

"He's cold, get him slivovica." And a bottle came over the rim of the firelight, an old green bottle from someone's larder, and the swig of the slivovica was comfort in our throats.

We awoke by the ashes of the fire with autumn sunlight filtering through the beech tops, and Djuritsa and I, leaving for the Fruška Gora in the woods to the south, were ready to go. Northward, across the Danube, the pale meadows of the Bačka lay half-hidden in the morning haze, silent, misleadingly at peace, their meadows land-marked with the white stone towers of churches. For a while, it was the last I saw of the Bačka partisans. But what they and their movement had already taught me I seemed unlikely to forget.

2

That summer we began to see that partisan war in these plains was nearing its end, for the Russians to the east were storming westward from Roumania, and the frontline would soon cut through the Vojvodina. As this developed the fighting here grew more intense, with the Germans trying to improve security in the immediate rear of their retreating frontline units. Against them the Srem *odreds* scored various successes, especially in vast destructions of the railway line. But the Germans meant to try and hold Srem, as it rapidly grew clear, since losing it would mean the outflanking of their many divisions in the mountains to the south. These divisions would have to come northward out of Greece. If they were going to get out they would have to go on north through Srem.

So they set out to clear the Fruška Gora. It is a story that I have told elsewhere,* but the upshot was that they failed. In a first stage, late in June, they encircled the Fruška Gora with several thousand troops, and tried to close all doors to escape by the partisans then in those narrow hills. These numbered a hundred or so, but they had many hundreds of unarmed volunteers from across the Danube in the northern plains. As the encirclement closed, all but a handful of partisans took all these volunteers across

*In *Partisan Picture*, see note on sources.

the plains to Srem to the woods of Bosut, and so onward to the Bosnian mountains. The few who remained behind, including myself and George Armstrong, pushed into the thickest woods and hid. But the hiding places were scarcely going to serve—ours was a hole in the bank of a stream—and so this little group crept south through the encirclement, one night, to the strongly partisan villages of south-eastern Srem, near the capital of Belgrade.

Behind us we left some severely wounded fighters with their nurses. All were found by the enemy, and all were shot. Proclaiming the annihilation of the partisans, these German units then withdrew their encirclement. At which the fighting *odreds* returned to the Fruška Gora and went over to the offensive again. This brought the Germans back, but this time they got better than they gave, and retired in confusion.

But now we had a particularly rending problem: out of all this fighting the *odreds* came with fifty or sixty men with severe wounds, and few of them could walk. The prospect was for more fighting against large German units, and the Germans had just demonstrated, once again, what they would do with wounded men and nurses whom they found.

A better solution was required than holes in the ground. Could we British not evacuate them by air to southern Italy? This was already being done with wounded in the big units among the mountains: why not do it here in the plains as well? We decided to try that. The enemy might stand in great strength inside Belgrade and around its outskirts, but here a few miles to the west we could rely on staunch partisan villages and an heroic loyalty.

Duly requested through base in Bari, the Royal Air Force was also willing to try; and I take my hat off to them even in retrospect for it must have seemed, at any rate to them, a very chancy business. They agreed to land Dakotas about fifteen or twenty kilometres west of German-held Belgrade, stipulating only that they first dropped a flight-sergeant to approve the landing strip we could offer. Flight-sergeant Macgregor descended one night with a pet dog to which our village hounds took violent exception, but was otherwise made welcome.

We took him to a long flat field between the villages of Karlovčić and Ašanje: if you land nowadays at the international airport of Belgrade, that field lies about twelve kilometres to the west. Lala our commissar organised a team of peasants to fill in holes and runnels until Macgregor said it would do. Carts were mobilised to bring up the wounded at a moment's notice from their hiding place.

Early in August Macgregor signalled to his command that "Piccadilly Phyllis" could take aircraft.

They came on the first night expected, two Dakotas winging in through the glow of enemy lights in Belgrade, and landed on "Piccadilly Phyllis" as though they had done it a dozen times before. Casual in khaki shorts, their RAF crews gave me a leap of the heart as they got out and strolled from their planes: here were my own people at last. I explained to the pilots that they were very close to major enemy forces, and that they must be gone well before dawn, but they took all this in their stride and seemed to think nothing of it. They were in no hurry to leave, being veterans who had already lifted to southern Italy many wounded from the big units in the mountains. Such was their confidence in the partisan army that they wandered round our field on the outskirts of Belgrade as though there were nothing in the least to worry about.

We liked this but did not share their lack of anxiety. We hurried; but even so it was a couple of hours before the planes were filled with wounded and had taken off for Bari. Then everyone dispersed so that the enemy, rushing out next day to find whatever could be found, would discover only the ashes of the signal fires that Lala's team had built and lit.

To SOE's man for Hungary, here by default of his mission having failed, these and later airlifts of the same kind were a profound satisfaction. They showed what right policy could achieve in the unlikeliest time and place. They carried British backing for the partisans, and in a sphere of great humanity, not to speak of risk, right into the heart of the enemy's position. It was a good blow struck for our fighting alliance and for decent friendship in the future.

Meanwhile, relieved of the worry of their wounded, the Srem *odreds* were able to redouble their actions.

Then, with the autumn, it came time for me to go. Coming from the east, the Russians were about to near Belgrade; and here behind the frontline a little to the west the place was getting crowded.

We had moved up into the Fruška Gora again, and one night three Americans arrived, landing unannounced but happily unhurt amidst a field of vineyard stakes where only supplies were expected. There also came from base in Italy a curious reinforcement, if that is what he was supposed to be: a gentleman wearing a bright red regimental cap who, it soon transpired, had come straight from Selborne-land. It also transpired that he was a gentleman of the landed interest who expected full rights of feudal service from our peasants.

They were good humoured about this to begin with, and all the more from believing that he must be a Russian by the colour of his cap. But later on they had to be asked for patience. Not by me, however: for it now became a high priority with me to take myself somewhere else. The new arrival reminded me too closely of a version of Slogger Coppers, and the necessary sense of humour seemed to be in short supply. I had forgotten that there were such people, an error that was to be smartly corrected in the sequel.

Happily, my old friend General Kosta now arrived in the Fruška Gora to take over command of the Vojvodina in this period when it was about to shift from the periphery to the centre of major operations. He was eager to get to the other side of the frontline so as organise new regular units from existing *odreds* and new volunteers.

He came at a good moment for me. Within days he had made his preparations. He called me in and said: "A plane is coming tomorrow night. It will take me to the Banat, north of Belgrade. Over the frontline. Come with me, and bring your wireless operator. Yes, and bring the Americans."

The plane duly came, a DC3 with a Soviet pilot, and carried us some fifty kilometres to the east, landing us in Bečkerek, a town since renamed Zrenjanin after a partisan hero of those parts. From some way to the south a rumble of gunfire told us that the assault on Belgrade had begun. Other Soviet troops were marching north-westward through the town, heading for Hungary and what was shortly going to be the assault on Budapest. They were the first Soviet troops I had seen, hard men who had come all the way from Stalingrad and through a score of devastating battles, and they carried with them, along with their smallarms and their gear, their machine-guns on wheels, their horse-drawn transport and their trucks and tanks, the tone and temper of a most valiant army. It was the army that had torn the heart out of Hitler's legions, and we stood on the sidewalk and watched them with curiosity and respect.

In those few days, when one extraordinary experience followed another, Kosta took up headquarters in the town hall before going on to meet Tito in the nearby town of Vršac. He saw to it that we Western allies should have a comfortable apartment on the main street. "Have you got a flag," he asked me, "and has the American? Hang them out, then, from your windows." So we hung out the Union Jack and Lieutenant Ryder flew the Stars and Stripes beside it while the Soviet infantry went marching by below, and we all felt suitably ambassadorial; it was beginning to be that kind of thing. In after years I understood better the sense of Kosta's wishing us to show our flags.

There was really nothing more to do here, and base, applied to by George Armstrong and his transmitter, thought so too. Having said our farewells, we took the train for Belgrade and got there a few days after the battle for it. Now I saw this battered city once again, three and a half years since running from it, and the sight was grey and saddening. But the time was not for sadness. Somehow or other, we were a stage nearer home, and still alive. Here, too, was Fitzroy Maclean, as thoughtful and as courteous as ever.

Arrived himself the day beforehand, Fitzroy listened to my tale with a wry lift of the eyebrow and made sure that I should feel welcome, taking me with him to a victory dinner given by Marshal Tito for the generals of the Soviet divisions which had helped the partisans to liberate Belgrade. A mere major is out of his depth on such occasions, but the Soviet general of artillery next at table, a shortish man with the look of one who can never be surprised, had all the sympathetic air of Tolstoy's gunner captain in *War and Peace*. He knew as little English as I Russian, so we exchanged toasts for want of words.

3

Maclean took me in his aircraft to Bari in southern Italy. Here I found SOE again, but I also found Marion, who had skilfully got herself transferred months earlier from Cairo, knowing that if and when I returned it would be to Bari; and she was now working in the map room of the SOE back-up organisation for the Balkans. Much of the brass was at Bari, but this back-up organisation had its being in a nearby seaside village called Torre a Mare, a heavenly place I found it. There we slept through long and quiet nights and woke together in the morning with a shy astonishment at finding each other where we actually were. Marion was wonderfully calm and patient with the returnee from sixteen months' absence, but what should we make of our lives together? As for countless others, it was a question that remained to be seen.

Meanwhile we were given a week's leave, and wangled transport across Italy to a village clinging to the cliffs beyond Amalfi. There at Positano the British town major, a friendly soul from some war-fractured regiment, found us somewhere to stay, and we ate at a restaurant near the foot of the cliffs called the Buca di Bacco; maybe it is still there, it certainly deserved to be. This was not the end of the war, but it felt like that.

This in fact was still November 1944; and it was not the end of the war. What next? We could both go home, having each done five years' service overseas; but that was not the spirit of the times. Returned to base, I applied for guidance to my seniors.

"You can," they said, "go to Vietnam."

"Never heard of it."

"It's somewhere in Asia."

"Well, I think I'd rather not, what else is there?"

"As a matter of fact, there's northern Italy. We've got things going there now."

"You've got things going there?"

All right, they conceded, things were going there; and why be bolshy about it? Still, a man returned from all that time with partisans could be forgiven for being a trifle wrong in the head. They hoped I would recover. And by this time, which may have helped, I had become one of the most experienced men they had.

Such a person was required to head a liaison mission with the partisans of Liguria, far up in north-western Italy beyond the frontline. Others were going to other regions in the north, but Liguria was not yet "filled".

"Or it may be," they said. "Peter Macmullen is thinking of going there. Ask him, you'll find him at Monopoli."

This was not a game of chance but a nearby town which held the base for the SOE Italian organisation. I found Peter at Monopoli and warm agreement took two minutes. We were old friends. He would go as number one and I as number two.

We had known each other in Cairo during the Keble period. Then I had gone to Jugoslavia and he had gone to southern Greece, where, it appeared, he had spent some nasty and frustrating months with a bunch of "nat bands". This had evidently confirmed in him certain strongly held views as to the general undesirability of foreign populations. "I wasn't sure," he said, "but if you'll come—"

He was the best of men to go with. Our task would be to join the Ligurian partisans as soon as possible, carry out the usual tasks of liaison and supply, and gather information on the rear dispositions of enemy units. This information would be for the benefit, or so it was hoped, of American 5 Army on the western side of the front, the eastern side being the sphere of British 8 Army.

Reinforced by George Armstrong, who had come with me from the Vojvodina and Belgrade but needed no persuading to go at once to northern Italy, we soon had our little mission in shape. It was less good for Marion, not because she disagreed with this decision, but because I think we made a big mistake. Talking it over, we decided that she should go home to find somewhere to live in London when the war was over, and I said goodbye to her at Christmastime in Naples. The army had told us nothing of fly-bombs, still supposed to be a deadly secret though falling all over London for months, and she got to London in time for the V2s. She could valuably have stayed in Italy; but the army, of course, could not be expected to bother itself over a detail like that. I wince with that mistake to this day.

Peter and I duly proceeded to American 5 Army headquarters near Florence. There Peter ensured that we were briefed with whatever useful information they had, which apparently was precious little; and after that we were ready to go. We had meant to go in December, but the partisans in Liguria signalled an enemy offensive and could give no dropping point. So we went on 16 January 1945.

The journey was short and comfortable. No long-distance dropping at night any more, but a leisurely start after breakfast from an airstrip near Leghorn. No hours of crouching in a stone-cold fuselage, but twenty minutes' pleasant flying up the coast beside the shining blue Tyrrhenian, 1,500 metres below, before turning inland with an umbrella of four British Spitfires larking overhead. And then across peaks and folds of frozen mountains, climbing from the riviera, until the pilot found his signals on the ground and slowed and fell to 170 metres or so. And at last a leap and sunlit drop to a land of lovely snow.

A group of partisans was waiting in the snow.

PART V

ONE

I

OUR PILOT HAD dropped us well on target, but the whole wild landscape seemed empty, except for this little group plodding to us in a waste of snow.

One of them was a large man in a rumpled windjacket, civilian trousers and skiboots. "Miro," he said; and we had his name already as the commander of all this zone. Another was of much the same age, rising fifty, and this was Marzo, the zonal chief of staff. Neither had any marks of rank or even uniform save for a red scarf, but both were armed. While Miro was full of easy-going welcome, Marzo said little; and the thought occurred to me that here was another Slobodan who would find our British presence hard to accept. But it turned out differently.

After we had exchanged greetings they led us along snowbound slopes to a huddle of cottages hard frozen with the cold, the Capanne di Carrega. Here on the upper slopes of Monte Antola they had their temporary base in a cottage less narrow than the rest; I rather think it was some kind of peacetime hostelry. It was in any case frostily cold, but they gathered us around a table with food, the mash of roast chestnuts that we were to get to know far better than we wished; and small embarrassed speeches were made as they always are on such occasions, at least in my experience. We inspected each other cautiously, even covertly, which is another thing that people do on such occasions.

A little was explained, but it would take us time to get the hang of things. Later, when we had, we could accept that this zone, the sixth partisan zone of Liguria, was the largest and most effective in all the coastal mountains that reach westward round the Bay of Genoa to the French frontier, and southward for about eighty kilometres in the rear of Hitler's frontline. After Miro and Marzo, Colonel Umberto Lazagna was deputy chief of staff, another veteran in his fifties, and Rolando was commissar. Not present for reasons which became clear later, Rolando was represented by a golden-bearded metalworker called Attilio, whom I judged to be about my own age. Most of the fighters, as in Jugoslavia, were around twenty or so.

We learned of their positions and problems, then and in the days after; but it will be useful here to go back a little.

As long before as May of the previous year of 1944, the Allied commander-in-chief, Field-Marshal Alexander, had informed *The Times* that partisans in German-occupied Italy were engaging as many as six of the enemy's twenty-five divisions then available. Intelligence at 5 Army headquarters had told Peter and me that these partisans had increased their strength during the summer of 1944. Few details seemed to be known, but the partisans had evidently become a major element in the military balance behind the enemy frontline. Spread all the way from the western Alps to the eastern hills beyond Venice and in the provinces between, the partisans had become a useful ally. It appeared that the enemy could now use his principal lines of communication only by an unrelenting defensive effort almost from the gates of the big cities, while inside those cities the enemy was further harassed by city units, partisan "action groups" who were also numerous.

All these units were said to be under the same overall command, that of the committee of national liberation for northern Italy, established secretly in Milan; and all of them, it further appeared, acted as part of the same six-party political movement. There were said to be dissensions among them, notably between the Garibaldi brigades led by communists and the "Green Flames" brigades led by Christian-democrats or "non-politicals". The latter, however, were somewhat few and far between, while these dissensions, it was thought, were held in check by the generally close coherence of the top six-party committee in Milan and its subordinate regional six-party committees. And all this, we found in due course, was generally how it was.

2

The summer and autumn of 1944 had been filled with battles. Alexander was obliged to begin them under a new handicap. An Allied landing in the south of France, launched in August 1944 from North Africa, had called for reinforcements from the Italian front, and Alexander had to lose six American and French divisions. With what remained to him he opened a major offensive on 26 August and pushed the Germans north through Tuscany and the Adriatic Marches. But what remained to him proved insufficient to push them further. Late in October his offensive petered out. The Germans were able to build a strong defensive line, in depth across Italy, which they called the Gothic Line. They would clearly hold this line until the spring of 1945, six months away and perhaps more. But meanwhile, behind them and among them, they had the partisans to deal with.

The Germans still had plenty of fight left in them, and they used this interval. They knew that they would have to face another Allied offensive in the spring. So they turned on the partisans with more military strength and fury than ever before, aiming to crush this menace in their rear before the spring offensive could begin. Intelligence at 5 Army seemed to think that the Germans might be well on the way to doing that. One operation after another, *rastrellamentos* as they were called, had struck at every large partisan zone. Men escaping southward through the frontline spoke of the ferocity of these offensives. The question was: what, if anything, now remained?

Post-war analysis has shown that by October 1944 the Italian partisan fighting total had expanded to about 50,000 Garibaldini, with another 15,000 or so in other useful brigades, and perhaps a further 15,000 in a scatter of more or less ineffective units, or some 80,000 altogether. We also know that far more volunteers were to hand, but there were no arms for them. So what was the situation in January 1945?

Here in "our" zone, things were soon revealed as being a lot better than 5 Army had prophesied. Trying to get our grip on things, we listened sceptically to Miro and Marzo and their comrades; but gradually, as we lived ourselves into the situation and began to understand the terrain, we saw that they told the truth. We also began to recognise similarities from our own experience elsewhere.

The main difficulty of adjustment for me, I think, was the extraordinary difference of terrain. I was used to open plains with the next enemy-held town or village almost always in sight. I was used to moving only in the hours of darkness. I was used to leaving a village at one end with the enemy coming into it at the other, or shifting from one concealment to another, or fighting as it were with the enemy at arm's length. But here we were in high mountains, peak after peak, with the enemy altogether out of sight. The change was hard to assimilate.

Yet we could see, as we went along, that the basic elements were not different. We had dropped in the wake of one major enemy sweep across these mountains, and, as we soon found out, on the eve of another. In all this, for one thing, the nazi-death equivalent was just the same. Troops under German officers now aimed not so much at destroying partisan units, which they found difficult, as at robbing the partisans of village support by terrorising the villagers, which they found easy.

Most of these enemy troops on the scene were described to us as Mongols. That was the name they had among the villagers: *i Mongoli*. In fact, as later interrogations confirmed, they were a mixed bunch of brutalised Kazakhs, Turkomen and Volga Germans, men of the Soviet Union's ethnic minorities, who had been taken from German prisoner-of-war camps with the offer of escaping death in those camps if they joined the German Army. And perhaps because there was no way back for them, they were very pliant tools in nazi hands. They were also very tough tools.

While partisan units manoeuvred in the mountains of the zone during December and early January, these troops under German officers shoved into villages and burned down houses and shot old men and raped women and purloined whatever property they could carry off. To these tales we also listened with scepticism at first, but we soon found out that they were true.

As we went through the first weeks after our arrival, it became further clear that the antidote and its effects were the same. This enemy tactic of driving a wedge of terror between the peasants and the partisans was a failure. But it failed above all because the peasants, by this time, had identified whatever was humanly decent, life saving, or even minimally hopeful with the example and cause of the liberation movement. Once this identification was made, further terror could only strengthen it: even if many had to die and some, to save their skins, betrayed.

Then there was a third element that was both the same and different, although only the sequel could fully demonstrate it.

This third element consisted in the underlying contest of intentions between the liberation movement and the Allies. Or, rather, between the liberation movement and the Allied command with SOE and SOE's American equivalent, the OSS or Office of Strategic Services. If I have said little about the latter, this is because the rôle of the OSS in the Italian campaign was generally in second place to that of SOE, but its policy, so far as I know, was just the same.

This contest was in play by early in 1944, but out in the open only towards the end of the year. The same in kind as in Jugoslavia and Greece, this version of the great equivocation in Italy was nonetheless different in its local context, in its balance of power or influence, and in due course in its outcome.

The Jugoslav partisans were going to carry the day for their liberation movement and the new society they wished to build, because they were far too strong and wisely led to be overthrown. Not even a major Allied landing in Jugoslavia could have overthrown them. Their Greek equivalents were going to fail because they were strong but not strong enough to withstand that kind of effort to destroy them, and, in their politics, they were not wise enough either. The Greek liberation movement was duly wrecked in December 1944 and after; and then, foreseeably enough, there followed years of misery and strife.

In Italy, by contrast, the outcome was to be surprisingly something else again. Probing the secrets of the avenues ahead and raising two fingers in blessing by the sacred law, James might have had something to say upon the subject; but James was nowhere to hand. So the avenues remained mysterious in so far as we bothered to inspect them: which was not much, for the next *rastrellamento* now began and gave us other matters to attend to.

TWO

THERE HAD BEEN at first, for me, something of the sense of anticlimax. Perhaps, after the Vojvodina, anything of this kind must have engendered it. Besides, we were now a headquarters staff and were not supposed to see the enemy: or rather, the enemy if possible was not supposed to see us. Miro had his units placed in a wide spread guarding the approaches to the zone; and the information on his map, as he explained it, looked sensible and well conceived. But at first it all seemed oddly far away. The new *rastrellamento* of the end of January, really a second instalment of the one in December and early January, proved a convincing correction.

It came in from several directions, and was aimed at chopping the zone into several compartments so that each could be dealt with in turn. The answer to this was to refuse to be "compartmented". Reacting, we all moved: hastily and far and often, shifting from one slope of Antola to another, ploughing through the snow. There was the usual confusion.

There was also much to learn. I remember getting very hot one night, arriving in some mountain hamlet whose name I no longer have, at finding there were no sentries posted down the trail behind us. It was explained to me, I think by Paolo, that there were no sentries because none was needed: down the trail behind us, towards the valley of the Trebbia, a partisan ambush was in position. No enemy would get up through the snow during the hours of darkness. I was not convinced, but Paolo all the same was right.

The details do not matter, and were much the same as always in situations of this kind. Movement and dispersal were the watchwords, and the gauging of the moment when counter-attacks could usefully begin. Gradually, a pattern emerged. There being no chance of receiving parachuted stores till the worst was over, Miro arranged that our small mission, Peter and George and me, should cross the Trebbia, away from the slopes of Antola, and shelter in the villages beyond. He gave us an escort of two or three fighters, and we marched.

We came down east from Antola into the gorge of the Trebbia, a mountain river like the Wye in the hills above Hay, and got across the road south of Loco where the enemy had a strong post. Then we climbed the hills on the other side, seaward from Santo Stefano, and pushed through Barbagelata, a village burned down in the *rastrellamento* of five weeks' earlier and still, like the villages of Srem, stinking of charred timber and of death. Here or hereabouts we turned back west again towards the gorge of the Trebbia, having no mind to go too far from Miro and his command who were still on the slopes of Antola. There we found a cottage tucked into the cliffs above the Trebbia gorge, steep and narrow at this point with its highway winding at the bottom.

All this taught us the terrain. Its advantage to guerrilla operations lay in its shape and size: you could walk round one side of a mountain while the enemy was searching for you on another, and you could come on his patrols with a huge impact of surprise. Here in our cottage, for example, on most days we could see the enemy moving along the highway far below, but the enemy could in no way see us. Yet the advantage had a price, and the price was a high one. These mountains held very few people; and this absence of population meant three shortages severe in all partisan warfare. It meant a shortage of local political backing, a shortage of shelter, and a shortage of food. The notion that ideal partisan terrain is a range of wild and empty mountains is almost the reverse of the truth.

We learned a lot from that *rastrellamento* although little that we could usefully tell base, and George worked his set sporadically. By the middle of February couriers from Miro found us with the news that his units had passed to the counter-offensive. Reaching him again, we learned that there had been plenty of hard fighting around Antola, up the valleys leading from the plains and from Genoa. We had seen nothing of that, but at least we had learned the terrain. We were beginning to feel at home in these mountains.

The news was good, and I will tell it in due course. But not all of it was good, and some of it was painful. Once again, as on a dozen times since 1943, the enemy had taken his toll, and once again in the ways that this enemy preferred. The case of Don Bobbio has its place here.

THREE

I

DON BOBBIO WAS the Holy Roman priest of a lost little mountain hamlet in the hills behind the blue riviera. He was one of those who had to face this final winter.

Those hills were harsh and hungry, as they still are, and their people then lived much to themselves, being well supplied with chestnuts for a staple food and a grave suspicion of the outside world, but with precious little else. You reached Don Bobbio's kingdom, the hamlet of Valletti, by a muletrack stumbling away into the hills above Varese, which is the village capital of this backland high behind the sea. But when you had climbed to Valletti the string of cottages beside Don Bobbio's church seemed barely worth a name. Still, there were a dozen of them and more than a score if you added their stonebuilt barns; and the little place, being at the upper end of a muletrack, might handily serve for a partisan bivouac.

As it happened, Valletti was seldom that. Its peasants were for some time reluctant to help, partly from fear of losing in enemy reprisals the little that they had, partly from preferring that the world outside should turn around without them, and perhaps because Don Bobbio was averse to their helping. Their priest was by reputation as withdrawn as his flock, and far more shy than any of them: a shy small man in body, almost a miniature man, for whom the duties of his kingdom filled his life. Attached to Heaven through an immediate superior in Varese, he knew of another, still more superior, in Sestri on the seacoast; but beyond that other there was only the bishop in Genoa, the Holy Father in Rome, and God Himself. Other authorities could not concern him.

Organising for the movement, Marzo had come to Don Bobbio's kingdom in the spring of 1944. He had walked up the muletrack in his old fur cap and red neckscarf with his pistol in his pocket, and knocked first at the door of the manse, which is what he always did on such visits. At Valletti he had to knock patiently and often before an anxious Don Bobbio half-opened the door, and then Don Bobbio could barely wait till Marzo, being made to understand that there was nothing to be hoped for here, gave up and went elsewhere. Other priests were inclined to listen and even help, and at least two had already quit their homes and churches to join the Garibaldini units of Cichero as military chaplains. But Don Bobbio was not of their kind.

Things get around, though; and Don Bobbio became known to possess a rare treasure. This was a pair of binoculars. Needing binoculars for an action against high-tension masts near Statale, where the job was to be done in open ground and earliest sight of enemy approach very desirable, Marzo returned to Valletti. Don Bobbio required smooth persuasion, but eventually lent his binoculars on condition of receiving a written receipt stating that the liberation committee had taken them by force. If anything went wrong, Don Bobbio could then argue that his binoculars' being found in partisan hands was not his fault. The bishop would forgive him.

Wondering at so much anxiety, Marzo departed with the binoculars, the masts were blown up, and the binoculars restored to their owner. But soon after, through that summer of 1944, Don Bobbio was discovered by the bedside of a sick partisan who was lodged at Valletti for lack of anywhere else to put him, and then at the bedside of other sick or wounded men. Grateful for these unexpected attentions, partisans going through Valletti on a Sunday, or stationed nearby, took to attending mass at Don Bobbio's little church. Then came the big *rastrellamento* of December.

With that, the partisans near Valletti pulled back into still more remote places. Coming up the muletrack in due course a fascist unit entered Valletti and seized the first able-bodied men they happened to find there. These were two. Neither was a partisan, though one was a sympathiser, but both were fairly young. The Blackshirts accordingly shot these two in what passes for the main square of Valletti, and then they went into the church. Here they found Don Bobbio, who was kneeling at prayer. They put a hangman's halter round his neck and dragged him away; a famous painter called Renato Guttoso, after the war, would make a picture of the scene as the peasants described it. Hauling Don Bobbio with the rope around his neck, these fascists then went back along the muletrack to Varese, and down to the coast by truck to Chiavari.

On this occasion there was a trial. Don Bobbio was accused of the crime of celebrating mass for partisans. It is not clear what might have happened if Don Bobbio had denied doing this; and perhaps the bishop could have intervened on his behalf. But Don Bobbio gave no time for any intervention. He replied that the accusation was true, and that he was content with what he had done, and that doing it was his duty as a priest.

Next day the executioners took Don Bobbio to the cemetery, with a cluster of people following as close as they dared; and there they showed him a waiting grave. Then they stood his flimsy figure with its back to the grave, and the commander of the firing squad told Don Bobbio that he could have a minute or two to prepare his conscience. But the priest of Valletti was seen to stand as straight as the stick of a scarecrow and was heard to reply, unafraid, that he had no need of time for that, his conscience was at rest, but he would pray for them. They shot him as he raised his hand in blessing. The people who were there, the record adds, took to their heels from fear of being forced to bury him.

Executions were a common thing in those days and the fascists made a habit of performing them as publicly as possible. These Italian fascists, like others elsewhere, were in no sense shy of admitting their equivalence with death: on the contrary, they insisted on it as a policy, and were even proud of it. They had no gas chambers, for they lacked German means and method; but they did their best with what they had.

2

Even so, not everyone taken by the fascists or the nazis died in public. A number of political prisoners were found afterwards to have vanished without trace. Efforts were made to find what had happened to them; and this became one of Marzo's self-imposed duties as soon as the war was over. At one point when beginning his search, he found that the records of Genoa's Marassi prison, where many politicals were held in 1944 and early 1945, contained a mystery. Twenty-one politicals had been removed on 2 December 1944. But as to what had become of them the records were silent. The warders knew only that fascists had removed these twenty-one and told them that they were to be exchanged for fascist prisoners in partisan hands. This was credible, for by the end of 1944 such exchanges of prisoners in the sixth zone, above Genoa, had totalled some 400 prisoners of both sides. Yet there was no partisan or other record of any exchange of these twenty-one.

Then the liberation forces in Genoa laid hold of Spiotta, one of Liguria's Blackshirt leaders who had failed to get away with the Germans. Questioned, Spiotta swore at first that he knew nothing of the missing twenty-one, but finally admitted that they had been taken to Portofino. Whatever might have been done to them at Portofino, he said, was the responsibility of his boss, Faloppa; and Faloppa had escaped to Franco Spain. But the little harbour of Portofino was still there; and Marzo thought that perhaps its people might be able to help in solving the mystery.

He went there to ask, and was disappointed. Living in the old stone houses that pile in clustered terraces above the blue depths of this most beautiful of all the sailing ports of the riviera, there were those who remembered that they had heard something unusual on the night of 2 December 1944. But the night had been dark beneath clouds and rain; and all they could tell, vaguely, was that a truck had arrived from the landward end of the seagirt point where Portofino lies, and that German soldiers, some time later, had opened fire towards the sea.

Marzo persevered: someone must know more. Asking around, he came upon an elderly mechanic long settled at Portofino with his pension. Giuseppe Silicani told Marzo that he had worked for the local German detachment on an air compressor that they used. That December evening he was ordered to keep the compressor working through the night, and not to let it stop. Doing this, he saw German soldiers driving a gang of prisoners along the quay towards him. He counted twenty-two as they went by, and they were near enough for him to hear above the din of the compressor. One of the prisoners kept shouting that it was all a mistake: he was not a partisan, he was a thief, he had thought they were going to be exchanged, that's why he had joined himself to the politicals. The Germans, said Silicani, drove all twenty-two to the end of the quay and a little beyond, moving them round the base of the cliff crowned by the old castle of Portofino that is nowadays a picture gallery; and there they shot them all and thrust the bodies into deep water with weights attached. So one mystery was solved, but another, the reason why they died, remained where it was; and nobody ever bothered to question it. Such murders were part of the prevailing death; they required no particular motive. The only odd thing about the massacre at Portofino was its secrecy; yet perhaps it was simply that the executioners preferred not to dig graves.

That midnight slaughter was otherwise a small event in the

measure of those times. There were larger ones. A new partisan group of early 1944, half armed and ill led, took refuge in a cave near Voltaggio and were given away to searching enemy troops by the barking of a dog which they had kept with them in their inexperience. Their exact total was never established, but it was about a hundred. Obliged to surrender, all were shot down outside their cave. The prevailing death was decomposed only in the rotting of the corpses, which lay where they had fallen till peasants buried them.

Such killings went together with every lesser disease of debasement, whether in theft or rape or merely material destruction. But more than courage was required to stand against this epidemic of moral collapse. The hardcore fascists, like the hardcore nazis, also had courage. To produce and use the antidote effectively it was necessary to develop a stronger courage than the enemy: a courage, that is, steered by moral purity. The words may sound strange today when violence for political ends, or supposed political ends, has so often become fruitless, stupid, or merely criminal. Yet they apply very well to the great liberation movements, whether then or since. The anti-nazi war had to be fought, not suffered in silence or evasion: but fought on terms altogether different from those of the nazis and their kind. Nothing can otherwise explain the style and tone to which whole populations rallied in spite of fearful enemy reprisals.

The treatment of prisoners was one aspect of this. As in Jugoslavia, the usual treatment shown by the nazis and their kind was a firing squad, invariably after torture if the prisoner were thought able to give information. Facing death in this way men and women responded as they could; and it was noticed that even the least heroic could respond as Don Bobbio responded. Many such cases became known. Again in our zone there was the case of Cucciolo, a peasant lad of sixteen who had walked up to the partisan command and told Marzo that he was eighteen, which Marzo disbelieved. Cucciolo was allowed to stay, but without arms and to mind the mule of a small detachment, a *distaccamento*, in the hills behind Rapallo. These men were surprised one day, and taken. All were destined for execution, ten of them I think, save only Cucciolo who, being without a weapon and very young, was to be spared death.

But Cucciolo refused to be parted from his companions, and loosed off a string of insults at his captors until they shoved him into a truck with the rest. They drove the truck towards the valley of Fontanabuona till they came alongside the wood at Fregaia: today the place where the eleven were shot is marked by a tablet with their names, including that of Rinaldo Simonetti, who was Cucciolo. Arriving there, Cucciolo asked to send a line to his parents, and the lieutenant in charge of the firing squad agreed. The letter has survived. In it Cucciolo, whose writing skills were not much, asked his parents to forgive him and wrote that he was dying for the salvation of Italy: *muoio per la salvezza d'Italia*. Very high-toned, no doubt: but try it before a firing squad.

This kind of answer to the disease of moral collapse came in such ways and in small ways like the sharing of cigarettes, food, chores and risks; and it became as the months went by a trial of self-respect, a personal test of one's own value. It came also in the partisan treatment of prisoners. Early in April 1945 a group of German troops based on Torriglia had the idea of raiding on bicycles up the valley of the Trebbia: a bad idea from their point of view, for they were stopped and encircled in the riverside hamlet of Loco. But they were led by a sergeant-major of marines of a quite remarkable arrogance, and this I know because I interrogated him afterwards, who refused to surrender. Back and forth shooting continued till the next day when they gave in, by this time having several wounded, and one severely. Now at Loco there happened to be an ambulance, abandoned there by some previous enemy chance. The Cichero partisans put this severe German casualty into the ambulance and sent him down to Genoa with a note to the SS commander there. "This man," said their note, "can be saved by immediate surgery. We can do none here. We send him to you gratis, and without asking for the usual exchange." It was not the only partisan action of its kind in our zone.

The Cichero partisans certainly shot some of their prisoners, and as many as thirty-seven, I think, of the "Mongols". But they shot their prisoners only when these were found guilty of atrocities. Their answer to terror, in short, was not a counter-terror but a disciplined and even a judicial application of the antidote. They also applied this to themselves. There was the grim case of Dino, a Genoese communist who became a deputy commander of one of the Cichero divisions of Garibaldini and looked after divisional stores. Late in March 1945 Dino was found to have stolen several kilograms of coffee and chocolate from stores earmarked for the partisan hospital at Rovegno, a village above the Trebbia remarkable in architectural history for its baroque church tower in carved stone, and, at that time, a secure partisan base. Coffee and chocolate were precious, but Dino had taken very little and he had taken it not for himself, but, as he explained during his trial, for his family in Genoa. His family were near starving at the time, as was confirmed by appropriate inquiries, and Dino's idea had been that they should sell what he had stolen on the black market.

Rapidly known, the shock was considerable. A large and likeable man of about thirty-two, Dino was admired for his steadfastness and record. You felt about this happy character that nothing would ever go seriously wrong with him; and yet Dino had done what nobody would forgive, and he a communist into the bargain. He would have to be punished, possibly put under arrest, in any case disgraced and made to work his passage back to a decent reputation.

But the communists of the sixth zone took another view. Four of their leaders formed the judicial tribunal, insisting that they should not avoid this obligation because Dino happened to be one of theirs. The officer for the defence was Colonel Lazagna, by politics a Christian-democrat and a lawyer in civilian life. Dino confessed his guilt, and defending counsel argued extenuating circumstances: the man had thought only of his family down in Genoa. But the tribunal sentenced him to death, and on an excruciating dawn, which none of the judges certainly ever forgot, Dino was taken out for execution. He made a short statement. If they had given him this extreme sentence and refused mercy, he said, it was because he was a communist.

I think that this was true. Even for those ruthless times the sentence was excessive, and the judges, as one saw, were among those who thought so; but they would have passed it on each other, if such a case could be imagined, just as they would not have passed it on a non-communist. In that situation the application of the moral antidote acquired an inevitability, however grim; and nobody that I heard spoke against its use, not even those who otherwise spoke against the communists. Even their political opponents appeared to have accepted that it was the communists among them all, first and foremost, who must supply the moral rigour that the times required.

Another contradiction of the anti-nazi war emerged in this development, and one that was obvious at the time even if little discussed. How could communists achieve moral leadership—it is a question you may well wish to ask—when still fiercely loyal to the claims of Stalin's State and its system? What was the part of Stalinism in all this? A full answer, if indeed it can yet be made, would call for a full history. But the anti-nazi war offered some clues.

What the anti-nazi war revealed, among other things, was that the communists did indeed achieve a moral leadership: not always, of course, but more often than not. The chief reasons at the time belonged to the virtues of courage and self-sacrifice. The reasons in hindsight add to these. Here in Italy and Jugoslavia, and no doubt elsewhere, it was partly that the nature of Stalin's régime was unknown: what was known instead, and foremost in many minds, was that Stalin's armies were smashing Hitler's armies. Partly, again, it was because these communists set aside dogmatic aims, and, while remaining distinctive to themselves, sank themselves in the community of the movement of liberation.

Not easily, of course, and again not always. A lot of time and painful truth, later on, were going to be required for them to recognise this contradiction as something other than hostile propaganda. But realities worked on them. On one hand, they were stuck with their doctrine about revolution's having to impose a "dictatorship of the proletariat": a real and direct dictatorship, that is, not just a cultural or political hegemony. On the other hand, ringing through their daily experience like a peal of bells in full swing and clamour, came the absolute demand of the liberation fight. This was that democracy should prevail, and be seen to prevail. Success could come only from the voluntary participation of masses of ordinary people in their own liberation.

The working out of this contradiction was to become part of a later history and a long one. After the war the communists were to pay a stiff price for their Stalinism; and others were to pay a stiff price, too. The bullying arrogance of arbitrary rule marred and scarred the immediate post-war years in Jugoslavia. Much was done then that was afterwards regretted, and even bitterly denounced: as, for example, their persistence until 1952 in the Stalinist policy of forced purchase of peasant crops. And Italy's communists would still be settling their accounts with their own Stalinism till late in the 1960s.

But during the war they were simply obliged to shove their theory aside. For what theory of dictatorship, however glossed, was going to lead great numbers of men and women to fight and suffer in the anti-fascist cause? Who but sectarians or fools wanted anything smacking of dictatorship after decades of fascist repression? Who was going to follow these communists unless they denied, in practice, the dictatorial reputation they had long earned in theory?

The questions were awkward, but they had to be faced. Being faced, this armed resistance did in fact achieve by 1945 one of the greatest of democratising insurrections of European history. And this achievement stood foursquare within the tradition which has linked, and which still links, anti-authoritarian and anti-colonial ideas and aspirations with the belief that freedom, the rule of law, is a supreme good in itself.

Far from shaping towards a new dictatorship, this self-liberation in Italy laid the foundations for a possible democracy after the fascist years. It carried much further the unifying process begun in Italy a hundred years earlier. It moved that unification out of the categories of the merely territorial or administrative, and into a profoundly innovative development within Italian society. Italy's post-war successes all derived from this wartime source, just as all of Italy's failures, so very evident by the 1970s, came from a fouling of that same source, from a denial of its ideas and aspirations, and from a return to sectionalist and sectarian conflict under the banners of a self-proclaimed Christian-democracy.

Whenever led by communists who were already in sharp dissent from Stalinist orthodoxy, even if they could not or would not admit so terrible a heresy, all the insurrections which counted during the anti-nazi war had every essential in common. This is not to award some kind of certificate of merit, or, again, to suggest that everything was well done: for myself, I neither thought so at the time nor have thought so since. If history could have been different, much would have been better done.

But it is to say that each of these great insurrections against one or other form of fascism depended on the voluntary participation of very large numbers of people who were "non-political" in any party sense. Each therefore depended on overcoming sectarian dogmas, as well as on overcoming the provincial chauvinism of the donkey's bray. Each depended on building unity among all ethnic groups and regions, on giving people the right and freedom to change their own realities, and to make their own history.

3

But if a lead towards unity was indispensable to wartime success—and I take the argument a little further here—what other policy could succeed in the peace that was going to follow? To this too the resistance gave its answer. When Marzo and his handful of companions celebrated Christmas 1943 in the cottage at Ramaceto they numbered two communists but the rest were Christian-democrat or nothing at all. And when they talked over the future, as Marzo has recalled in his memoirs, "we all agreed that we should defend the freedoms we had conquered and bring about renewal and equality before the law, such as could guarantee the social peace and welfare of all Italians". Their country, they agreed, "should be for everyone without distinction, communists or not, Christians or not, where every idea except the fascist idea would have its due place, respecting its own faith and the faith of others."

This democratising theme may be followed through all the public declarations of the liberation movement, as through all the private ones available in archives. Some were six-party declarations, others were declarations by one or other constituent party addressed to its members, but all that mattered spoke the same language then. In July 1944, for example, it was ordered that democratic administrations were to be created in every liberated zone of any magnitude, and by this time there were quite a few of these. The stress was on democratic representation as an immediate guarantee of mass participation in the struggle during the war, but also as a liberating model after the war.

"What matters," said these orders, "is to create organs of people's power in every village as soon as the nazi-fascists are chased out of it. These organs must emerge directly from the mass struggle and its institutions: from partisan units, peasant committees, factory committees, youth movements, women's defence groups." Each local committee was to evoke participation to the possible maximum. There was to be no question of renaming existing bodies or organisations simply because these existed, or of treating such existing bodies as the organs of people's power. On the contrary, the broom was to sweep clean, and in the space thus provided the men and women who had most clearly committed their lives to the building of a new society were to be assured a leading influence.

All this was difficult to realise. Very large numbers of young men and not a few young women joined the communist party, for example, when they joined the armed resistance, and became at once enthusiastic for maximalist and even utopian aims. The old world of parental misery was at their feet, wretched in its ruins: walking free upon the hills, they would build a new world tomorrow and at once. There was the case, so characteristic of many others, of the Garibaldini brigades of the Montefiorino district, formed initially by a carpenter and an ex-student. "Hundreds of these young volunteers donned a red shirt and the badge of the hammer and sickle," a communist organiser of that time has recalled, "and were very determined to call themselves communists." Unity might demand a much wider loyalty and understanding than any party confinement: but wasn't that a way of betraying the revolution for which they wanted to fight? "What we had to explain," runs the same contemporary account, "was that it was not a question of telling them to take off their red shirts, which in any case were also in the tradition of Garibaldi and the union of Italy, but of taking off their hammer and sickle badges, and of replacing these with the Italian tricolour. Because that epitomised the national character of the struggle: as much for us communists as for anyone else."

Opportunism or worse? So it was said by some at the time, and by others later. In fact it corresponded to the needs of mass participation in armed resistance. And these needs had an irresistible dynamism of their own, for it became ever more clear that only this kind of mass participation would enable Italian society to change itself, develop out of its parochialism, overcome its historical backwardness. The clearest minded saw this with a stark understanding. Nobody put it better, perhaps, than a young Milanese communist called Eugenio Curiel who was taken and shot by fascists in 1944. Only through the actual fight for national freedom and unity, Curiel wrote, would committees set up by the liberation movement be able to form the militants, forces, and organisations capable not only of confronting fascism but also, after that, of "replacing the apparatus of a corrupt fascist state, and of giving strength to progressive trends and a government of national union": so that, in peacetime, Italy would be able to achieve "the democratic institutions of a new state". Without the partisan struggle there could be no true liberation of the Italian people.

Liberation without that struggle would simply be imposed by

Allied victory; and nothing, essentially, would have changed in the hearts and understanding of the people at large. Yet this same partisan struggle must also fail unless it became the instrument of building a new political and moral consciousness through the countless channels of an individual participation in collective change. Working to that end, all sectarian or sectional ambitions must be worse than useless.

Many scenes of the anti-nazi war could be brought in evidence, even within my own experience. They would all, I think, depict an inner wrestling and striving for the realities of a companionship that could both unite and develop. Here were sounded all those decisive themes to be found in other liberation movements then and since: inside Europe, or outside Europe. Nothing in this could be easy, need one repeat; nothing could be guaranteed. Gains were repeatedly negated by old habits of mind, old suspicions, old but reductive loyalties, not to speak of the fallibilities of human nature. Yet the outcome, by and large—and what in the annals of social change can ever be more than by and large?—was a remarkable success. This outcome may be said to have ensured that the ideology of political insurrection should now move forward into the entirely larger dimensions of democratic development.

Elusive truths, no doubt, and yet profound ones; and alongside them the meddling and the calculating of outside powers had the impact of bulls in china shops. For it was a general fact that all the outside powers, if from political calculations often very different and sometimes plain contradictory, took up the same essential attitude. Let the "occupied peoples" fight and die, but always as a convenience and only under strict control. It is a hard saying, but harder still to deny. That was one of the pains of the anti-nazi war.

FOUR

I

ALL THIS BEGAN to emerge in Italy around the latter months of 1944. In October the big British and American offensive north of Rome slowed and then stopped for want of reinforcements. It had been hard fought, and costly in casualties, and now another winter must be faced; all the same, as everyone could see, the spring would bring a new offensive and then the war in Italy would end. So what to do about Italian post-war politics?

The king and his lot, it seemed, would have to go. But they were deeply in the mud with Mussolini and fascism, and nobody was going to shed many tears. Who would take their place? The democratic politicians in Rome seemed a rather dismal and divided bunch and were also, after all, the men defeated by Mussolini and fascism. As for the communists among them, they were obviously going to do whatever Stalin might decide. And if Stalin was carefully saying nothing about Italy now, and even advising communists to behave like good democrats, what guarantee could there be that he might not say something far less pleasant in the future? It was a serious question, and it was taken seriously.

In October 1944 Churchill went to see Stalin about various matters concerned with the conduct of the war, and also about the likely political balance after the war. Knowing that Stalin understood the realities of power, though it might be far from clear what else he understood, Churchill offered him a deal which was to become famous: not indeed as any kind of formal treaty, but as a rough understanding on a share-out. Russia should have ninety per cent of post-war influence in Roumania, with the West having ten per cent; and just the reverse in Greece. Jugoslavia and Hungary should be shared as to fifty-fifty in post-war political influence, while Russia should have seventy-five per cent in Bulgaria and the West twenty-five per cent. Churchill wrote this on a sheet of paper and shoved it across the table to Stalin who looked at it for a few moments and then ticked the paper with a blue pencil. Afterwards, things turned out variously. But one point that was sure at the time was that Italy was not in the deal.

This could only confirm, for Western policy-makers, what they had already decided. Italian committees of liberation might stimulate partisan warfare and continue to help in destroying the enemy. But they were not going to be allowed to govern Italy afterwards, being all too obviously the fruit of letting politics loose among people who could not be trusted. Orders were accordingly issued to prepare lists of suitably convenient administrators for all areas where the committees might claim to rule, and these were to serve Allied military government in occupied territory as soon as the war ended. Meanwhile, as the summer offensive petered out, partisan units in contact with Allied troops were downgraded in any way that offered. Most of these partisan units were eager to continue the war after their regions were reached by the advancing Allied armies; instead, they were disarmed and told to lose themselves. And in mid-October 1944, signalling a whole bag of implications, the Allied propaganda executive known in Italy as the Psychological Warfare Bureau or PWB was instructed "to play down very gradually the activities" of patriot forces fighting behind the German frontline.

This burying of the partisan movement was then found to be a little premature: it raised problems, political as well as military. Allied policy might already want post-war political power in Italy to pass to a Christian-democrat party sponsored by the Vatican, led by a skilful Vatican politician called Alcide de Gasperi who would be safe for all respectable and proper people, notably those with money. But de Gasperi's party still had to win wide popular support; and this meant, of course, that it could not yet appear in public as the highly conservative body which it mostly was. Like the communists, the Christian-democrats were members of the six-party liberation alliance, and they had to stay members, just as they also had to support the armed struggle behind the German lines whatever their misgivings. Any other course would sink them before they could swim. They had to "play left" or disappear. As de Gasperi himself remarked in November 1944, "a great part of Italy is anti-communist, but we cannot use anti-communism as our rallying call, because then we should risk being identified with reactionary forces".

But if the Christian-democrats had to support the liberation movement behind the German lines, so too must the Allies: otherwise the Allies would damage their preferred candidate for the post-war succession. Besides, there was the military factor. The partisans could still be very useful in harassing the German rear and soaking up whatever spare troops the Germans could still field. It would be militarily unwise for the Allies to ignore the partisans, and plain silly to act against them. On the other hand, building up the partisans meant building up the communists. What to do?

The answer, when it came, was the now familiar compromise. Aid and recognition should be given to the armed resistance: but cautiously, and only on condition that all partisans came under Allied orders and control. Liaison officers, British or American, would be sent in to make sure of this. These officers would direct partisan operations and insist on the political directives of the Allies; and in this way the Allies could have their cake and eat it. The partisans would fight, but they would lose all claim to be running their show. As mere auxiliaries, they and their six-party committees could be discarded when the fighting ended.

Now this compromise was well enough when written into the happy language of official memoranda, but quite another matter when you applied it on the ground. The military wing was perfectly aware of this, given its Balkan experience: or, at least, that part of the military wing where SOE had first-hand knowledge of the problem. You might promise the politicians to help the partisans only in the measure that you controlled the partisans; in fact, the promise was likely to be worthless. You might send in officers to give orders, but the orders would usually be ignored. In Jugoslavia the chetnik bands of Mihajlović continued to collaborate with the enemy no matter how many Allied orders were issued to the contrary, while the Jugoslav partisans merely laughed at any British officer sufficiently innocent to imagine that he could give them orders. It was not much different in Greece, except that there the "nat bands" thought up by Tamplin were more biddable, though not much less ineffective or expensive than Mihajlović's chetniks; and all this was known and understood by the British officers concerned. Most of these officers were themselves highly conservative, and some of them would later on make great conservative careers. But meanwhile their duty was to win the war, and the genuine partisans, who laughed at or evaded their orders, were certainly helping to do that. If the price for helping these partisans had to be the fiction of British control, then let the politicians worry over the results of that.

In Italy, besides, there was a safety net. Unlike the Balkans, all of Italy would be occupied by the advancing British 8 Army and American 5 Army at the end of the war. These powerful armies would entirely dominate the scene, and the Allies would be able to dictate whatever should happen next. There could be no "second Tito" here. Even so, it still appeared wise to take precautions, and agree beforehand about who was going to govern a liberated Italy, especially in the north, and how.

On 14 November 1944, having gone secretly from Milan to Switzerland and then to Allied-occupied southern France, a delegation of leaders of the senior liberation committee for northern Italy flew into Rome. They were bidden to reach agreement with the Allied supreme command on the status and future of their political movement and its tens of thousands of fighters in the field. Talks were held at the Grand Hotel in Rome. An agreement was signed on 7 December. Its contents were bitingly clear.

The Milan delegates argued their case. They showed that their committees could take over political control of all northern Italy as soon as the war was over, and that they would be doing this in the name of the properly constituted Italian government in Rome. They explained that they would exercise this control according to agreements already reached within the six-party alliance. They would guarantee a peaceful transition, and in every sphere of public life. They would lay firm foundations for a democratic Italy purged of fascism.

But General Sir Henry Maitland Wilson, speaking for the Allied side, had nothing to concede. The Allies would help partisans fighting north of the Gothic Line upon one condition. This was that the Milan committee and all its subordinate committees and commands must undertake to carry out whatever orders the Allies might now give them. Afterwards, when the fighting had ended, they must make full and immediate submission to the representatives of Allied Military Government. They must then agree to the immediate disbandment of all their fighting units, and the surrender of all their arms. Effectively, they must disappear.

2

Imposed rather than negotiated, this Rome agreement was not the armistice of September 1943 all over again, but it was still something like that armistice. A new Italian Army formed in the south was now fighting gallantly alongside the Allies, and its performance in the battles for Monte Cassino was only one reason for admiring it. Yet the anti-fascist army of the partisan brigades, which should have formed a central part of this new Italian Army, was to be destroyed. Worse, all those multi-party organisations and forces which stood for democratic renewal after fascism, and unitedly now, were to be set aside and consigned to dissolution. Just to confirm that this would certainly be so, the Allied side showed the Milan delegates a list of persons selected for administrative posts under Military Government. None of these was a nominee of the liberation movement; few had any connection with it.

All the same, the Milan delegates had to sign. On one side, the new Italian government in Rome, led by an elderly liberal called Bonomi, lacked the means or the will to give them any encouragement to resist. On the other, General Wilson now showed them how the Allies would deal with recalcitrance. On 5 December, two days before the Milan delegates brought themselves to sign, a British expeditionary force was sent into Greece to destroy the main body of a recalcitrant liberation movement. And while that destruction got into its stride in Athens, the Milan delegates swallowed their bitterness, and signed.

Surprisingly, as it may seem, the Foreign Office in London was far from pleased. Reading the small print, they rightly saw that the Milan delegates had not gone away with entirely empty hands. They had at least secured Allied recognition of their committee—the senior liberation committee of northern Italy, or CLNAI—as the due and proper representative of the Italian government. This was found alarming. Wasn't there a danger, Sir Orme Sargent was writing to Foreign Secretary Anthony Eden three weeks later, that the Italian partisans might become "recalcitrant" now that the Rome agreement had regularised their status? The fear was quite baseless, but Sargent had the Greek recalcitrance very much in mind. "The picture in Northern Italy," he advised Eden, "is in fact reminiscent in the strongest degree of Greece and we may, as in that unfortunate country, be helping to build up not only a rival to the Italian government in Rome, but also a rival to the Italian Army now fighting on the Allied front. . . ." Eden agreed with him. "I am afraid," he wrote to the prime minister on 9 January, "that there is much in this story which reminds me of Greece. We must watch it carefully." And the chiefs of staff were duly ordered to keep "a close watch on developments".

All that is water over the dam, but interesting water all the same. It flowed along channels which were to lead straight into the "Cold War". It showed just how uncomfortable it was for British conservatives to support a war in occupied Europe that had to go, and necessarily, so much against their ideological preferences. Wide of political reality in the run-up to the anti-nazi war, they remained in that position; and, all too understandably, it did not make them happy.

As it was, in this case, the chiefs of staff could do little with their "close watch". As in Jugoslavia, they had to forfeit a good military ally or else let things take their course and hope for the best. Besides, this was a game that two could play. On the face of it, the Allies were bound to win: they had imposed an agreement, and they were going to have overwhelming force to ensure that this agreement was eventually carried out. Yet the question still remained as to how far and who would carry it out in the meantime; and there, on that elusive ground, the two sides were less unequally matched.

Thus apprised of the fate reserved for their movement by the Allies, the Milan committee and its dependent committees and commands also knew that they had five or six months in which to put in hand their counter-dispositions. They set about appointing their own "shadow" administrations for all the cities and principal towns of the German-occupied north. Everything would then turn, after the coming of the spring offensive that would end the war, perhaps in April or May 1945, upon installing these administrations before the Allied spearheads could arrive, or, at least, in the moment of their arrival.

This in turn would have to mean a whole series of successful insurrections in these northern cities and towns. Choosing the moment for such insurrections would be hard and risky: too soon, and they would be crushed by the Germans: too late, and they would fail of their purpose. But if the insurrections were successful, then the Allies would find the nominees of liberation in control and command, backed beyond any doubt by the vivid enthusiasm of a large majority of the population. Would the Allies then care to throw out these democratic nominees in favour of their own? If not, the liberation movement could save real substance from the wreck.

None of this was admitted on the Italian side, any more than the Allies ever spoke of their intention to destroy the liberation movement; but the game in play could afterwards be seen to have been well understood on both sides, even if only at or near the top. The big question meanwhile was: what would the coming winter of 1944–45 do to the partisans? Would the partisans be fatally weakened by its rigours and by new enemy offensives against them: or would they survive, and in surviving, repeat the experience of the previous winter of 1943–44 by growing stronger in numbers, fighting value, and prestige? If so, what could the Allies do to parry the plans for insurrection?

How far the leaders of SOE asked themselves such questions, and what answers they may have found, are matters that remain unknown, for the relevant archives are closed to all inspection. Dropping into Liguria in January 1945, with most of the winter still ahead and the spring offensive months away, Peter and I received no briefing on the subject; and it seems unlikely that other liaison missions were better instructed. Even so, a few broad hints were already on the scene.

The first had come a little earlier than our arrival, and proved far from friendly.

For months before that, right from the outset of the spring of 1944, broadcasting stations under Allied control or influence had sent out appeal after appeal for patriotic fighting action in the regions held by the enemy. This was military policy, and the political wing could say nothing against it. British and other Allied casualties in Italy were high all through that spring and summer and autumn: who was going to spurn whatever extra fighting help that could be found? And all through those months, as we have seen, these appeals were answered, and a quarter of the enemy's forces had to be detached to deal with partisan fighters. Another "gigantic guerrilla" had come upon the scene, and it was greatly welcomed.

To this the Germans and their fascist puppets in the Republic of Salo replied with bigger raids and persecutions, with the torture and execution of captured partisans, with the burning down of partisan villages, and with a wild bloodbath in towns and cities. In all this the gap between the two opponents, the liberation movement and the nazi-fascists, widened to an abyss. The "middle ground" entirely disappeared. Those who took to the hills knew that they must stay there and fight it out, or else accept destruction. There could be no going home, no compromise, no evasion by concealment. The iron law of all successful partisan warfare was going to apply here as everywhere else: partisans who do not fight are partisans who wait only for their own destruction.

Then came the news from Allied radio stations which told that Alexander's summer offensive could not be the last, and so another winter must be endured. This coming winter of 1944–45 might be easier than the last to the extent that the partisans were many times stronger and more numerous. By the same token, it would also be more difficult in the supply of food and mountain shelter.

In the northern Apennines the Cichero divisions set about adjusting to this prospect, as did other divisions and brigades elsewhere. Their staffs picked out village bases that could possibly be held, protected these with roadblocks and permanent ambushes on lines of approach, laid in such provisions as were possible, and drew up lists of enemy objectives of a kind that snow and ice would still allow them to attack. Their problem was to conduct an offensive from what would have to be defensive positions: a difficult but entirely necessary task, and one that depended, just as much, on whatever the enemy had in mind. Fighting to survive was in any case their only option. There was no other way except disaster. They knew this and accepted it.

What the enemy had in mind soon became clear. Informants told Miro's command, but so did the enemy. During an exchange of prisoners supervised on the Cichero side by Attilio, Rolando's deputy as commissar in our zone, his German counterpart made an offer of immunity if the partisans would surrender. Attilio responded with an answer that became famous. He said that the partisans would fight until the Germans were on the other side of the Alps. Angered by this, the German officer said they would regret it. They had, he explained to Attilio, a new division ready to send against the partisans, a division of Mongols. "They've been in the Val d'Aosta, and there they've burned and raped and shot whatever and whoever, they'll do the same to you." It was the first news of the coming "Mongol" offensives of December 1944 and February 1945.

One other question now stayed for an answer: how much material aid, how much moral encouragement, could the partisans expect from the Allies in this fight for survival?

To this the answer came on 13 November. It took the form of an "order" from Field-Marshal Alexander, and was broadcast, as though by irony to rub it in, over Radio "Italia Combatte".

In good Italian, available as much to the enemy as to the partisans, this "order" as well as told the partisans to pack up and go home. Mud and snow, it explained, had stopped the Allied northward drive. There could be no further advance until the spring, maybe five months or more away. This being so, all patriotic fighting forces must now desist from any large-scale actions, conserve their ammunition, expect no parachuted supplies or few, and sit back for further orders. However differently intended, this in effect was an invitation to the partisans to disband, and to the enemy to come up and finish them off while they were doing it. Given the circumstances, no other interpretation seemed reasonably possible.

Was this proposal for disaster a mere naïvety on the part of Alexander's advisers: or, if not, what else could explain it? Down in Rome the indomitable Action party leader, Ferruccio Parri, demanded to see the field-marshal himself. Alexander, according to Parri's account of the meeting that ensued, was sorely embarrassed. All he had done, he told Parri, was to ask a Protestant clergyman on his staff of PWB, the Psychological Warfare Bureau, to say "something" to the partisans now that these were going to have to endure another winter.

One can easily believe that. Alexander's Protestant clergyman may have had a whole hive of strange bees buzzing in his bonnet, psychological or otherwise, but Alexander himself was far too good a soldier and human being to have conceived any such "order". Its military unwisdom was patent to any experienced eye; and such eyes, at least among the British, were not rare by now. Was it just that the PWB clergyman wanted to save partisan lives by sending them home to wait for the spring? If so, it was simply daft. Or did it reveal the plans of the political wing, the further working out of that devious game between the Allies and the liberation movement, the placing of a "move" that would kill off any chance of insurrections in the cities of the north after the spring offensive had begun? There were those in command of the liberation movement who thought so; and their suspicions were powerfully confirmed when, three weeks later, they had to accept General Wilson's dictation. One day the historians will be able to tell us.

However all this might be, the "order" was ignored because it had to be. Only a few brigades of worthless fighting value obeyed it, these including none of the Garibaldini or Justice and Liberty formations. The partisan military command concealed in Milan sent round an ingenious gloss on the "order" which proved that it meant the reverse of what it actually said; but this, too, was not required. Being in no mood for suicide, the partisans were going to fight. Cucciolo and Don Bobbio and many more were going to die, in battle or in front of firing squads. But it was not going to be for nothing, it was not going to be for some avoidable and crass defeat.

FIVE

I

PETER'S MISSION ARRIVED in the northern Apennines in nice time for the second "Mongol" offensive of February 1945, giving us a couple of weeks, as I have described, to get our bearings and measure the problems. The outlook, for the moment, looked both worse and better than expected. Worse because the weather was appalling, but better because the partisans were numerous, evidently well led, and in no mood for advice from psychological clergymen. Mid-winter though it was by now, their morale was good. They could see the end in sight, somewhere not far ahead, and meanwhile they had the measure of their work.

Yet there was still plenty of time for defeat. That also became clear as we found our bearings and probed the situation.

It was said, and this seemed likely, that the enemy had begun to lose his nerve. The fascists were losing it because they saw that the Germans, who protected them, were going to be beaten; and the Germans were losing it because they saw that they were going to have to eat dirt or fight on their own German soil, or both. Interrogating German prisoners, I heard them speak in misery of their families suffering at home: already the days of fighting the war at the expense of foreign peoples were good and finished.

But if enemy morale was no longer as laced with arrogance, it remained formidable. The fighting machine still worked; and often it could work, as we discovered, remarkably well. And among those with guilt on their minds, as many had, the anger of defeat increased brutality against civilians. The shootings, as at Portofino, became more frequent, if possible more senseless. The cruelties multiplied.

All the same, measuring one thing with another, we saw that this enemy had lost his overall initiative in these hills behind his frontline. He could still launch tactical surprises or what he hoped would be such, but he could no longer exercise any long term control. The strategic initiative had passed to the partisans. The Cichero divisions, like others among the best, had come through the December "Mongol" offensive better than they had feared but had needed time to recover. We now saw them come through the second, that of February, without losing any of their coherence. They were able to save a lot of villages from enemy assault or burning, and rapidly return to the attack. By the last days of March, with enemy offensive action petering out, these Cichero divisions were back in control of most of their mountain zone. The partisan "Republic of Torriglia" emerged again. Liberation committees came out of their refuges and grasped the reins of civil administration once more. Pressing outward, partisan units edged ever closer to the suburbs of Genoa, bivouacking now in the very outskirts, besieging and ambushing the enemy under the wings of the city itself. The partisan offensive now was from offensive positions. This offensive was against Alexander's "order"; but the wisdom of ignoring that was well and truly confirmed.

All this brought in prisoners whose interrogation was among my jobs. I used to have them brought in one by one, their eyes blindfolded, and then would cock my pistol and put it on the table with a clump; but this was to save precious time more than anything else, and none of them was beaten or otherwise tortured or shot. In any case, they all said what they knew with little argument. From this information Peter was able to compose an "order of battle" of enemy troops in our mountain sector, and this we radioed to 5 Army.

Most prisoners now were sad enough. Only a handful, nazis still, answered with the minimum of words. Two or three Austrians even volunteered to join our ranks. As for the "Mongols", there was no language that I knew to talk to them, but luckily we found among them a Volga German who was able to interpret. Some of these "Mongols", identified by peasants as criminals who had raped and burnt and shot, were duly tried by the legal organ of the sixth zone and were shot; and that went for the worst of the fascist prisoners too. But otherwise the procedure was gentle after the all-out bitterness of Jugoslavia.

One prisoner was unusual. A patrol operating far out into the plains of the north ambushed a German staff car whose single passenger was neither killed nor wounded, and seemed to be an officer of some kind. They had a lot of bother with him, for he was furiously annoyed at being taken, and above all outraged at being taken by a handful of ragged lads of an average age of twenty or so. But they brought him in, as ordered, and marched him hard across the hills to the hamlet where I was then, the Capanne di Carrega I think it was, astride the upper slopes of Monte Antola. He was still angry when he came in, but arrogant no longer. Meeting a British officer managed to make him even quite polite and with this, though blindfold, he seemed to think his troubles over. "Talk," I said, obliging him to stand.

2

He proved to be an interesting specimen of that type of German regular officer who was clear in his mind that the nazis were a gang of lower-class thugs but useful to Germany, worthy of support, and likely even to win the war. He was not, he explained, a nazi himself: a captain in the German Navy, for such he proved to be, was above that sort of caper. But Hitler had saved Germany from chaos and bolshevism, dealt with the Jews and other forms of insect life, and led the German people to a greatness that even the high days of Kaiser William had not known. This must surely be for everybody's good? As for the war with England, that was Churchill's fault and a mistake.

Expanding a little, he was inclined to give me a word of praise for speaking the language of the master race, and to sympathise with my position. We British used the partisans, he could understand that: after all, Germany had used the nazis; but it wasn't, he wanted to explain, in any way my fault that a captain of the German Navy should have been captured in this absurd demeaning fashion. On the contrary, he was moving around to say, it might be pretty much that we were on the same side now: or, if not quite yet, then soon? This particular war could go one way or the other, though personally he thought that Hitler would never be defeated. But then in any case there were the Russians, and we and the Germans were surely going to need each other for the next round? And so on.

We got down to business. Name, rank, unit? No trouble. Mission, task, reason for travelling by staff car from X to Y? But on this he stuck. He was visiting a friend, an insignificant matter of staff liaison, practically an accident. I brought the interrogation to an end; and Peter, duly informed, wirelessed 5 Army that we had a senior naval captain probably connected with the SD and what should we do with him? Base came back crisply and with some excitement: send him out under absolutely safe escort, and at once. No, we replied, impossible under weeks and in any case not safe. Then, said 5 Army, we will send an aircraft for him; clear a landing strip.

Though easier said than done in those rocks and gorges, Miro's command found and cleared a level of grass among the peaks round Santo Stefano d'Aveto, and there in the midst of a night of howling wind and seething cloud a singularly bold British pilot arrived in a flying cockleshell of the kind called Lysander. He landed this like a leaf in a storm, and for some rending moments it seemed that he and his craft must go over the side of the cliff. But they didn't, and men got hold of its wings. Our prisoner was bundled in and the pilot got away by another miracle, or so it looked, and landed safely at the other end. A lucky man, that naval captain: but after the war, with his opinions, he no doubt found himself a great deal luckier still.

As for us, our work prospered better than we had dared to hope. The Cichero divisions confirmed the first impression they had made. Not only did they stand off the February *rastrellamento* in good order, but they hit back hard as soon as its punch was thrown. They took in volunteers. They formed new units. They attacked new targets. And now there came a sense of rising climax as the snows thawed and the spring came close. We were all nearing the biggest test, and we all knew it.

Meanwhile, agreeably, parachutes rained down, or at least they dropped from the Dakotas in numbers considerably larger than we had expected. I think there were diverse reasons for this reinforcement of supplies. Top army command naturally wanted brisk action behind the Gothic Line at a time when preparing to assault that line head-on. And SOE, as to its military wing, was just as naturally enjoying a success, even a big success. The whole fighting movement here in northern Italy had taken fire in a burning mixture of anger and revenge, hope and political sound good sense. Here was another "gigantic guerrilla" that was paying off.

But for whose eventual benefit? The question was neither asked nor even admitted to exist, at least in public, but it stood there very solidly in private, and leered over our shoulders with a suitably cynical grin. Am I remembering the thing more clearly than it really was? No: because many hints and shifts showed that the partisan command were acutely aware of that question's presence. Any lingering doubt they may have had upon the subject was removed in February, when the zonal commissar Rolando dropped back by parachute after a trip to Rome. He had walked out through the lines in December or early January so as to find out what went on. A man of few words, audacious, a tough survivor of many adventures, Rolando was one of those Italian communists who, like Marzo, had seen the vision of a new companionship but knew, as well, how difficult it must be to win and carry through. Rolando said little to us about his trip save civilities, but he must have been able to tell the partisan command a great deal about what was in the wind. It was also certain, by all the local signs, that preparations for insurrection in Genoa now got fully into their stride; and of this we received some interesting evidence.

Miro produced a message from the Ligurian committee of national liberation in Genoa: its delegates would like to meet the representatives of Field-Marshal Alexander. They would come up to a village in the Val Brevenna, some way over the long slope of mountains that falls from Monte Antola directly to the city itself.

3

Answering this call, we walked one February day across the top of Antola, Miro and Attilio, Peter and myself, and two couriers, through the dawn of an unforgettable glow of distant light. Standing for a breather on the flank of Monte Buio, we had the snowlit rim of the Alps out there along the northern horizon, the slim point of Monte Rosa rising in a pinnacle across the hidden plains of Piedmont, and then, to the south and far below, there was the sea haze around the city that had now become the central aim of all our thoughts. It was one of those moments, rare enough in partisan life and yet perhaps impossible in any other, or impossible in this degree of poignancy, when you felt that nothing could defeat you or match your strength or outbid your skill: the eternal feeling, no doubt, of Robin in the Greenwood but one, I also think, that can be reckoned on the better side of human nature.

Brushed by the dawn, white and pink and pallid saffron, the peaks of that distant snow rim signalled every kind of good promise, and we smiled at each other with a sudden happiness and chatted for a while: Miro square-standing on his ski boots and his strong face puckered with its familiar air of mildly ironical surprise, Attilio with his beard glowing and his blue eyes bright with frost, Peter delighted at this marvel of the mountain peaks and myself much the same.

Later on towards the spring but somewhere in about the same place, there was to be a different kind of moment.

We were walking then through a late afternoon and a snowstorm that blew a gale among the last of the winter's messages. Carrying a portable radio receiver, Attilio invariably listened to the news, another duty of a commissar. The news told us that President Roosevelt had died. We stopped in the gloaming of that afternoon and stood for a while; and it was a shared feeling that we had lost a good friend. For us British Roosevelt was the man who had brought America to our side even before the Japanese had bombed Pearl Harbor and when we were otherwise quite alone: we knew nothing of the details, nothing of all that history, and nothing else about Roosevelt, but we knew he had done that. For the Italians, he was the man who insisted that the Atlantic Charter, the only war aim that was known save destruction of the enemy, should bring liberty to all peoples: liberty to choose the government they wanted, liberty to shove the past behind them; and this too was quite enough. That aim stood out through all the doubts and equivocations, and now the man who was most powerfully associated with its existence and its meaning was gone from us.

I can't think that we said much upon the subject, standing there in the blowing snow, but I am clear in my mind that we felt sadly bereft. We walked on again, and Attilio fell to singing the Ligurian partisan song that had come with Manes from Imperia where the purple mountains rise into France:

> Tira il vento
> Soffia la bufera
> Scarpe rotte
> Pur bisogn' andar. . . .

a simple kind of song that was both lament and cry of defiance, sentimental in any other circumstances, not sentimental here. It was not in the least sentimental here: and as Attilio blew its tune into the fury of the snow it seemed no bad exhortation, not least because Attilio, perhaps above all others, was a man who loved truth.

This was a loss still some weeks ahead on the morning that we came over the flank of Buio and went down through cold gorges to the Val Brevenna. Down there, beside a leaping torrent, a straggle of homesteads were lined along the hillside, the village of Pareto.

Attilio had charge of the arrangements and led to a small house, gave our couriers an order to watch outside, and pushed open the door. Two men in civilian clothes stood beyond a table covered with a cloth in stitched colours. The Italians embraced each other, and we two British were introduced. The room was warm, but the cold tension of the city's life, arriving here with the delegates from Genoa, was also present.

They were Parini and Maffi: or, as we learned later on, Enrico Martino of the liberal party and Secondo Pessi of the communist party now representing not their parties but the six-party Ligurian committee of national liberation, or CLN as it was universally known. They had slipped up through the night, and were pale with loss of sleep but also, as we found, with the news they had to tell.

There was much news, and from either side. Miro and Attilio spoke of the situation of the Cichero divisions, already turning from the February *rastrellamento* to their own offensive operations, and sketched the outcome that would now obtain. Within a month, if all went well and the signs were that it would, the Cichero divisions and their ancillary units would be standing in a tight half-circle round the whole arena of the city from the hills above Savona on the west to those above Neri on the east. They would have Genoa and its enemy garrisons surrounded. Then they spoke of the supply position, and the help now being received from the Allies. They spoke carefully of this, perhaps because the help was more than they had thought likely, or we either. But nobody wanted to mention that.

Parini and Maffi résuméd the situation inside Genoa, talking now chiefly for us. The six anti-fascist parties in Genoa, surviving underground, had joined in alliance on the day that Mussolini had fallen, 27 July 1943, nearly two years earlier. On 9 September of that same year, the day after the armistice, this committee had transformed itself into the Ligurian CLN, just as other anti-fascist alliances were doing in other cities and towns of enemy-held Italy. A little later, with the onset of partisan warfare in the hills, the CLN had set up a regional military command, again composed of representatives of the six parties. Nearly all its fighting units in Liguria were Garibaldini led chiefly by communists; but the communist party, as one with five others, had no more than its share of political and executive power.

Here was the groundwork for democracy in Italy. It had proved hard to stand on, but not because of party dissensions. These existed beneath the surface but were kept there, while the joint effort of companionship through nearly two years of clandestine work and struggle had driven these dissensions into an unwanted area of distraction. Parini and Maffi conveyed this, but other evidence confirmed it. The groundwork of democracy had proved hard to stand on for a different reason. German firing squads had taken a high toll, and German concentration camps, and fascist spies, and the ill-famed cellars of the Gestapo prison in Genoa's Casa dello Studente.

Now these losses had become worse still. Four members of the military command had been taken in December, and were at present in the Casa dello Studente but likely to die there; two others, also taken, had already been shot. In their stead a new military command had been named. Parini and Maffi went into the details. For many weeks now, given these conditions, all members of the committee and command inside Genoa—a few of them, like Miro, were with the units in the hills—had lived a hunted life, shifting their quarters each night or so and yet managing to retain their links and to continue with their work.

Were all conceivable leaks now stopped?

Parini and Maffi hoped so, but they spoke with a dignified scepticism. Who could ever be sure? Meanwhile they were calm and even serene, taking fear for granted, two middle-sized men in bourgeois clothes of an adequate respectability, a lawyer and a man of artisan background who tomorrow would go back into their city and again take their chance with the rest. The morning light came in through that cottage window and slanted icily upon their faces while they talked of the underground grip which they of the CLN had taken on their city, and how they had organised its illegal life, and built an administration to save the city from enemy destruction and then govern it.

But here was the crux of the drama: what would happen when the Allies opened their spring offensive? Now that the CLNs in northern Italy were the duly accredited representatives of the government in Rome, what attitude would be shown by the Allies who had approved that government? Parini and Maffi let those unspoken questions stay unspoken. Instead, they inquired what tasks the Allies wished them to perform? It was a tactful way of asking the same thing.

A little gingerly, all being aware of the ambiguities involved, such questions were considered at this and later meetings. Our own orders at this stage were brief and clear about tasks to be carried out. So far as Genoa and its installations were concerned, these were to secure maximum effort by the CLN and its fighting units in an enterprise called "anti-scorch". This meant the planning and eventual carrying out of actions to prevent enemy demolition of ports, railways, tunnels, public service installations and the rest. As all experience had so far shown, above all in western Russia, the Germans systematically wrecked everything they could when retreating for the last time. If they were able to do this in northern Italy, the problems of post-war government would become immensely heavier. Allied command was urgent on the need to reduce enemy demolitions to a minimum. This would be difficult, since on the best of hopes an interval must come between German withdrawal and Allied seizure of the terrain. It was in this interval that the CLN and its fighting men must act.

But "anti-scorch" was another piece of ground on which all could stand together. Parini and Maffi explained that "anti-scorch" was already at the head of their priorities. The German command inside Genoa had mined Italy's biggest port and all its installations, and was ready to sink large vessels across points of entry and exit. Out from Genoa, to north-west and north and south-west, railways ran through many tunnels: these too were mined for demolition. If carried out, these demolitions could wreck the city's life for years to come.

To prevent them the CLN had mobilised a force of some 3,000 urban partisans in small groups available at the shortest notice: but these had very few weapons. Could we British arrange for special drops to meet this shortage? If so, how soon could we do it? Beyond that, the CLN had also organised teams of anti-demolition experts whose task, already in train, was to shadow the German demolition teams, understand the details of the mining, and stop their explosive charges from being detonated. For these units, too, arms were needed. Next, military reinforcements would be needed from the brigades in the hills as soon as the decisive moment came: the urban partisans would fight, provided they had arms, but they lacked experience and numbers.

All this was good and true, but there was naturally more behind it. Where could anyone draw the line between a successful effort to prevent these wholesale demolitions, and an insurrection which would put the CLN into power before Allied spearheads came upon the scene? Who could save Genoa except the CLN: but if the CLN saved it by taking power through a necessary insurrection, how could the Allies object? Were we to reply that the CLN was to act but also not to act? We had no such orders. Not even Alexander's clergyman had thought up anything so bizarre or futile.

As it was, though we did not know it at the time, the Milan military command's leader, Luigi Longo, settled the issue decisively with an order of 10 April: an order, this time, that was going to be obeyed. Coming exactly one day after the spring offensive opened against the Gothic Line, this order called for all-out action at the appropriate moment against enemy strongpoints; and this all-out action was to be combined with mass insurrections in the cities of the north. Strikes, street demos, and every other possible form of agitation were to gather at quickening pace into insurrectionary movements capable of carrying whole populations into control of "whole sectors": better still, of "whole cities and zones".

Though communist inspired, this order was issued with the full support of the other five parties. Only the newly-appointed commander of the Milan senior command, General Cadorna, was against it: he took the Allied viewpoint, but his opposition was pushed aside. In Genoa, as it came out later, there was a similarly complete agreement among all parties and commands. Some of the Church dignitaries, notably in Genoa, still hoped to avoid an insurrection with its unavoidable outburst of democratic politics, and were already trying to secure a German withdrawal by some kind of agreed compromise. But the partisan leaders of the Christian-democrats, who also knew that their future credit must stand or fall by their attitude now, gave their full consent to insurrection and took their part in it when it came.

SIX

I

THEN SUDDENLY IN shafts of sunlight the spring arrived; and with it there began the Allies' last offensive. This opened on 9 April along the Gothic Line from Tuscany to the shores of the Adriatic: still a long way from us in Liguria, but it found Miro's units ready. Already, in March and early April, they had closed in on isolated enemy positions of any strength, destroyed or driven out those of small strength, and begun pushing from our mountains into all the periphery of the northern plains.

We had watched this process. Peter greatly marched about our zone, inspecting, listening, arguing; and he liked what he saw. Partisan politics might be the nearest road to the devil, but partisan patriotism and morale chimed directly with his own ideas of right and justice. He took their cause to his heart, though prudently, and, what was a considerable bonus, he got on famously with Miro. Marching around, he also took shortcuts and risks in spite of his Greek-taught experience, fruit of Tamplin's otherwise fruitless "nat bands", that you'd be "nabbed" if you did; and one night beyond Bobbio, or so he afterwards affirmed, went so far as to stay with an elderly contessa who provided "hot water *and* sheets on the bed". In short, he liked and was liked in return, and there was no trouble between the CLN and the "representatives of Field-Marshal Alexander". Not all partisan zones were fortunate in this respect, and least of all Piedmont to our northwest.

Then "anti-scorch" came usefully in; and this, even given our good relations, was just as well. For on 13 April, hard on the heels of the first big batterings at the Gothic Line and before that line was fully shattered, another Allied order came across the public radio. This time it came not in the name of Field-Marshal Alexander but in that of General Mark Clark, commanding American 5 Army on our western side of the front. As a directive to partisans, it was not quite as daft or potentially disastrous as the one issued in Alexander's name the previous November, but it thoroughly gave the game away for anyone who might be still in doubt upon that subject.

At a moment when all effective partisan units were necessarily on the attack, reinforcing their actions to a maximum so as to hamper the enemy's movements and upset his plans for demolition and retreat, General Clark saw fit to tell them to do exactly the reverse. Referring to partisan brigades and divisions as "bands" just as though nothing had changed in the last twelve months, this order said that apart from "certain bands" which had received "special instructions"—and of these we had none in our zone—other "bands" were to "maintain their strength and be ready for action". But they were not to act, save in minor operations, until so instructed. They were to stand by, in short, until General Clark found it convenient to make some use of them.

This was the writing on the wall in language that nobody could misread, and it was not misread. All serious units operating across the enemy's rear acted against the order, and went into action on the biggest scale they were able. The eventual pattern was first established in the great inland city of Bologna, though we learned of this only later: advancing into Bologna, on 21 April, American 34 Division found the city firmly in the hands of its CLN.

Am I reading into Clark's order a will to undermine the liberation movement, and in the moment of its greatest possible success, that was really not there? It seems unlikely, for the corresponding orders to Allied missions were clearer still. In our case, as I recall, we were told to instruct the Cichero divisions not to go down into the towns, and above all not to go down against the enemy in Genoa.

Peter had to take these instructions to Miro and his command, and of course he took them and argued for them as well as he could. It was bound to be a rather delicate occasion, since Miro's command had already given us their operative "Plan A", finalised about a week earlier, which provided for full-scale partisan assault on enemy positions in all the towns of the riviera and above all in Genoa. Peter delivered his orders which amounted to the exact opposite of "Plan A", and these were duly heard, apparently without surprise, by Miro and his command. Then it was that "anti-scorch" came in to save the day.

"How can we save Genoa from destruction," they asked, "and the railway tunnels, and all the rest, unless we take offensive action before the demolitions can begin? How can we save the port of Genoa with 'small actions of anti-sabotage'?"

A plan developed. In a long radio message to 5 Army, the only one of our signals that I somehow still possess, Peter recommended agreement on a rising within the city, aimed at anti-scorch, that would be backed by the rapid infiltration of 300 picked fighting men from the mountain units. "The plan," said this signal, "would take five days to lay on from the date of your approval and cannot take place before 20 April. Standby signal would be thorough bombing of coastal batteries. Action signal naval demonstration. You to fix code name. Grateful your comments soonest repeat soonest." I cannot recall that we ever received any comments, favourable or otherwise; and the rising in Genoa began and then continued upon the quite different and altogether larger "Plan A" of Miro's command. It stands on the record that British warships did in fact make a naval demonstration off Genoa on the third day of the insurrection. Though too late to be of any use, this was the Allies' sole contribution to the whole remarkable affair.

Meanwhile things were hotting up. News from the CLN inside Genoa became more detailed, pinpointing enemy targets, reporting on further enemy plans for massive demolitions, and asking for air support in the form of bombing of key points. In our zone, we got rather more of this air support than we cared for. American fighter aircraft came wheeling over and hit at anything that moved on our roads, so that use of these roads which we controlled became a risky business during daylight. Recriminations grew understandably bitter. But no appeals to 5 Army made the slightest difference. Given their orders to hit "anything that moved", peasant carts, people on foot, whatever, those pilots carried them out: why should they worry? But all this was soon swallowed by the onrush of events.

2

The big battles along and through the Gothic Line were in the centre and east, and not in our western mountains, and we knew nothing of them. The record shows that as early as 14 April, five days after the offensive had begun, the German commander von Vietinghoff reported to Hitler that he could hold neither the Gothic Line nor any of its rear positions. Only immediate withdrawal to a line north of the river Po, he urged, could save his armies. On 17 April Hitler turned down any such idea.

"Under no circumstance," von Vietinghoff was told, "must troops or commanders be allowed to waver or to adopt a defeatist attitude, as a result of such ideas apparently held in your headquarters." And Hitler's commands continued with a characteristic threat, adding that "where any such danger is likely, the sharpest counter-measures must be taken". Every inch of northern Italy had to be defended to the last. "I desire to point out," Hitler concluded by way of his chief of staff, General Jodl, "the serious consequences for all those higher commanders, unit commanders or staff officers who do not carry out the Fuehrer's orders to the last word."

But no threats could help Hitler now. The front was broken, and on 20 April von Vietinghoff ordered a general withdrawal to the line of the Po. His retreat became a rout to a point where even General Heidrich, commanding 1 Parachute Corps, was able to reach the northern side of the Po only by swimming for it.

But the Allied advance went more slowly on our western side of the front. Here a variety of American, Brazilian and other divisions began shoving into the northern Apennines after 12 April but made little progress. Only on 23 April did they begin to bite into the hills of the Ligurian riviera. And only on that day did the German commander in Genoa, General Meinhold, make up his mind to try to extricate his 7,000 German troops and 7,000 Blackshirt and other fascist auxiliaries, as well as several thousand more positioned outside Genoa. He sent a courier to his garrison at Serravalle, a little way north of Genoa on the only possible escape route, and ordered its commander, a Lieutenant Udet, to negotiate a deal with the Cichero divisions. If they would let him through, he promised through Udet, he would order no demolitions.

The deal was refused, and the CLN took its fateful decision.

The nearest Allied spearheads were still upward of fifty miles away, down the coast road to the south. Inside Genoa large groups of Meinhold's troops stood under commanders who had made it known that they would refuse Meinhold's orders, on the grounds that compromise with the partisans was betrayal of the fatherland. On the chances of a successful insurrection, the local situation was hard to judge. It could still go either way.

But later on that same day, 23 April, the CLN judged that it would go their way, and sent out their call for a general rising, while at the same time moving their anti-scorch teams into action. Midnight saw the greatest maritime city of the Mediterranean in full upheaval.

Scenes from the Anti-Nazi War

Up in the hills, on the next morning of 24 April, we entered Torriglia, evacuated by the enemy the day before. Torriglia is a little market town at the southern head of the valley of the Trebbia: down the other side, towards the sea, the roads fall into Genoa as though diving for its heart. Already the foremost mountain units had dived with them, and were fighting in the city. Now the insurrection was at full blast, with the bulk of the Cichero divisions well into it as well. But there was a problem.

One thing that is fairly certain about all warfare, so far as anyone has ever been able to show, is that it develops in confusion. It doesn't get reported like that afterwards, of course; and to read the memoirs of leading generals you would easily imagine that confusion was the last thing that they, as distinct from the generals on the other side, ever suffered from. Never mind: at the time and invariably, in my experience, confusion reigns. The only interesting question, and it may be very interesting for those actually involved, is whether the confusion is much or little: after all, their lives are going to depend upon the answer.

On this occasion, I would say, the confusion was about average: which, considering the circumstances, was very much a plus for Miro and his staff. Infantry in regular armies, even in those remote days, were linked from forward units back to other units behind them by shortwave radio equipment; and it was generally possible, even in high-rise confusion, to know where forward units had got themselves to. Miro and his staff had no such equipment: the legs of their couriers and occasional cars or bicycles were the most that they could manage. And communications between the CLN hidden inside the city and Miro's command in the mountains high above were naturally even worse.

So the problem, for Miro and his staff on that day of 24 April in Torriglia, was to know just what was going on in Genoa. Had they sent the Cichero divisions down too soon? Or worse, unthinkably worse, had they sent them down too late?

A direct liaison was obviously vital; it was also urgent. The zonal deputy commissar, Attilio, would take a car and motor down and make it.

Here was a job, I said, for me; and all agreed. A radio link between the fighting inside Genoa and 5 Army, still miles to the south, might help. This meant taking George Armstrong, but there was no need to press him. As unmoved as ever, just as in Novi Sad during another enemy defeat the previous October,

George took to our little plan as calmly as crossing the street. He wasn't going to miss out now.

Late that evening, 24 April, we piled into an elderly car acquired from some sedate civilian retirement, Attilio and a driver, George and me; and we set out.

Steering down beneath a canopy of stars through an otherwise pitch-black night, we let that old car go as it would: which, considering that it was going down the side of a mountain, was really quite fast.

Climbing above on either side, as we dived into the night, the lamps of mountain hamlets winked and glittered with the stars.

Somewhere down below us there was Genoa, and a battle for its life.

SEVEN

1

CITIES ARE LIBERATED from enemy occupation, as the troops go in, with cheering crowds and flowers, and maidens casting kisses to the happy few who get there first, and matrons remembering their youth. The day is kind with generous abandon, and there is wine for free in every tap.

It has always been like that; or so they say.

But the liberation of Genoa was not like that. It began as a desperate affair on the evening of 23 April; and it continued as a desperate affair. Only three days later did it climax in a final and a huge success.

2

"You must tell me about it some time," said the AMGOT brigadier several weeks later, "once we've got things, I mean, tidied up."

An elderly sort of person who reminded me of a genial version of Tamplin, this brigadier represented Allied Military Government in Occupied Territory: in territory, that is, occupied not by the enemy but by the Allied armies. It seemed an odd way of labelling territory, here in northern Italy, where Italian action had done so much for its liberation, and it was resented. Long swept into oblivion, this was the kind of detail that had importance in those days. As for the name AMGOT, I am bound to recall that the good and democratic British Army held it to be a Turkish word for camel-dung: which, of course, it may or may not have been.

In the weeks following this liberation we soon saw, in any case, that the label "occupied territory" was an accurate one. Shoving aside the committees of liberation and all they stood for, AMGOT made it clear that it meant to govern that way. There were consequent scenes of protest, even anger. Caustic words were said. But Manes and Maffi and Scappini and the other hardliners of the Genoa CLN and its military command saw no point in any of that. They had liberated their city but they knew about the Rome agreement and its clauses dictated by General Wilson; and they long understood that resistance would be worse than fruitless. So relations eased, and the old gentleman who represented AMGOT, finding that his course in how to govern Italians had left several ends untied, was suitably relieved.

Soon he was positively happy. Within weeks of liberating Genoa and the whole region of Liguria, all the divisions of Cichero and comparable units were being rapidly disarmed, disbanded, and got rid of. The committees of national liberation were being dissolved with the same reassuring speed. From running loose among the people, politics was being clutched back under safe control again. As for whatever might have happened in Genoa during the great insurrection or before, eager figures never seen before were coming forward to explain their crucial and heroic actions, so that posterity should award the credit to the right and proper persons. Sound and respectable versions were on the make; and in some of these, I think, even the priest of Saint Rock would have taken a decent pride. Never backward at ingenious invention, he could scarcely have done better himself.

As things went on like this, the AMGOT officers began to threaten us with friendship. I was somewhat mollified, being innocent. But Peter saw further and more darkly. "Time we got out of here, and got out quick," he announced with customary decision, and set about the necessary preparations. Soon there would be talk of transforming us into AMGOT officers: who knows, with promotions from half-colonel to colonel or beyond, and a cushy villa on the coast thrown in. After all, we were well in with the natives, weren't we, we'd surely find that comfortable? On the Italian riviera, with summer coming soon?

We should find it no such thing. But how to get out of here, how to go home? It looked a tough one, even impossible. With the fighting finished in Italy, going home was a popular idea and transport by sea bound to be long, slow, and much obstructed; the queue would be enormous. As for transport by air, not even the priest of the shrine could have thought that a workable idea.

Muttering fearful things, Peter departed for the distant south where all our seniors were, and was absent for a while. When he came back he announced that we should go home in three days, or in four. He had barked through half a dozen military bureaucracies, and casualties must have been high. But he had done the deed.

We completed such duties as remained to us, which chiefly consisted in Peter's making sure that William got his girl, that other dependants were suitably looked after, and that George Armstrong had all the movement-orders he could possibly require. Gathered unofficially, the Ligurian CLN gave us a handsome dinner as well as the freedom of the city, and said those pleasant words of friendship that only Italians can say and also mean.

And that was that. We made our farewells, or such as we were able. I seem to remember that Marzo was still wearing his partisan scarf while he went about his duties as one of Genoa's two deputy mayors, appointed by the CLN and duly confirmed in office by AMGOT. I can't say if he ever gave a thought to his momentous journey over the Mont Cenis, twenty months earlier, and all that had followed from that courageous bid; but I should doubt it. Now he was busy chasing other problems, running to catch up with the future. And, as it happened, I missed him in the moment of our departure. He was said to be down at Portofino, looking into some matter connected with missing persons.

We departed for our headquarters, then in Rome, and there we were politely received. This seemed to me so out of character that even I became suspicious. But the wheels of fame were turning faster than we could know or guess. A courteous British ambassador even went so far as to invite the two of us to lunch. And after that, with one miracle jostling another, we were given immediate air passages to England.

I saw it must be true when we refuelled in Paris under a slate blue northern sky such as I hadn't known in years, and were flying on again. Enormously privileged, we were really going home by the fastest route, leaving whole armies clamouring behind. Perhaps like all such gifts, this one was disconcerting to the beneficiary; or I at least found it so. I had longed for England through these years and yet now, going home like this, England seemed to retreat in front of me. What would it be like, this country that I scarcely knew? How would I possibly fit in, what would I do?

Odd questions, you may think, to be fussing with at such a time. Perhaps not so odd. The England I had known was a country which had seemed to have no use for huge numbers of its citizens, and mere survival was the best that you could hope for from it. I'd learned to despise all that because then they'd taken us into war, blunderingly, miserably; and we'd gone to war, misgivingly, badly led, hugely handicapped, and somehow we'd made sense of the confusion and fulfilled the promise of our old traditions.

We had taken on whatever challenge that offered, however tough, and we had dealt with it. Is it any surprise that we had learned self-confidence and self-respect? For many, and myself among them, these five and a half years were in a large sense the whole chance of a lifetime. It was not a chance to have wanted or welcomed, but we had taken it and we had turned it to good purpose.

Now we were coming back and we should want a different world, a new and decent one; and who need doubt that we could build it? We should want simple things, but necessary things, and we should want the old men to step back and concede. Am I inventing a state of mind that didn't actually exist? Many years have passed, but I think not. It was merely an official myth of after years, when the drive and pride of that time was lost in the fogs of greed and subservience, and self-confidence was gone, that the armies which left England came back again, or those who were still alive to come back, in the same state of mind as when they had gone. The evidence may be elusive, but it still insists that they came back in a different state of mind. And who need be surprised? For they had suffered grievous disasters and yet won great victories; and all that kind of thing, if you can manage to survive, tends to be educational. With a proper military pessimism we scarcely expected, I should think, to be made particularly welcome, or those, at any rate, who had long been absent overseas; and least of all did anyone expect to live in a land of milk and honey. No: but in a land capable of showing what our people could really do when the opportunity was there.

In expecting this, moreover, events would soon show that those returning were at one with a majority of citizens at home. The general election of 1945 showed that. Then it was seen that the "war effort", in other words the active participation of vast numbers of ordinary people in defence of their homes, their cities, and their fellow-citizens, had crashed through many ancient barriers of class and caste with a rude egalitarian joy, and had given this embattled people a sense of unity and useful purpose not known before. The histories say that this was the state of mind that took all leading politicians by surprise. If so, it could only have been because leading politicians were gravely out of touch with their electorate, especially the Forces' electorate. The armies coming home wanted a sack of good things, such as getting back to wives or the prospect of wives, shedding uniforms, living again.

But somewhere down the line they also wanted social change, political change, even radical change if that was what was needed. A country free of cursed miseries, of dole-queues, dead-ends, glaring discrepancies of wealth and poverty, and all the despair at the bottom of the heap: wasn't that the sense of all that all of us had done?

Blessed innocence, you will say, yet at least a doubt crept in as we entered northern skies, now serenely falling into dusk, and came over England and landed at the RAF base of Northolt, west of London, and got out and called thanks to the crew and walked to the sheds.

Then there was simply the happiness of being back.

The gift continued, and took us through every remaining hazard, even as to explaining to Security who we were and why we had come and by what obscure military wangle. World-weary men in sergeants' stripes, Security looked at us and shook their heads; but they let us into England.

Taxis were there or something of the sort, I can't recall. Peter got into one and motored away to his family outside London. I got into another and went into London to look for Marion, and found her.

It was 6 June 1945. It was going to be a new world.

I thought: "It's going to have to be one. . . ."

3

Now if this were a tale about myself, here would surely be the place to end it. But as it is not, there are one or two matters still calling for attention.

You may be wondering, for one thing, how our journey to England was possible, given that it had to beat the competition of so many thousand other energetic home-goers. No doubt Peter's drive was decisive. Yet there was also something else. The wheels had turned to powerful effect, and myths are strong medicine when their makers put their mind to it. On this occasion, I might even say on our occasion, they hit the highest register.

Did I say myth? Six years later, this "something else" became enshrined in sound official history. His Majesty's Stationery Office then issued the fourth and final report on the Italian campaign by the Supreme Allied Commander in the Mediterranean, Field-Marshal the Viscount Alexander of Tunis.

Drawing on all relevant and internal information, this résuméd the course of Alexander's great offensive that smashed the Gothic Line and drove the Germans to surrender. Seven lines in its sixty-six pages were devoted to the action of the partisans north of the Gothic Line. Not many, you may think; but we in Genoa got one and a half of them, no less.

On 27 April, these words affirmed, getting the date wrong by only two days, the German commander in Genoa "surrendered the Genoa garrison to a British liaison officer". Good official history; and so it must be right. So right, in fact, that Winston Churchill duly affirmed the same in the fifth volume of his war memoirs. And then you wonder why Peter and I were given air transport to England ahead of all the army in Italy? My dear friend, heroes deserve a little something now and then: why grudge them that?

But leaving aside sound official history, the actual story is not a myth. It owes nothing to the priest of the shrine if a good deal, no doubt, to the sacred law. It forms my last scene from the anti-nazi war, and may be the most instructive of them all. For it says much about the great equivocation between what was said and what was done, what was promised and what was intended; but it also says something, and not a negligible something, about the limits of the influence of that equivocation. It says that if the anti-nazi war didn't exactly make a new world, all the same it made an end to a lot of the evil of the old world as well as pointing, as we saw, the way to make a better one. Or so, I think, you may reasonably allow yourself to believe: given the evidence, that is; and unless, of course, you are altogether sold on sound official history.

EIGHT

I

WE RAN ON down through the night, Attilio and his driver, George and me, with our ancient car doing its humble best and our weapons, for anything they could be worth, held ready at its open windows. The CLN in Genoa had judged this the right moment to launch their insurrection, but did the partisans possess the strength to pull it off? The old car slid on downwards, groaning at the bends with what sounded like the repetition of a more than reasonable doubt.

On the great pass of the Scoffera we found nothing; but this was known. The Germans had left it yesterday, or perhaps this morning. Then the hairpin turns to Genoa began to plunge and spin, the old car grinding wearily, and as they did so there were mountain hamlets climbing above us with their lanterns in the night. We ran on down into a gulf of darkness, and then at last there were figures on the road ahead. The first roadblock, but ours; and this too was known. Beyond, it was all discovery.

Roadside villages grew into suburbs, and now there were the scattered outskirts of the great city itself. Another roadblock; and ours again. Then another and another, civilians with guns, solemn with the doing of what they had never done before, peering, nervously questioning Attilio, little groups in ambush by the roadside.

So far, the CLN had pulled it off: all these approaches were in our hands.

Then the city itself. Few lights. Canyons in the gloom. More partisan roadblocks, but now, towards the port, the rattle of small-arms fire and the odd thump of grenades.

The inner city was also in our hands.

"Bini should be here."

He was. We found him in the printing house of the *Corriere Mercantile*, bringing out the first number of his party's daily, *Unità*: pale and thin as ever, journalist, educator, survivor of years of clandestinity and partisan war, tense with the sweat of fatigue, abundant with news. The port was still intact, but large enemy units were besieged within its buildings. The fight against them continued, but also the fight to bring the city back to its own life again.

Newspapers had to be part of that. Sharing the same print-shop as the communist *Unità*, the Action party had just run off the first issues of its own new daily, *Italia Libera*: its splash headline said that the CLN had taken over the government of Genoa and military power throughout Liguria. There were details, but no time to read them. Bini came second with *Unità* and a headline saying that "Genoa begins a new life, democratic and progressive".

"And the other parties?"

Yes, the socialists and republicans were sharing the *Lavoro* print-house, and the Christian-democrats and liberals that of the *Secolo XIX*. By the small hours of next morning, 25 April, each would have papers on the street, say in five hours' time.

"And the Germans?" I asked Bini, "the Blackshirts, all that lot?"

But Attilio was rightly anxious to get on, for it was urgent to find the committee. He pulled at my arm. "Ah, let's get on, Colonel." I had lately been promoted to lieutenant-colonel, and Attilio liked to be formal in his more anxious moments.

So I followed him into the night of that city of closed doors and we motored through more canyons, shuttered in their glistening April darkness, up and round and up and round the terraced streets of Genoa, until we came out on what appeared to be a promenade. I caught a glimpse of a starlit view opened upon the sea far below, but there was no time to admire it. Attilio stopped our driver beside a long building of the blind ecclesiastical appearance that they have in Italy. Inside there might be a vivid spiritual life; outside there was only this façade. We left the car and went inside what I later learned was the monastery or episcopal college of San Nicola, and marched through corridors of silence and obscurity. Suddenly, as we came, a door opened with a flood of light falling from a chandelier, and here in this parachute of brilliance there were familiar faces: Maffi, Parini, others. The CLN was in session: or those of its twelve members, two for each party, who were not momentarily absent.

An explanation and a precise view.

The CLN had taken full powers as the recognised delegate of the government of Italy. They had done this early on 24 April, some sixteen hours before. Subordinate CLNs in other Ligurian towns and cities, Savona and the rest, were now following suit.

The CLN had also published its nominees for all senior administrative posts. Parini was prefect of Genoa; others were mayor, police chief, port director and so on, each with a deputy: again a total of twelve, with two from each party.

And the fighting situation? In hand, and the port so far intact, even if enemy units still held its major buildings. A good success, but not yet a sure one, not by any means. They questioned Attilio. Where exactly were the mountain divisions not detailed for the city? Had they occupied X, Y, and Z? Attilio exploded with information. All major units had advanced on their objectives. All the tunnels to the north, the great tunnels linking Genoa by road and rail with Milan and the north, were in our hands. Another success.

Once more, not final. The CLN told us that the German commanding general, Meinhold, had informed them that he would destroy the port of Genoa if not given safe passage for his troops through the partisan blockade. He still had the strength to do that, even though anti-scorch teams were already on the job. But the CLN had stood firm, refusing any bargain. They had demanded Meinhold's unconditional surrender.

Couriers in and out of the monastery, messages, the usual rush and scurry of commanders trying to keep up with events and even steer them.

Three in the morning now. Go and sleep. Beds were found for us two British. Hard monastery beds, yet soft with the comfort of having got here. And in the morning, such are the fruits of victory, coffee for breakfast and fresh hot rolls: better even than cheers and kisses.

The CLN proved the soundness of its judgment on that next day, 25 April. This day made history.

A major enemy grouping tried to fight its way out of the port, but was held: none of it got through, and the port was still intact. Other large groupings were barricaded in powerful buildings, refusing to surrender. There was much back-and-forth shooting.

Yet the battle for the great city, clearly by that late afternoon, was being won. Meinhold might still try to fight his way out, but he had lost Genoa. If he did try to fight his way out, he would run a savage gauntlet: the brigades astride of every road to the north would see to that.

It was high time to tell all this to Number One Special Force, then somewhere near Florence. They would tell 5 Army HQ, and

5 Army would tell their troops advancing on Genoa from the south. George had his suitcase transmitter on a table in our room with an aerial run up through the window to the floor above. He tapped away on his key. But nothing replied from the other end.

We had done this kind of thing in strange places over the past twelve months, from the plains of Srem and the Bačka to the back streets of Novi Sad. Now we were as safe as anyone could wish, and there was no contact. We needed contact as never before, but no contact came.

"They don't answer."

"They've got to."

"Well, they don't."

Later that night, with a contact still to be made, someone came to fetch me. I went away down the corridors of San Nicola, cursing wireless telegraphy. Here there was no risk that a radio-tracking crew would park along the promenade outside San Nicola and pin down our little suitcase transmitter as it bleeped and whispered on their dials. Here we could transmit all day and all night with no problem of security. And here we were with vital news for once: vital for the armies as well as for us. And there was no means of telling it.

I walked down the corridors and wondered what next. Some way along a door opened on the same vaulted room as yesterday, and here were Scappini, communist leader of the CLN, and his liberal companion Martino-Parini. They were sitting at their table as I came in. They looked up and Martino-Parini said: "The Germans have surrendered. To the CLN, to us."

And it was so. At seven that evening General Meinhold had signed a full capitulation to the CLN of himself and the 7,000 German troops under his command. All these he had ordered to surrender to the nearest partisan units under the sole condition that they would be handed to the Allies whenever the Allies should arrive. Four members of the CLN signed this document, while Meinhold and his chief of staff signed for the enemy.

The document was there on the table. I read it in the yellow light of a chandelier, two copies, one in Italian and the other in German. I hope that I said something appropriate.

What I certainly did say, back in our room again, was "George, listen to this. . . ."

But George threw up a hand, his other tapping the key. "They're getting me. Now we can tell them."

And we did tell them, furiously encoding, furiously sending, far into the small hours of that morning of 26 April. Did those signals make things absolutely clear? Distrusting my memory I looked the other day for confirmation in the files of the Public Record Office, and found surviving there a number of my decoded messages, including those sent from Genoa that night. They did make things absolutely clear.

Signed that evening, the capitulation came into effect at nine the next morning, 26 April. Most of the fascist units gave up at once or tried to dissolve into hiding; some of the German units also obeyed Meinhold's orders, but others refused. From one of the biggest German groups there came in two officers under a white flag. They brought a strange message from their commander, a naval captain called Berninghaus. Their message said that Berninghaus had assembled a court martial and sentenced Meinhold to death as a traitor. This mattered little, for Meinhold was now safe in the hands of the CLN. What did matter was that Berninghaus refused to surrender, and was threatening to bombard the city with his big guns on Monte Moro if the partisans continued their attack. But the mountain divisions were now on the scene and went into the assault at once. It took them most of that day to reduce the Berninghaus group, and more casualties were suffered. Altogether, the liberation of Genoa was going to cost the partisans some 300 killed and 3,000 wounded.

Another sizeable German group was holed up in a tall building at the Foci, a little to the south-east of the port itself. They were showing no fight, but they were also refusing to surrender: not, at any rate, to a bunch of partisans. They were going to wait for the Americans.

"Come and help shift them," Manes suggested.

So we got hold of a white shirt and walked down the middle of the street to that building near the Foci, Miro and Manes and me, and turned a corner and came into a boulevard with not a soul in sight, but ahead of us, some eight storeys high, a building with enemy troops who seemed to be at every window. One exaggerates at such moments, and it may be forgiven. We thought they were several thousand, with their weapons like a serried frieze on every level of that building above us; but later it was shown that they were only 1,500.

In a lonely kind of way we came to their wire, and their guards behind the wire looked at the three of us and we looked back at them.

"Ask them," Miro said, "to tell their commander."

I made the best of what parade-ground stiffness I could manage, and the guards listened. One of them went into the building and after a while came back and said that his commander would receive us inside.

"No," I said, "tell him to come out, we shall not go inside."

This time the wait was longer, and the joke began to get the better of Miro, for he and Manes had no means at all of forcing those Germans out of their building: without, at least, a long and bitter fight. But Manes managed to look stern, and I tried to.

At last he came, a plump naval officer with an understandably worried face. His own position was not exactly easy, for his troops had had enough, but German officers could not surrender to partisans. Yet he listened to my proposal and agreed to come with us: whereupon Manes, a veteran of the Spanish war, needed no further hint. He led briskly into the first house down the boulevard, danced up a flight of stairs to the first floor, and hammered on the door of a flat. The poor lady who lived there opened up in terror but was fluttered into silence by Miro's smile, and we all took chairs around her sitting-room table.

The naval captain required some convincing. He would surrender with his troops, but only to the Americans.

"The Americans are far away, they won't be here for days. And I'm instructed to tell you that the patriot forces will attack you at dawn."

But would they? He looked at me uneasily, not saying this doubt but evidently trying to think it. He also had the air of a man caught out in some dreadful social blunder.

"They'll put in a fullscale attack at dawn, these two commanders confirm it. You haven't a hope. Why invite needless casualties, you've heard of Meinhold's capitulation?"

Yes, he'd heard of that, and unlike Berninghaus, it seemed, he wasn't a furious nazi.

"Well, you've got Meinhold's order to surrender to the patriots, you'd better obey it."

He agreed at last, stipulating only that he would not surrender now, with the night coming on, but early next morning, the morning of 27 April.

Miro and Manes consented. It was good enough, and we parted.

This and other capitulations rounded things off. The great insurrection had fulfilled all the plans of the CLN. They had liberated their city. They had forced the enemy to surrender to them. They had reversed the fearful disasters of 1943 when Italian generals had destroyed another Italian Army. They had finished off the fascist years. They had made good the promise of the partisan struggle, and justified its losses.

All the same, a pressing question remained. Where in fact were the Americans? They could come now at any time they liked, and perhaps it would be as well to tell them so. But how? My radio messages were getting through to Number One Special Force, and so presumably to 5 Army, and so onward to the spearheads of 5 Army moving up the coast to Genoa. Yet who could know what delays and doubts might lie between? Once again a direct liaison became urgent.

I think it was Marzo who found the answer. The telephones were still working down the coast. Indeed, pretty well everything was working. On that day of 26 April the traffic police were brought back on duty, the power stations were mostly in fair order, the new administration had taken over. The city was under its own command, and the only serious problem was a shortage of food in the shops.

The Americans were said to have reached Rapallo, some thirty kilometres down the coast. So telephone them; and Marzo got through to a well-known café on the main road. He handed me the receiver. An Italian voice at the other end said: "The Americans? They're outside, they're everywhere."

"Go and get one, any one, any American."

And like that, from one American to another, we reached an officer who listened.

At this point Peter came into his own. I have never known anyone half as capable of conveying authority and conviction; and just now it was evidently useful to convey both. He decided to motor down to Rapallo that night. He came back towards nine the next morning, sitting on the bonnet of a Jeep. He had the chief of staff of General Almond's 92 Division in a seat behind him. Someone took a photo of him, and I have it still. He is even looking pleased.

And after him, in due course and without delay, there flowed into Genoa a multitude of Jeeps and trucks and tanks and all the ironmongery of war: 92 Division of 5 Army entering Genoa exactly three and a half tremendous days since the CLN had taken its decision. They came in without a single casualty, and they were rightly in good heart, signalling their relief with an hour's shoot-out against suspected snipers on roofs. I don't know if there were any snipers, and it was lucky nobody got killed; but all this was swallowed by the general happiness. It was also swallowed by the surprise, for 92 Division turned out to be no ordinary outfit. Its infantry were all black Americans; its motorised units were all yellow Americans, being Nisei Japanese from California; and its tank crews were all white Americans: a layer cake of different colours. Nobody had seen anything like that before; but the happiness, all the same, was more than the surprise.

And so the war ended, here at any rate, and there was nowhere else to go but home. This is what the histories tell; but there were still one or two things that the histories have not told.

Before it ended, there occurred a little misunderstanding. The commander of 92 Division, General Almond, proved to be a tough but kindly fighting soldier of experience: his ability to get things done was impressive when we came to know him in the days after his arrival. But he arrived under a disadvantage. Staff at 5 Army headquarters had seen fit to tell him nothing useful, we learned, about the liberation movement and its partisans. Weren't these, after all, a bunch of "bands" waiting helplessly around until told by General Clark of 5 Army what they were to do next? More of a nuisance than anything else? Even something of a joke? My detailed radio signals about Meinhold's capitulation to the CLN and about subsequent events, sent back over George Armstrong's transmitter in San Nicola, had entirely failed to reach him: either because they were signals of British origin or for some other reason connected with the amities of war alliance. General Almond spoke of this failure in friendly communication with the patience of a man accustomed to it, given the nature of military staffs. But he also showed himself a fast learner. It was certainly a help.

The CLN and its military command were of course eager to receive General Almond with a due formality. They arranged to do this in a handsome salon on an upper floor of their head-quarters in the Hotel Bristol. Its tall windows gave on an ancient street flanked by arcades whose successive arches loop down towards the port, and all its ambience had dignity and history, both being felt at this moment to be tokens of the triumph of the insur-rection. Being taciturn Ligurians, as well as tempered by years of clandestinity and danger, the members of the CLN were short on words. But they were also Genoese, citizens of the Proud

Republic of medieval centuries, heirs to a stubborn tradition; and they wished on this occasion to say what they had done.

They wished to inform the Allied commander of their liberation of the city and its province, and of their care to bring Genoa back to normal life. They wished to give him an account of the fighting, of the provisional total of prisoners they had taken, of the quantity of enemy arms they had captured, and of other interesting matters. They wished to run through the chief headings of their civilian work, relating to the restoration of law and order, public services, food supplies, newspapers, and much else bearing on the welfare of the population. They wished to introduce to him the men they had appointed to govern Genoa, the prefect and the mayor and the others. Lastly, they wished to welcome the American general, and assure him of full co-operation in their city which they had delivered from the enemy.

They gathered in this marvellous room filled with April sunlight, and sent for me as their interpreter.

We waited for the American general whom all of us had yet to meet.

Having got into the city an hour or so earlier, General Almond came punctually, a sturdy man of middle years, with one or two of his senior officers.

Parini or Scappini, I forget which, opened with some words of welcome, all standing, and the general listened to my translation. Then he turned to me.

"Tell them," General Almond said, "that my troops have liberated their city, and they are free men."

A silence followed: which continued.

The general looked at me with some surprise: couldn't I speak the language?

Then Providence intervened, or the sacred law, or whatever you prefer to think may now and then take pity on the frailties of humankind and stop collisions in the avenues of time. There came, from outside that room, the sudden din of shouts and uproar.

We rushed through the floor-to-ceiling windows to a balcony giving on that street of arcades.

Looking down, we saw far up that street the dense fore-ranks of a crowd of advancing men, and then we saw it was a column, a column of German prisoners a dozen or more abreast, hundreds of them, thousands of them, marching down that street unarmed but with armed partisans on either side. Had Manes arranged it? Had

Miro? Or was it an accident that they came exactly now? I still have no idea. But if ever a most convincing proof of partisan success appeared upon its destiny and moment, this was it.

At my elbow, General Almond said nothing; but he looked. The prisoners came on down that street, an endless column, for it turned out afterwards that more than 14,000 German and Fascist prisoners had been taken in Genoa alone; and the people in the arcades continued to clap and cheer.

Then we went back into the salon and General Almond gave me a measuring glance and said, "All right." And then he made a speech that warmed the heart. He had known nothing of what to expect; but of this he said no word. Instead, he praised and thanked the CLN for what they and their troops had done. He spoke handsomely of their work. He promised that his own troops would interfere as little as possible. And he ended by stating that he was well aware of the difference between the fascists and the people of Italy.

Then the CLN said what they had wished to say, and the meeting concluded with Parini, the new prefect of Genoa by nomination of the CLN, proposing that all stand in a minute of silence in memory of the late President Roosevelt. After which General Almond enlarged a little on what he had said before, generously, and affirmed that the friendships won by President Roosevelt would surely be continued by his successors, and notably by President Truman. Harmony reigned.

Yet the great equivocation, in this case between saying that you were fighting for a democratic renewal in Italy and doing in fact nothing of the kind, was not going to take this kind of thing lying down. The partisan units of the committees of liberation had freed Genoa and all its region, and had installed a democratic government there, or the nearest thing to a democratic government that anyone could reach in those days. Coming into Genoa without the need to fire a shot, General Almond with his 92 Division were suitably pleased.

Yet all this meant that politics had got seriously loose among the people; and besides, the partisans and their committees had done all this against the recent and specific orders of the Allies. They had not stood helplessly around, waiting to be told what to do next: as it proved, waiting for orders that never came. They had taken matters into their own hands. Now they were going to have to meet the bill for doing this with something else than casualties in battle.

Scenes from the Anti-Nazi War

The Rome agreement imposed the previous November was still in force. It stipulated total and immediate submission and disbandment. And not long passed, about two weeks I think, before the men to enforce the Rome agreement arrived in Genoa, as in other northern cities of Italy. They were the representatives of AMGOT; as I said, of Allied Military Government in Occupied Territory.

The elderly British brigadier was seconded by a not-so-elderly American colonel. They informed us briskly that they had come up from Sicily where, it was explained, they had completed a do-it-yourself course in how to govern Italians. Apparently it required only a few weeks to learn everything that a sensible Anglo-Saxon could need to know about that. In any case they had the power of decision; and the power they had was no laughing matter. It consisted in the overwhelming force of General Almond's division, as well as that of any other Allied divisions which might become necessary if the CLN and its partisans should prove recalcitrant. They began by demanding to see the CLN and its administrative nominees who were governing Genoa.

Prefect Parini and his colleagues of the CLN at once arranged a meeting. It took place, as I recall, in a stone-faced building of the fascist era. It was going to be a very different sort of meeting from the one with which they had welcomed General Almond; and perhaps a stone-faced building of the fascist era seemed the right sort of place to hold it in. Here they told the representatives of AMGOT what they had done, were doing, and proposed to do in the matter of governing Genoa.

Neither the British brigadier nor the American colonel, naturally, could speak Italian; the course in Sicily had not provided for it. Speaking Italian, after all, was scarcely a thing you would require in order to govern Italians. You had interpreters for that, and so they called on me.

Having duly listened by way of my English to what the natives wanted to say, the British brigadier smiled patiently and looked at me with the bland blue eyes of rectitude and innocence. He was determined to be worthy of the best imperial tradition. He would be tolerant of funny foreign ways. But he would be firm. You should begin, in such situations, as you mean to go on.

"Tell them, will you please, that the committee, this committee, is dissolved as from tomorrow. All their functions cease. All their responsibilities are assumed by AMGOT."

Now this was what was in the Rome agreement. But I took a deep breath and looked at the committee, the survivors of all those grim months and years of clandestine struggle, the liberators of their city and their region, the architects with others like them of any possible democracy in a postwar Italy; and I felt ashamed. Then I told them what the brigadier had said.

Those severe Ligurians listened in silence. They barely replied. They had reckoned with its coming. That was one large reason why they had launched an insurrection and carried it through.

2

And they were right. What the CLN had foreseen, this CLN as well as other CLNs, held good. AMGOT officers might have all the force of the Allied armies at their call, but it proved beyond all practical powers of AMGOT to remove the democratic nominees now placed in positions of responsibility. In the weeks that followed our CLN even extracted AMGOT consent to the formation of a partisan security police, much needed in those days of turbulence, under the command of Attilio. The brigadier and his colonel didn't like it, but they had to agree. Their own nominees could have achieved precisely nothing; they would have been ignored. The democratic nominees were confirmed in office, and they remained in office.

Disarmament of the partisans was then the big issue. This proved to be AMGOT's most anxious concern. The brigadier and his colonel had arrived, we learned, with a great and even desperate fear that the partisans would not disarm, would not accept the peace, but would make off into the hills and prepare to fight the Allies in the name of red revolution, or, at least, would conceal their weapons with the intention of fighting for that in the future. AMGOT had the recent "lesson of Greece" very much in mind. There, in the previous December, the British had met with a recalcitrant resistance movement in control of Athens, and had found it necessary to send in a British army to destroy it. AMGOT's orders, backed by American 5 Army and British 8 Army if required, were to make sure that nothing like "another Greece" could occur in northern Italy.

"Make them disarm," was AMGOT's first order in Genoa. Of course we could do no such thing: we could only report on the process of disarming already set in train by the CLN and its military command. "How many weapons have they handed in?" then became the daily question thrown at us. "Send them home, get rid of them, let them disappear": such was the constant burden of the AMGOT directives.

This may seem excessive in retrospect, even comical; it seemed outrageous at the time. The armies of the Allies would have liberated northern Italy from the Germans in any case. But without the partisans and their committees of national liberation the Allies would have liberated a most frantic chaos and destruction by the enemy. Only the partisans had prevented that destruction in the critical last days of enemy retreat. Only the committees of national liberation had stood against chaos, panic, wild revenge or all the other devils that wait always in the wings of war, and had launched the beginnings of democratic renewal. The CLNs and their partisans had done all this and much more; and what applied to Genoa applied elsewhere as well. Leaving their own claims aside, there is the evidence of what the British thought at the time.

A staff report on the purely military side, written in July 1945 by Colonel R. T. Hewitt of Number One Special Force, recorded that the partisans north of the Gothic Line took some 40,000 prisoners while the Allies were assaulting and destroying that line from the south. Overall partisan contribution "to the Allied victory in Italy was a very considerable one, and far surpassed the most optimistic forecasts. By armed force, they helped to break the strength and the morale of an enemy well superior in numbers. Without the partisans' victories there could not have been an Allied victory in Italy so fast, so complete, and with such light casualties." Their own casualties were not light, whether in battle or in prisoners shot by enemy firing squads. An official Italian report of 1946 gives a total of partisan dead, from first to last in this war, as 44,720, but of partisan wounded fewer than half that number, or 21,168. Much more than reversing the ratio of killed to wounded that is normal in regular warfare, when wounded prisoners are not shot, these figures speak for themselves.

But the Rome agreement had to be carried through. The democratic nominees were not eliminated; but they had to assist in the elimination of their movement. The CLNs were set aside and left to vanish in futility. Their fighters were sent into unemployment or whatever peacetime niche they could find. The democratic party alliance which had powered the resistance was able to survive until 1947; but then the "cold war" brought it to an end and there followed, almost at once, a stiff repression of the Left.

The process of burial went fast ahead. When not distorted or miscalled, the memory and meaning of the great Italian resistance was reduced to an adventure, even a squalid one, and twisted out of recognition. There were some strange distortions. The partisans of Liguria had liberated their region and their city, saved the port of Genoa and its rail and road tunnels, installed a democratic administration in advance of Allied arrival. All this had been reported in detail, at the time it was happening, over my radio link in the monastery of San Nicola, and was afterwards confirmed by the American commanding general on the spot. Yet sound official history, by 1951, could still assure posterity that the Germans had "surrendered the Genoa garrison to a British liaison officer".

Could things have gone differently? Could this liberation movement have won the peace as well as winning the war? Winning the war was already very much: but was it ever possible, along those avenues of time, to win more than the war itself? Wading through the get-rich-quick confusions and anti-democratic conspiracies of Italy in the 1960s and later, after long years of government not only without the Left but consistently against the Left, there would be Italians of another generation to answer with an angry or impatient yes. The partisans, they would say, should have resisted the Allies; the communists should have fought on for revolution. Those who would say this were in the realm of fantasy. Nothing of the kind was ever possible, nor did any serious person suppose it was. The war was wonderfully over: who in their senses was going to start another? Even if the communists had been so forgetful of reality or of their own policy of democratic unity to have attempted to fight on, what proportion of partisans would have followed them? Perhaps a handful, certainly not more; and for how long? Liguria was traditionally "red", and nearly all its effective fighting units were Garibaldini under communist leadership. Yet even in Liguria the possibility of resisting the Rome agreement, and fighting the Allies, did not exist. The only possibility was to save what could be saved, politically and morally; and this was done.

What the Italian resistance made possible was not a revolution for socialism or anything that might be called socialism. This was never on the cards. What it made possible was the basis and the groundwork for an anti-fascist democracy; and in this it did not fail. Every social and cultural advance in Italy since then can be seen to have its roots in that wartime companionship and common struggle for the decencies of life. Obscurely or directly, the revival of self-respect and of democratic attitudes and ideas were the work of the resistance. Its fifteen little "partisan republics" of the north were brief, spread around between the Gothic Line and the Alps; but their influence was not ephemeral. That at least could not be buried. The notion of a workable democracy lived powerfully on. Not powerfully enough? And the eventual results were meagre? It is not so sure; but even if it were so, the fault can scarcely be laid at the door of those who built and defended the democracy of liberation.

And the case of Jugoslavia is clearer still. The country that fell apart in 1941 in fear and hate and civil war, half a dozen civil wars, was put together again. Not from the top, not by orders from on high: but by the unity of life against death, the unity of countless people "at the bottom", the unity of working for a different future.

That was the essence of what came out of the war in Jugoslavia, no matter how one may judge the wisdom, value, or desirability of this or that post-war policy. It is a theme that takes me beyond my brief; but in the Vojvodina, to go no further, the nationalities today live together in an amity and integration such as never existed in the past, as anyone may see who goes to look (as I sometimes do); and together they build a society, along with other Jugoslavs, that is as different from the Jugoslavia of the Triune Kingdom as day is different from night.

Was the war therefore in some way worth while, somehow a good thing in spite of all its tragedies? Is this what I am suggesting? Not for a moment. The war was a catastrophe in all its aspects, a nazi-fascist catastrophe compounded by old betrayals and equivocations—such as, for example, the fatal Munich sell-out to Hitler in 1938—and it could never be anything less than a catastrophe. The sufferings it inflicted will never be made good; and even their size and horror are beyond all computation, perhaps above all now when memories grow dim. If Europe and other smitten regions stumbled from that war with any feelings left that men call human, then the conclusion can only be that human nature is somehow better than it should be.

There could not be a problem, on our side, of pretending that the war was anything except disaster for all it touched. The problem on our side, as Amílcar Cabral was going to say in just such another situation, was to know how to turn weakness into strength: to know how to extract from disaster, if that could possibly be done, the chance of removing the causes of disaster. Not completely, for no one yet has reached utopia. But sufficiently: sufficiently, that is, to extract the chance and make it good.

This is what the great movements of resistance, in their essence, set out to do. And this is what in their development they did: in spite of their proclaimed enemies and deplorably often in spite of their proclaimed friends as well. They extracted hope and human value from the misery of war. They cleared a space for civic decency and even progress in all the brutish squalor of those years. They held that space and used it. Plenty of other miseries came after. But whatever good came after was first given shape and life in that crucible where every man and woman, before the end, had to be for one side or for the other, for submission to evil or for resistance to evil, and where so many, before the end, took the side of resistance.

That is a fact to be altered by no shuffling of bureaucratic feet or distortion of the record by any canting crypto-nazi crew. And it can alter nothing of the same fact that the victory was incomplete, often painfully so; for this kind of victory can never be complete until we all grow wings. Now, in our own time, the old contest is there again. Self-appointed super-patriots of the far right, acting for themselves or for unadmitted paymasters, try to reduce the democratic upsurge of the anti-nazi war to a dubious or squalid episode, and croak their froglike voices to the tunes of a victory which, they would have us believe, was theirs: whereas, in fact, the truth was precisely the reverse. New "national fronts" clamber on the scene, no smaller or more stupid than the nazis were when they began. Old equivocations are replaced by new equivocations, just as apparently "respectable and proper" as the old ones were.

They are all things to resist. Now as then: but sooner, this time. A lot sooner.

NOTES ON SOURCES

IT MAY BEAR repeating that this book refers only to one region of the liberation struggle in Jugoslavia, and to one in Italy. Those countries had other regions, in Jugoslavia many other regions, where the scale of effort and self-sacrifice was comparable; while other countries over-run by nazi-fascist terror could show the same, though on a smaller scale except in western Russia. But I have written here of these two regions of Jugoslavia and Italy for reasons obvious in the book itself; and the sources here are listed accordingly.

Readers who are also historians may object that mine is no proper kind of history, neither fish nor fowl nor guid Scots herring; and the objection would be reasonable. Yet the anti-nazi war in some of its leading features and many of its phases, above all perhaps those considered here, was just that kind of anomalous and unsatisfactory creature; and its trail through that six-year blizzard, if followed only by travel through the archives (or, that is, the available archives), will be more than hard to follow. Some insight into elusive or ambiguous motives and emotions will be useful; and these are the aspects of the truth that I have wished to offer. Of this truth, in so far as I have known and understood it, I have withheld nothing and distorted nothing save three or four personal names, all of minor figures, and these only to avoid any risk of hurt feelings for surviving relatives. Otherwise I have tried to tell it *wie es eigentlich gewesen*: simply as it was.

As for the sources of this truth, they are chiefly in the oral testimony of participants, sometimes collected by me and sometimes by others, whether at the time or later. They are of course restricted to certain dramas and decisions within SOE in southern Europe, and to the Vojvodina and Liguria: but these were "cases", I would argue, that may be considered as characteristic of a far wider experience in those years.

No few of the participants referred to, or upon whose testimony I have drawn, lost their lives in fighting the anti-nazi war, and others have died in the many years since. If this book has a special dedication, it is to them. Many others are happily still going strong. Among these I desire especially to thank Aka Kovačević and the Savez Udruženja Boraca Vojvodine for generous friendship on many occasions, and, for Liguria, Gio'-Batta Canepa; while asking all of them to bear with and forgive the many shortcomings of my story. Marion Davidson and Edward Thompson generously read the text, as I was going along, and made suggestions for improvement; and for help at various points I also wish to thank Leo Abse, Julian Harber, Mervyn Jones, Richard Kisch, John Saville and Michael Stenton.

For archival records in respect of this volume of an eventually larger work, to be entitled *Chance of a Lifetime* and including later years, I have chiefly used the FO 371 and WO 202 series in the Public Record Office, to whose kindly officials I also give thanks. There is much of relevance in these series. WO 202/142 has many (decoded) signals from my Jugoslav mission (code-named "Savanna"), while comparable signals from Col. Macmullen's Ligurian mission (code-named "M 12") are in FO 371/49798, in WO 202/9387 and, most usefully, in WO 202/7299, this last containing the more important of my signals from Genoa during the insurrection. Of these the clincher is No 522 of 26 April, received from me at 3 a.m. on 26 April by No 1 Special Force, which reports: "Have had meeting with CLN. Meinhold has made unconditional surrender to CLN of all forces under his command. . . ."

SOE

M. R. D. Foot is the only historian till now to have received access to the SOE archives, or to such of them as may still survive, and he appears likely to remain so. His admirable *Resistance in France* (HMSO, London 1966, revised edn., 1968) has a corresponding detail and authority. There is no regional survey to compare with it, at least for SOE in southern Europe, and Foot's more general *Resistance* (Eyre Methuen, London 1976), which does have materials on southern Europe, is comparatively sketchy and not unfree from error, being notably deficient on the Italian campaign. In this situation the Auty-Clogg symposium of the Cumberland Lodge papers and discussion of 1973, listed below under *Jugoslavia*, is indispensable reading; it covers, however, only Jugoslavia and Greece, omitting Albania, Bulgaria, Roumania, Hungary and Italy. So far as Hungary is concerned, I wish to thank the Foreign Office for kindly extracting for me some brief but useful notes on the work of Section D during 1940–41.

Italy

The Italian bibliography of the Italian resistance is copious and many-sided, while the English remains almost non-existent save for fragmentary memoirs. A start may be made with the following, listed alphabetically for convenience (and including the Ligurian written sources I have chiefly used):

Alexander, F.-M. Viscount *The Italian Campaign (12 Dec 1944 to 2 May 1945)*, HMSO, London 1951

Amendola, G. *Lettere a Milano 1939–45*, Editori Riuniti, Rome 1973, 1976

Battaglia, R. *Storia della Resistenza Italiana*, Einaudi, Turin 1964

— *Risorgimento e Resistenza*, Editori Riuniti, Rome 1964

Canepa, G.-B. *Storia della Cichero*, ANPI, Genoa 1946

— *La Repubblica di Torriglia*, ANPI, Genoa (n.d. but 1946); third edn., Di Stefano, Genoa 1975

Cassinelli, G. *Appunti sul 25 Luglio 1943*, SAPPI, Rome 1944

Churchill, Winston S. *The Second World War*, Cassell, London 1950, five vols.

Deakin, F. W. *The Brutal Friendship*, Weidenfeld & Nicolson, London 1962

Genoa, Comune di *Revista del Comune*, annual series, esp. for years 1946–49 and for 1975

Lazagna, G. B. *Ponte Rotto*, ANPI, Genoa 1946 (and later edns.)

Liguria, CLN *Documenti*, Ist. Storico della Resistenza (Liguria), Genoa 1947

Longo, L. *Un Popolo alla Macchia*, Mondadori, Milan 1947

Napolitano, V. *25 Luglio*, Vega, Rome 1944

Pietra, I. *I Grandi e I Grossi*, Mondadori, Milan 1973

Secchia, P. *L'Insurrezione nel Nord*, Unità, Rome 1945

Spriano, P. *Storia del Partito Comunista Italiano*, Einaudi, Turin 1975, esp. vol. 5

Taviani, P. E. *Breve Storia della Liberazione di Genova*, ANPI, Genoa 1948

Jugoslavia

The Jugoslav bibliography of the liberation struggle is very extensive in accessible archives, histories, memoirs, and visual materials collected in a large number of well-organised museums and libraries; the bibliography of English sources is also relatively rich. I give below a short list of the more important works that bear on my narrative. Apart from a few of general application, those in Serbo-Croat are limited to books bearing on the Vojvodina and adjacent areas. In this last respect the two books by Jovan Veselinov are indispensable; while, for the British side in general, so, as already mentioned, is the Auty-Clogg symposium.

Readers should note that the view of General Mihajlović given in this book, and of British policy towards him, has continued to be the subject of political controversy, usually by persons who were absent from the scene. Largely, it has consisted of accusing those British officers who were concerned in the "switch" from chetniks to partisans, the actual story of which I have told here, of being liars or betrayers of their trust. The plain fact remains that the "switch" was made on purely military grounds, as I have explained, and would in any case have been otherwise unthinkable. Nothing that has since come to light has in any way invalidated that military justification. Those who wish to follow the argument in detail, and as set forth by a number of responsible British officers, notably Colonel Gordon Fraser, may do so in a series of issues of *The Times Literary Supplement* (above all, for 22 Oct 1971; 14 April 1972; 11 May 1972; and 26 May 1972). A recent restatement of "the case for General Mihajlović" is in D. Martin, *Patriot or Traitor*, Hoover, Stanford, Cal., 1978. This adduces no new evidence, makes many baseless and indeed libellous assumptions about the British officers concerned, and can be accepted as no serious contribution to the subject.

Auty, P. *Tito, A Biography*, Longman, London 1970
Auty, P. and Clogg, R. (ed) *British Wartime Policy towards Resistance in Yugoslavia and Greece*, Macmillan, London 1975; and, notably therein, contributions by S. W. Bailey, Elizabeth Barker, F. W. Deakin, Fitzroy Maclean, and George Taylor
Barker, E. *British Policy in South-East Europe in the Second World War*, Macmillan, London 1976
Buchheit, G. *Der Deutsche Geheimdienst: Geschichte der Militärische Abwehr*, List, Munich 1966
Churchill, Winston S. *supra*
Clissold, S. *Whirlwind*, Cresset, London 1949
Davidson, B. *Partisan Picture*, Gordon Fraser, Bedford 1946
Deakin, F. W. *The Embattled Mountain*, Oxford 1971
Dedijer, V. *Dnevnik*, Državni Izdavački Zavod, Belgrade, three vols., esp. vol. 1, 1945, and vol. 2, 1946

Djilas, M. *Conversations with Stalin*, Hart-Davis, London 1962
— *Wartime*, Secker & Warburg, London 1977
Maclean, F. *Eastern Approaches*, Cape, London 1949
— *Disputed Barricade*, Cape, London 1957
Nadj, D. *Kad Su Sremci Krenuli*, Progress, Novi Sad 1964
— *Tsvet Nikao iz Smrti*, Dnevnik, Novi Sad 1967
— *Kosta Nadj: Vojnik Tri Armije*, Proleter, Bečej 1971
Nadj, K. *Ratni Susreti s Titom*, Privredni Prigled, Belgrade 1977
Savić-Kolja, S.: Josip Broz Tito, *O Svenarodnom Revolucionarnom Ratu* (collected speeches and writings on and around this theme), SUBNOR, Novi Sad 1977
Savić-Kolja, S., Kekić, D., and Milin, V. (ed) *Sećanja Komandanata Vojvodjanskih Brigada*, SUBNOR, Novi Sad 1975
Seton-Watson, H. *Eastern Europe Between the Wars 1918–1941*, Cambridge 1945
Tadić, Ž. (ed) *Vojvodina u Borbi*, SUBNOR, Novi Sad 1963
Thayer, C. *Guerrilla*, Michael Joseph, London 1964
Tito, Josip Broz *Zbornik*, Vojnoistorijski Institut, Belgrade, esp. vol. 1, 1949
— *Borba za Oslobodjenie Jugoslavije 1941–45*, Kultura, Belgrade 1947
— *Selected Military Works*, Vojno Izdavački Zavod, Belgrade 1966
— see Savić, *supra*
Tomacevich, J. "Yugoslavia During the Second World War", in Vucinich *infra*
Vasić, G. *Hronika o Oslobodilačkom Rata u Južnoj Bačkoj*, Vojvodina u Borbi, Novi Sad 1969
Veselinov-Žarko, Jovan *Svi Smo Mi Jedna Partija*, Budučnost, Novi Sad 1971
— *Iz Naše Revolucija*, Pokrajinska Zajednica za Naučni Rad, Novi Sad 1974
Vucinich, W. S. (ed) *Contemporary Yugoslavia*, Univ. of California 1969
Vujasinović, T. *Ozrenski Partizanski Odred*, Vojno-Istorijski Inst., Belgrade 1952

Other
Albert Ouzoulias' (Colonel André's) story is in his *Les Fils de la Nuit*, Grasset, Paris 1975. Alexander Werth's description of Maidenek is in his *Russia at War 1941–5*, Barrie & Rockliffe, London 1964, 768, 890–7. For the fate of Niki Odescalchi and

some other Hungarians, see M. Károlyi, *Memoirs*, Cape, London 1956, 308, 325, 381; and also, in a slightly disguised account, J. Listowel, *Dusk on the Danube*, Chatto & Windus, London 1969, 34. Awaiting Richard Kisch's book on the subject, the best available account of the Cairo "Forces' Parliament" is that of the late D. N. Pritt QC, who with his customary courage went to the help of Aircraftsman Abse and others: *Autobiography*, (3 vols., Lawrence & Wishart, London) II, 1966, 113ff; and see also L. Abse, *Private Member*, Macdonald, London 1973.

INDEX

AMGOT, 257-8, 273-4
Abse, Leo, 157
Action party (Italy), 148-9, 264
Alexander, Field Marshal, 169, 214, 239-40, 261-2
Almond, General, 270-1, 272
Alpi Graie, 26
Ambrosio, General, 21, 22
André, Colonel (Ouzoulias), 74-5
Andrić, Leposava, 180. *See also* Baba
"anti-scorch", 249, 251, 252-3
Armstrong, Staff-Sgt. George, 205, 208, 218-19, 255-6
Atherton, Captain Terence, 86

Baba (Leposava Andrić), 180, 181, 193, 194-5, 200-2. *See also* Andrić
Badoglio, Marshal, 13, 14, 15, 18, 145; attitude to anti-fascists, 16
Barbato (Pompeo Colojanni), 34, 143
Belgrade, Hitler's bombing of, 61
Beltrami, Filippo, 34
Bisagno, 141-2, 146, 164
Bobbio, Don, 220-2
Brandreth, Staff-Sgt. Stanley, 42, 123-4
British aid for Greek resistance, 92; for Italian resistance, 234, 244, 249; for Jugoslav resistance, 44, 119, 173, 179-80; evacuation of Jugoslavs to Italy, 205-6
British dilemma over communist resistance, 98-9, 101, 103, 153, 237

CLN (Italian liberation committee), 236, 247-50, 254-5, 263-6, 272, 273-4
Cairo, SOE in, 79, 89
Campbell, Sir Ronald, 15, 64, 66
Canadian Jugoslav volunteers, 85-86, 122
Canepa, John-Baptist, 10-12, 19-21, 24-5, 28-32, 35; establishment of partisan band, 36-7; adoption of new name, 37. *See also* Marzo *and* band of Cichero
Cefalonia, massacre at, 23
chetniks, 43, 87, 90, 102, 105-6, 115, 183; British aid for, 106, 119, 127; collaboration with Germany, 116-17. *See also* General Mihajlović
Chrystal, Brigadier, 155, 156
Churchill, Winston, 16-17, 64, 102, 118-19, 120-1; meeting with Stalin, 232
Ciano, Count Galeazzo, 66-7
Cichero, band of, 37, 139, 142, 239; first attack, 140-1; disbanding of, 258
Clark, General Mark, 251-2
code-breaking in Britain, 116, 118
Colojanni, Pompeo, *see* Barbato
communism, in Greece, 93-4, 95; in Italy, 16-17, 23-4, 145-7, 150-1, 227; in Jugoslavia, 93-4, 95, 227
communist ideals in Southern Europe, 96-7
Crete, battle for, 61
Cucciolo (Rinaldo Simonetti), 224-5
Curiel, Eugenio, 230

Davidson, Basil, early career, 47–49; at start of war, 50–3; in Hungary, 54–60, 175; in London (1940), 76; in Istanbul, 77–78; in Cairo, 79; in Jugoslavia, 174, 177, 181; in Italy, 213–19. See also Dolinek, Rudolf
Deakin, Captain (afterwards Lt.-Col. Sir) William, 42, 117, 118–119, 126
democratic ideals in Italy, 229
Directive 44, 21, 22
Dolinek, Rudolf (an alias for B.D.), 181, 187
Dragutin, 199–200

Eden, Sir Anthony, 153
El Alamein, Battle of, 91
Ennis, Sergeant William, 42
Essaillon (fortress prison), 11–12, 19, 25

Feješ, Klara, 197–8
"Forces' Parliament" (Cairo), 154–7; (Deodali), 158
Fortress Europe, 63, 72

Garibaldini, 148, 168, 230
Gavrilovič, Rile, 187
Genoa, insurrection in, 254–7, 263–70
Glenconner, Lord, 103
Graziani, Marshal, 151, 169–70
Greek resistance movement, 78, 92, 93, 101–2, 153, 217; British destruction of, 236
Grulović, Ačim, 177

Hasluck, Mrs, 83
Himmler, Heinrich, 35
Hitler, Adolf, in 1941, 9; and Badoglio, 14–15, 18; bombing of Belgrade, 61; invasion of Russia, 68
Hudson, Captain D. T., 78, 86

Hungary, 54–60

internment of Italian troops, 24
Istanbul, 77–8
Italian Navy, 26
Italian politics, 13–16, 232–40, 247–50, 275–6
Italian resistance, 11, 16, 34, 36, 139–44, 149, 151; running down of, 233. See also Marzo and band of Cichero
Italy's surrender, 18, 22–3

Jones, Mervyn, 158
Jugoslavia, history of, 181–2; postwar, 277
Jugoslav resistance, 41, 42, 74, 86, 93, 96; British aid to, 119, 173, 179–80; British contact with, 122; British neglect of, 103–4, 105–6; conflict with chetniks, 103, 105; fighting against Germans, 116; militarisation of, 173; personalities in, 177–8; purposes of, 182–3; strength of, 217. See also Tito and odreds

Keble, Brigadier C. M., 106, 111–115, 116–17, 119, 122, 132, 134; and Maclean, 129–30; his death, 135
Keitel, General, 73
King of Italy, 13–14, 145
Klugman, Lieutenant (afterwards Major) James, 83–5, 86–7, 100, 111, 114
Kosta Nadj, General, 38, 41, 43, 207
Kragujevac, massacre at, 72

Leeper, Rex, 131
Lewin, Arthur, 155, 157
liberation movements, see resistance movements
Longo, Luigi, 147

MO4 see SOE Cairo
MacGregor, Flight-sergeant, 205–206
Maclean, Brigadier Sir Fitzroy, 129–35, 173, 208
MacMullen, Lt.-Col. Peter, 209–210, 251, 258–9, 269
Maffi (Secondo Pessi), 247–9, 264
Maidenek concentration camp, 188–9
Malatér, Paul, 175
Mandel, Georges, 50
Manes, 267–8
Marzo, 10, 11–12, 139, 164–5, 222–3, 229, 259. See also Canepa, John-Baptist
Massacres, at Cefalonia, 23; at Kragujevac, 72; at Portofino, 223; at Rača, 185–6; at Voltaggio, 224
Matić, Dule Petar, 177
Mihajlović, General, 87, 92, 102, 103, 104. See also chetniks
Milan, elimination of army in, 22
Miro (Antonio Ukmar), 166–70, 213, 218–19, 252, 255, 267–8
"Mongol" offensives, 216, 241–2
Moscatelli, Cino, 34
Mosley, Sir Oswald, 46, 161
Mussolini, resistance to, 11; fall of, 13–14; internment, 33; meeting with Hitler, 33–4

Nadj, General Kosta, see Kosta
nationalism, 102
nazi effect on human nature, 186–187
nazi "national fronts", 73, 143–4, 184–5, 187, 190, 278
Normandy landings, 172

Odescalchi, Prince Niki, 171, 172, 203
odreds, 173–4, 178, 179

Orović, General Sava, 177
Ouzoulias see Colonel André

Pallavicini, George, 171
Páloczi-Horváth, George, 56, 65
Parini (Enrico Martino), 247–9, 264, 265, 266, 273
Parri, Ferruccio, 148, 240
partisans see resistance movements
Pavelić, Ante, 65
Pearl Harbor, 62
Pearson, Colonel J. S. A., 121
Popović, Proka, 203–4
Portofino, massacre at, 223
prisoners, treatment of, 24, 224–6, 242
Psychological Warfare Bureau, 233, 240

Rača, massacre at, 185–6
resistance movements, 97, 152, 231, 278; British aid to, 44, 92, 101, 234; British mistrust of, 153; destruction of, 275–6; ideals of, 199; purposes of, 182–3, 196; women in, 195, 201. See also Greek, Italian and Jugoslav resistance movements
Roatta, General Mario, 15–16, 18
Rolando, 244–5
Rommel, Field Marshal, 89
Roosevelt, President, 62, 246
Rossi, General Carlo, 26
Ruggero, General, 22
Russia, invasion of, 68

Saint Rock, priest of, 54, 77–8, 79, 81–2
Salo, Republic of, 34, 35, 142
Sargent, Sir Orme, 121, 131
Savić, General Kolja Sreta, 177
Selborne, Lord, 99, 120–2, 127
Selby, Major Neil, 127

Seton-Weston, Hugh, 77, 82
Severino, 141
Simitch, Alexander, 86, 123
Simonetti, Rinaldo, *see* Cucciolo
Sleede, Captain, 79-82
Smuts, Field Marshal Jan, 17, 145
socialist ideas, wartime growth of, 155-7
Soleti, General, 33
Solomons, Private Harry, 156
Special Operations Executive (SOE), 53, 64, 67, 71-2; Cairo branch, 79, 89, 92, 107-9
Spriano, Paolo, 23
Stalin, Josef, 68, 232
Stalingrad, 91-2
Stojaković, Djordje, 192, 193, 196, 202
Student, General, 33

Tamplin, Colonel Guy, 89-91, 127
Thompson, Lt. Edward, 154

Tito, 42-3, 74, 86, 95-6, 98, 123-124; British aid to, 173; Capt. Deakin's contact with, 126. *See also* communism in Jugoslavia *and* Jugoslav resistance
Togliatti, Palmiro, 150-1
Tuzla, partisan capture of, 43-4

Ukmar, Antonio, *see* Miro
Ullein-Reviczky, Antal, 60

Veličković, Sveta, 180, 184, 190
Veselinov, Jovan, 178 (and see Notes on Sources)
Voltaggio, massacre at, 224
Vujasinović, Todor, 43

Werth, Alexander, 188-9
Wilson, General Sir Henry Maitland, 133, 235
women in resistance groups, 169, 195, 201
Wroughton, Sgt. Walter, 126